GRAVE ATTENDING

Grave Attending

A Political Theology
for the Unredeemed

For Cynthia
with deep gratitude
for all of your support!

Karen Bray

FORDHAM UNIVERSITY PRESS
New York 2020

Fordham University Press has no responsibility for the
persistence or accuracy of URLs for external or third-party
Internet websites referred to in this publication and does not
guarantee that any content on such websites is, or will
remain, accurate or appropriate.

Fordham University Press also publishes its books in a
variety of electronic formats. Some content that appears in
print may not be available in electronic books.

Visit us online at www.fordhampress.com.

Library of Congress Cataloging-in-Publication Data
available online at https://catalog.loc.gov.

Printed in the United States of America

22 21 20   5 4 3 2 1

First edition

In memory of Julia Deedee Agee Sprecher.

For Jackie, David, and Sean.

*And for all those who, having attended
to a world on fire, were blamed as the match
instead of credited as the alarm.*

CONTENTS

Grave Attending

CHAPTER I

Unbegun Introductions

Scene One: The Moment

"I'm exhausted."

"What's that?" I shout from Marie's pre-fab kitchen, where I've been making tea and sandwiches.

"I'm exhausted!" Marie, a friend in the beginning stages of dementia, says, half-hollering, half-sighing.

"Oh yes, sure, why don't you take a nap, we can eat later."

"I'm not tired, I'm exhausted. This is exhausting."

When I finally reach Marie's side she is looking at the social media site Facebook. It is the summer of 2016, and she has been scrolling through both Democratic and Republican political attacks. While Marie's cogency of mind has begun to wane, her visceral awareness of the moods behind what she reads and what is said around her has amplified. She trembles more forcefully when there is a tone of anger in the conversation; she weeps more quickly at a touching moment. The breakdown of mind and the breaking open of mood have been simultaneously illuminating and heart-wrenching.

"Yes, Marie, I'm exhausted too."

One might have expected a scholar of affect employing the critical study of emotion to political theology to have found the intensity of moodiness that percolated to the surface in the early months of 2016 exhilarating. As we inched closer to November, 2016 had turned out to be a particularly poignant political moment in which the race for the presidency showed us not only what the American people had been thinking, but much more so what we had been feeling. One might expect a sense of excitement at the fertile ground for a political theology engaged with affect such a prevailing mood had laid bare. But I, like Marie, did not feel exhilarated; quite frankly and unceasingly, I felt exhausted.

I continue to feel worn down by the well of resentment and the accompanying abhorrent policy decisions tapped into and perpetrated by Donald Trump. I cry over the explosive anger fueled by white rage and heteropatriarchal angst—emotions whose embers have been, for decades, stoked by right-wing pundits, Tea Party candidates, fundamentalist religious thought, and neoliberal corporate managers, but whose blaze has now been finally set free by Trump. Such political moodiness, however, began long before any of the candidates declared their intention to run. Forces of public feeling, those that I found exhilarating rather than exhausting, had already taken hold as what some have called the "New Civil Rights Movement"—a movement animated by such demands as "Black Lives Matter" and "Say Her Name"—and spread across the country.

A week after Michael Brown, an unarmed black teenager, was murdered by police officer Darren Wilson in Ferguson, Missouri, I find an Obama "Hope" postcard in a desk drawer, the contents of which I am purging to make room for a new semester's worth of ephemera. The iconic off-white, blue, and red image created by street artist Shepard Fairey during the 2008 U.S. presidential campaign strikes me, strikes at me, and stirs in me a particularly potent melancholy. What has happened to the hope? Or, more precisely, what might this potentially feel-good politics have been covering over, which the epidemic killing of black people by arms of a state have now revealed to those of us privileged enough to be out of the line of fire? Might the prevailing moods taking hold in both police brutality and the march of resistance against such brutality mark how this hope has not been fulfilled?

My sense of melancholy on that day was not, I would argue, a rejection of hope, but rather the insistence that it remains possible only if we let other emotions—those of grief, rage, depression, and anxiety—flood the streets as reminders of how much farther we still have to go on the way to a promised land and, more crucially, how much we might have to question altogether just what is being promised and where and when it should be found.

The emotional difference between the mood captured by the Obama "Hope" poster and that revealed in the lyrics of Lauryn Hill's song "Black Rage" is not insignificant. The song is sung to the melody of "My Favorite Things" from *The Sound of Music* and includes these excerpted lines:

> Black rage is founded on blatant denial/sweet economics, subsistent survival, deafening silence and social control, black rage is founded in all forms in the soul . . .

> Victims of violence/Both psyche and body/Life out of context is living ungodly . . .

> Try if you must but you can't have my soul/Black rage is founded on ungodly control/So when the dog bites/And the beatings/And I'm feeling so sad/I simply remember all these kinds of things/And then I don't feel so bad.[1]

Black rage, as expressed in this song, embodies what Sara Ahmed has called the political freedom to be unhappy.[2] It is a call, a lament—one that should provoke us to ask not why Hill isn't more hopeful, but rather what her mood, her black rage, might tell us about being forced to live a life out of context—one faced with blatant denial.

I played "Black Rage" for my students on the first day of a 2014 course on affect theory. The course began less than three weeks after Michael Brown's murder. For many of my students the mood of the song concluded the first day of their first college course. The deep tie between feeling and fearing so bad set the tone and defined, or rather reflected the atmosphere in which we would come to critically engage the study of affect and what such a study might reveal about how we have been *affected* by political moods and their emotional and ontological cultivation. Our collective study of affect began with the mood of lament over—and so hope for—black lives, because lament against injustice and its concomitant hope for justice are where the affective and the ethical most clearly intersect. At these moody intersections—those where lament and (a perhaps moody) hope meet—a political theology that is attendant to the prevailing mood of the moment and the temporal, emotional, and value shifts that might arise in resisting violence to both psyche and body is birthed.

This is a book about what it would mean to be a bit moody in the midst of being theological and political. Its framing assumption is that neoliberal economics relies on narratives in which not being in the right mood means a cursed existence. Its opening provocation is a diagnosis of a soteriological and theological impulse in neoliberalism that demands we be productive, efficient, happy, and flexible in order to be of worth and therefore get saved out of the wretched experience of having been marked as worthless. The theological underpinnings of neoliberalism offer a caged freedom in the guise of opportunity. Hence, I offer a critique of such redemptive narratives through constructions of what it might look and feel like to go unredeemed. To go willfully unredeemed might be to stick with those whom neoliberalism has already marked as irredeemable. In attending to what it is to be materially and affectually unredeemed, it is my hope that new theological and political landscapes of becoming together differently might be surfaced. At its core, this book attempts to construct a political theology attendant to moody and material life. It offers affect theory as a hermeneutical lens from which to reread contemporary political and postmodern theologies. It does not offer a definitive account of religion and affect. Nor does it propose a solution to all the ills within and troubled by political theology. Rather, it asks what new questions, insights, sources, and modes of doing political theology arise when we take affects, most particularly the moods of the unredeemed, seriously.

According to Melissa Gregg and Gregory J. Seigworth, the editors of *The Affect Theory Reader*:

> Affect arises in the midst of *in-between-ness*: in the capacities to act and be acted upon . . . affect is found in those intensities that pass body to body (human, nonhuman, part-body, and otherwise), in those resonances that circulate about, between, and sometimes stick to bodies and worlds, *and* in the very passages or variations between these intensities and resonances themselves.[3]

Affect theory might be considered the critical exploration of both what types of acts, knowledge, bodies, and worlds are produced in this in-between space *and* how we might better attend to affect's role in such a production. For example, think of the force of feeling produced when standing on the top of a mountain or in front of your favorite painting. Think of that first ineffable moment of terror that arises when you *feel* like something is off in your environment. Think of the spark, the tingle of expectation before a first kiss. It is the study of these pulsations, for which we do not have appropriate language, that affect theorists engage.

However, affect theory is also the study of those feelings for which we have many names: rage, anger, madness, envy, anxiety, boredom, joy, happiness, optimism, pessimism, depression, and ecstasy. The study of affect is also about how these feelings get coded within cultures or how they come to stick to certain types of bodies, objects, and choices. We can think, for instance, of which objects and subjects get coded as happy in the context of the American Dream. Here a blonde, white, able-bodied spouse (of the "opposite" gender), a white picket fence, a suburban home, 2.5 kids, and a golden retriever all become shorthand for happiness. Happiness, in this sense, while not being inconsequent to those ineffable pulsations we feel atop the mountain, takes a very particular shape—one that gets narrowly defined and associated with particular people. For instance, we might here call to mind the figure of the "Happy Housewife" versus that of the "Angry Black Woman." Affect theory, in this sense, can be considered the critical investigation into how others assume we should feel and how we are actually feeling.

There are multiple strains of affect theory one might take up in the study of affect and religion. Various theorists map the study of affect in various ways. According to Seigworth and Gregg, "There is no single, generalizable theory of affect: not yet, and (thankfully) there never will be. If anything, it is more tempting to imagine that there can only ever be infinitely multiple iterations of affect and theories of affect: theories as diverse and singularly delineated as their own highly particular encounters with bodies, affects, worlds."[4] For Gregg and Seigworth, affect inherently contains a multiplicity of forces whose effects multiply within bloom spaces created by interactions with diverse and particular forms of bodies, other affects, and worlds. Hence, a generalizable or singular theory of affect cannot suffice; such a theory would indeed rob affect of the slipperiness of its own stickiness; that is, that part of affect that, while sticking to certain bodies or worlds and therefore threatening certain bodies and worlds, also contains the promise that such bodies and worlds might get unstuck.

My focus on a political theology of affect, one concerned with the ethical resistance to neoliberal capitalism, leads me to frame affect theory through three interconnected and yet distinct lenses: the psychobiological lens, the prepersonal lens, and the cultural lens.[5] I suggest—perhaps contra Donovan O. Schaefer, who, in his work in *Religious Affects: Animality, Evolution, and Power*, distinguishes between phenomenological approaches to affect and prepersonal ones—that each of these strains has phenomenological inclinations.[6] The key divergences I find stem from the interpretive schema with which they approach the phenomena engaged. For the purposes of a political theology appropriately attuned to the unredeemed, I am most interested in the phenomena of how power and affect comingle in the formation of marginalized sensibilities.

Feminist and queer thinkers of affect, such as Ann Cvetkovich, Sara Ahmed, and Lauren Berlant, depathologize and deindividualize "negative" feelings. Instead of viewing these feelings as signs of sickness in the individual, they ask us to examine the diagnostic potential of such moods. How might envy, for instance, diagnose the mentality created in a society in which we are always striving, but failing to "keep up with the Joneses"? How might depression diagnose a society that asks us to be ever more efficient and productive, but cares little for the necessities of rest and reflection? How might rage diagnose what it feels like to have your life under threat or your intelligence under suspicion because of your race or gender? How might anxiety diagnose a society taught to be afraid of anyone who worships your god? It is this strain of affect theory—the critical examination of culturally produced emotions—that the current project most forcefully takes up as its guide for the rethinking of political theology. To understand such potential, it is important both to introduce key cultural theorists of affect and to lay out the contributions such theory might make in the fields of religious, biblical, and theological study. We begin with the former.

Queer and feminist affect theorists such as Heather Love, Berlant, Ahmed, Cvetkovich, and Michael Snediker approach affect through an epistemological lens; they seek to diagnose how both "positive" and "negative" affects shape our ways of being, knowing, and moving in the world. They identify how certain affects mark those who do not go with normative emotional flow as failures or threats. In the critical examination of the cultural production of affect and emotion, we are able to identify how options and spaces for becoming are opened or closed off through the interactions of affects not only between humans, but also within the matrices of relations between organic and inorganic actors such as food, labor, people, zoning laws, and aesthetic production.

Sara Ahmed's work resides within the canon of queer and feminist affect theory. For the purposes of the following project, her work in *The Promise of Happiness* is most salient. In order to explore the ways in which the promise of happiness shapes ontology, Ahmed outlines figurations she refers to as "affect aliens."[7] Affect aliens are those who do not fit the affectual script handed down by society. For instance, Ahmed notes that "to be a good subject is to be perceived as a happiness-cause as making others happy. To be bad is thus to be a killjoy."[8] The killjoy is an affect alien because she is unable to live up to the script of being happy so that others may be happy.

The Promise of Happiness invites us to consider what might be learned from pausing awhile and inhabiting the terrains tread by affect aliens: by the killjoy, the queer, or the revolutionary.

Ahmed is critical of "happiness" in its contemporary shape, but she by no means eliminates the possibility of joy. For instance, she suggests that "to become pessimistic as a matter of principle is to risk being optimistic about pessimism."[9] Rather than resting clearly in support of a particular feeling or its counter, pessimism or optimism, happiness or melancholy, Ahmed seeks to learn what might be found when we take more seriously the complexity of feeling. Methodologically, while this project at times may find itself tarrying longer with negative moods than their positive counters, it is not my wish to become optimistic about pessimism. Rather, following Ahmed's lead, I look to what moods have been covered over and which new places (including what joys) we might encounter when we let these moods—depression, melancholy, mania, anger, anxiety—reorient whom and what we pay attention to. I also look to what we might encounter when we let these moods teach us about how we might wander away from demands to be happy with a system that has caused such unhappiness. Revolting against demands to be happy is just one way *The Promise of Happiness* aims to tap into bad feelings as creative responses to an unfinished history. Through these creative responses, we might theologically rethink the neoliberal narratives of redemption that keep us chained to our misery, while promising us we will, through them, be happy and free.

Similar to Ahmed's work on happiness and the critical or diagnostic potential found in the willfulness of mood is Ann Cvetkovich's engagement with depression. Cvetkovich is an oft cited affect and queer theorist and a member of the Public Feelings project, a project which seeks to "[open] anew the question of how to embrace emotional responses as part of social justice projects. It is alert to the feelings that activism itself produces and with the ways that activism could change if it were to accommodate feelings, both positive and negative, more readily."[10] Hence, Cvetkovich's work provides a bridge between theory and activism. For instance, Feel Tank Chicago (a branch of the Public Feelings project) sponsors an annual depression march in which people wear bathrobes in the street and carry signs that read "'Depressed? It Might Be Political!'" The march, as well as the Public Feelings project in general, taps into the critical potential of negative moods.[11] More than any other theorist of affect, it is Cvetkovich's work on depression that has set the stage for the hermeneutic and the ethic nurtured by the political theology of this project.

In *Depression: A Public Feeling*, Cvetkovich engages a dual methodology. The first half of the book is a memoir of her own depression, what she calls "The Depression Journals." The second half of the book is a critical reflection on depression. Cvetkovich's writing moves beyond the diagnostic and to the realm of political. This vision engages with feelings of despair or disappointment to uncover radical ways of living. Cvetkovich envisions a resistant life lived in the face of depression through a sense of utopia found in quotidian acts of habit and creativity. While some of these spaces overlap with more public embodiments of subcultural life (for instance in the performances of queer duo Kiki and Herb), one of Cvetkovich's key contributions (along with cultural theorist Katie Stewart) to affect theory is an attention to domestic spheres that have gone under-theorized. In turning to the everyday, her methodology, which is in sympathy with the methodology of this project, "emerges from important traditions of describing *how capitalism feels*, but it also puts pressure on those left-progressive projects not to rush to meta-commentary."[12] She reminds us that each depression, while social, is also singular; depression's quotidian embodiment by a particular person prevents any easy narrative of what depression is or how it should or should not feel.

Further, in turning toward the domestic, Cvetkovich problematizes the binary between the public and private sphere; this becomes all the more essential when thinking through a life lived with depression, one which often engenders a feeling of being trapped in one's own home or mind. For instance, the wearing of bathrobes in public unsettles the seeming affectual calm of the civic streets and asks for the political freedom to be unhappy. This is not to say that Cvetkovich eulogizes feeling bad, but rather that she asks us, in dialogue with Berlant, to slow down enough to look at how people find ways to live better in bad times, including how we might counter "slow death" with "slow living."[13] Further, she notes, "If depression is a version of Lauren Berlant's slow death, then there is no clean break from it. . . . But just because there's no happy ending doesn't mean that we have to feel bad all the time or that feeling bad is a state that precludes feelings of hope and joy."[14] To move toward this joy, we must first depathologize and acknowledge the feelings of despair that may remain even in the midst of, or as a creative source for, pleasure.

Additionally, Cvetkovich finds these moments of hope and joy within the formation of everyday habits like crocheting, alter building, or brushing your teeth. For Cvetkovich, memoir writing is one of these everyday habits that "maneuve[r] the mind inside or around an impasse, even if that movement sometimes seems backward or like a form of retreat."[15] Once exposed to a critique of their roles in culturally coercive demands, joy and creativity can become for us strategies for life in the face of blockage. Cvetkovich provides perhaps the greatest amount of hope in what we might call a micro tactic of the self that has macro political implications. These micro tactics of the self are possible in part (and perhaps ironically) because Cvetkovich does not see the self as an autonomous static being. A self, formed in the between spaces of affect and desire, is one constructed through relation. Indeed, Cvetkovich's depressed subjects, herself included, have their identities shaped as "depressed" not merely out of an individualized mental illness but through an assemblage of worldly factors. The queer and feminist cultural study of affect reorients where we might find theological and ethical political counters to neoliberal politics not only in moments of revolutionary change, but perhaps even more so in moments that remain in the everyday.

Understanding such an assemblage between the most intimate experiences of self and larger worldly factors brings us back to the importance of affect for the study of religion. It is my contention that affect theory makes at least four key contributions to religious study. First, it helps us to resist what Schaefer calls, "the linguistic fallacy." According to Schaefer, "the linguistic fallacy [is] the notion that language is the only medium of power."[16] Affect theory reminds us of the ontological and epistemological significance of the nonlinguistic and the nonrational. Further, although we must stay vigilant against the study of affect and religion slipping too quickly into "the ahistorical metaphysical essentialism of Eliade or the politically attached individualism of James,"[17] this does not mean we must assume that critical investigation into the sociopolitical aspects of religion comes only from the linguistic or discursive. For Schaefer, rather, the phenomenological approaches to affect achieve a proper investigation into how the nonrational works from within and also shapes modes of power.

Affect theory implores religion scholars to read texts, rituals, and doctrines not only for what they claim to be saying or doing, but also for how they feel, what emotions they reveal, and how such emotions might complicate interpretation. Additionally, it is my contention that the queer, feminist, and critical race approaches to affect theory most successfully engage nonrational forms of power production, because such cultural lenses forcefully interrogate what affects *do* more so than what affects *are*. Theorists working in these modes, such as Jasbir Puar, Ahmed, Cvetkovich, and Berlant, remind us that such emotive epistemologies are also tied up with particular histories that must be addressed if we are to take seriously how different subjects have been formed in moody encounters with religious texts and practices.

Second, affect theory asks us to re-attend to material encounters. For instance, instead of beginning an investigation into what a religious tract (a historical pamphlet for proselytizing) said, we might ask how the encounter of being given the tract felt to particular people in particular moments in history. Indeed, phenomenological approaches to affect theory that engage a New Materialist lens (Chen, Bennett, and Connolly)—one which looks to ways we are affected by nonhuman bodies (both organic and inorganic)—further remind us that encounters with nonhuman religious material carry theological weight.

Third, reading for affect and recognizing religious sensibilities in certain affectual modes, such as a religious sense of prayer or lament within the moods of secular protests, helps us to rethink where ritual and faith are practiced today. For instance, we might recognize Hill's black rage as prophetic liturgy. Finally, affect theory returns us to that source of theology, the fourth in the Wesleyan Quadrilateral, after scripture, tradition, and reason, and the central animation of Spinozist tinged theologies and religious naturalisms: experience. Nonrational encounters with the sacred and the mundane have epistemological and ontological force.

As the aforementioned list illuminates, there is fertile ground for the theological study of affect and for the construction of affect theology. Yet while there are hints of entanglement between these fields of critical inquiry and philosophy of religion, affect theorists have rarely sojourned into the sacred sphere. Nor have they necessarily wished to entangle or be entangled with God. Additionally, theological, biblical, and religious studies have only recently and fruitfully engaged this web of critical theory, with philosophical and political theologians lagging even farther behind those in religious and biblical studies. This book hopes to add to other projects seeking to confront these lacunae and, particularly through engagement with queer, affect, crip, and Black studies and theories, to refigure theologically the political, the holy, and the salvific.

To remain with everyday encounters and to refigure what such moody encounters have to do with our salvation is also to open the archive of political and theological feeling to include sources we might normally overlook. The deployment of an alternate archive is the methodology of many of the thinkers listed earlier, and it is their lead that I follow. For instance, this book engages Robin James's reading of music videos by Beyoncé, Lady Gaga, and Rihanna, along with Elizabeth Freeman's reading of S/M practices to construct a Holy Saturday theology nurtured by what I name in Chapter 2 as *bipolar time*. The archive of Chapter 3 includes political theorists, along with horror films, a popular novel, newspaper articles, and poetry, to argue for a theology of unproductivity and the holiness of everyday utopias and crip ontologies. Attention to an alternative archive is a queer practice, one fundamental to the work of Michel Foucault, as touched on in Chapter 5, and to more recent projects like Jack Halberstam's *Queer Art of Failure*, which looks to Pixar cartoons, feminist performance art, and postcolonial novels (to name but a few) in its critique of the neoliberal injunction to be successful.[18] Instead of striving to succeed at a game that has been rigged against us, Halberstam urges us to fail more often, better, and together with all those whom colonial and neocolonial projects (including those of heteronormativity and white supremacy) have marked as failures: queers, women, people of color, indigenous people, the impoverished, transgender and gender queer folk, and the disabled.

I employ such nonbinary thinking and archival collecting as I engage affect in order to challenge and supplement contemporary political theology. By taking into account the socially mediated phenomena of affect in the world, affect theory returns postmodern philosophy to the significance of material and moody histories. Hence, might affect theory help us to return postmodern political theologies to the significance of the force of flesh?

It is the supposition of this book that such force of flesh (flesh here representing a porous ontology of self in which we are shaped through embodied matrices of power, à la the work of Mayra Rivera and Alexander Weheliye) diagnoses and challenges the affectual and material effects of the contemporary political economy. Affect theorists revivify critiques of neoliberalism by taking seriously the effects on real bodies within specific histories and cultures of a neoliberal economy, and the heteropatriarchy, white supremacy, and ableism that it forties and which fortify it. In this book such real bodies come most forcefully alive through the theory written out of marginalized positions—theory written from the position of queerness, cripness, and blackness. Hence, I employ the critical study of affect to interrogate neoliberal narratives of redemption under which to be productive, efficient, and happy is to be free. Affect theory helps us to ask afresh how people are really feeling, what kinds of bodies "good" or "bad" affects stick to, and what kind of salvation or freedom is actually on offer from neoliberal redemption narratives.

To achieve such refiguration, a critique of productivity and wholeness will be key. This critique draws on counter-capitalist projects undertaken by a strain of critical theory often aligned with that of feminist and queer affect theory: crip theory, or critical disability studies.[19] Crip theory, as expressed in the works of Robert McRuer, Anna Mollow, Tobin Siebers, and Alison Kafer, to name just a few, looks toward the non-normate body as a site of critical inquiry into a variety of hegemonic structures—supported by capitalism—that argue for the supremacy of "productive" and "reproductive" bodies. I seek to engage a crip sensibility in order to view madness and its concomitant affects (depression, mania, rage, and anxiety) not only as political affects, but also as sites of crip insight. Welcoming a crip insight, we might come to more sensitively experience God and society through a non-normate mind.

For McRuer, compulsory heterosexuality is actually dependent on compulsory able-bodiedness in that compulsory heterosexuality is built around concepts of normate bodies and sexual desires, which in fact create both the queer and the disabled as other, as those who are expected to answer the following question in the affirmative: "Yes, but in the end, wouldn't you rather be more like me?"[20] Hence, crip theory will (most prominently in Chapter 3) help us to ask both who is it that wants to be, gets to be, and benefits from being saved into becoming in the end "just like me," *and* who is the "me" whom we are supposed to become like. In other words, a crip sensibility—one critically engaged with the moods nurtured by capitalism—will help us to challenge neoliberal narratives of redemption in which the once "broken" (as in crippled bodily or mentally and as in made broke by neoliberal economics) can now become whole, happy, healthy, and productive.

McRuer and Mollow help to resurface those identities gone unseen by other disability theorists. For instance, even in Sharon Betcher's excellent constructive theological engagements with disability, Betcher has noted that just because there is a high rate of suicidal ideation amongst the disabled does not mean that they are mentally ill.[21] This move, like the ones Betcher worries about when metaphors of intellectual *blindness* pathologize the blind, is a plausible distinction, but one that can operate, beyond her intentions, to set up the troubling divide between proper disability and those whom other disabled people should be distanced from—in this case, the mentally "ill." Hence, this venture into these lacunae reminds those of us interested in constructive ethical work that even as we embrace and tarry with the vulnerability of relation and affect, we will still be at risk of creating our own abjected remainders, of affirming certain negativities at the expense of others (an issue most forcefully engaged in Chapter 6).

To counter such processes of abjection, Tobin Siebers has offered disability as a critical framework from which to question all definitions of aesthetic value and harmony. For Siebers, a "disability aesthetic" favors physical and mental difference over the replication of normative standards of beauty and health.[22] Disability as an aesthetic value counters the demand that the disabled be rehabilitated and redeemed. This aesthetic mood is woven throughout the following chapters in which, in resistance to the need to be redeemed into the productive social body, we might seek out the singularities of becoming that wander away from such coercive cohesion. These reformulations of identity and redemption provide fertile ground for political theological propositions.

With the aid of the literature—from affect, queer, and crip theorists—detailed earlier, this book counters what Betcher has called theologies of "whole(some)ness" by aligning with what we might consider theories and theologies of "broke(en)ess," as in theologies written from the sites of those both made broke and considered broken by the American hegemonic political system and, of course, global capitalism. I ask political theologians and particularly political theologians of a radical and leftist bent to take seriously the critiques of health, productivity, and positivity made by affect, queer, crip, and Black studies theorists. In doing so we may better inhabit our democratic potential.

Scene Two: The Room

I'm not supposed to be there; I am certainly not supposed to help her make the bed, but there would be no time to talk if I waited till her shift ended; she did not have a break. Odette was one of my favorite union members when I worked as an organizer for the hotel workers in New York City. She was loud and funny; in this way we were kindred spirits. Her Jamaican accent would boom across the employee cafeteria, a cafeteria like most hotel employee spaces, which lay in the bowels beneath the luxurious floors above. Over plates of rice and beans and Dominican chicken, food served by hotel chefs below and not above, she would tell me about her kids and her managers and we would talk about the union, its professional business, and good industry gossip. She was only in her mid-thirties, but she had worked at this hotel for twelve years. She was respected by her fellow room attendants and a little feared by her managers. About a year into knowing Odette, something shifted. She spoke more softly; when I would see her she seemed worn-down. Her voice no longer boomed; the jolt of a metal fork hitting a plate—as she raised her hand to her mouth so that food would not slip out when she laughed—no longer rang through the room. All of a sudden I could not find her in the employee areas, which were the only

areas where union staff were allowed to speak with our members. But a
contract dispute loomed and we needed to talk, so I roamed the floors to
which she was assigned. I found her in a king suite. She was holding the
small of her back as she slowly stood up after having reached over to pick
up some trash. We began speaking in hushed tones. I'll never forget what
it felt like to help lift the mattress while she changed the sheets on the king
size bed. After what the hotel industry called the "bedding wars" which took
place in the early 2000s, hotel beds and linens had become impossibly
heavy. Lifting just one made my shoulder twinge. I cannot imagine doing
whole floors of beds by myself. But of course this was what Odette and
many more (often older, and almost always women of color and immigrants) did every day. At some point after making the bed Odette briefly
broke down and, opening up, she told me that lately she had been utterly
exhausted. Her back had been killing her. She could not pick up her two
toddlers without wincing in pain. Providing comfort to strangers, servicing
them, she had little left to give her kin. Years later, I heard that Odette had
passed away from cancer, and I still wonder what role exhaustion played in
her death. The service of comforting, what it meant to have made such
comfort a commodity, has never left me.

That room, as it turns out, was the first time I became conscious of what
I would later (following Michael Hardt and Antonio Negri) learn to call
the "the affect economy."[23] While one product of Odette's physical labor
was a well-made bed, more fundamentally her work produced the affects of
comfort, homeyness, or a sense of being pampered for the hotel guests.
Hardt and Negri include such care-work in their definition of the affect
economy and what they call "immaterial labor." Immaterial labor represents a shift in neoliberal economics under which the economy, no longer
built on factories, within Western nations, has come to focus on service-
able exchanges of affects—comfort, excitement, sexual satisfaction—and
not "material" products. I began to ask questions: Which theologians were
reading these neo-Marxists? What proposals from within an understanding of the economy as an affect economy might they be unearthing? Was
affect becoming more prominently a proper object of theological study?
And might that study be political?

While I did not find much work on queer, feminist, and critical race
explorations of affect within political theology, theological engagements
with Hardt and Negri did open landscapes of theologically thinking the
economic, without necessarily needing a specifically Christian theological
ground. In my post-*Multitude* theological encounters, the field known as

"radical theology" was most prominent. The 2015 special journal issue of *Palgrave Communications* on radical theology describes the field thusly: "Radical theology as a field encompasses the intersections of constructive theology, secular theology, death-of-God theologies, political theologies, continental thought and contemporary culture. It expresses an inter-disciplinary engagement and approach dedicated to redefining the very terms of theology as a concept and practice."[24] In my encounters with radi-cal theologies I felt the beginning senses of a theological home. Radical theologians were writing about the economic and political; they were, for the most part, counter-capitalist and critical of neoliberalism; they were not confessional and many were not even Christian; and they expressed a desire to pay close material attention to immanent worldly (and perhaps holy) becomings.[25] And yet, this new home felt bare. For all the talk of imma-nence and materiality, this literature did not seem to be attempting to effect by affect. I was unsure where emotion fit within the discourse. Yet, in the eclipsing of affect in the theological redeployments of Hardt and Negri and other postmodern thinkers engaged in political reflection, the field of radical theology left open unmarked terrain across which this book now hopes to venture.

Radical theologians embrace the postsecular idea that there is a theol-ogy undergirding our secular politics and economics, and they work to uncover the dangerously conservative, absolutist, and providential theolo-gies behind the American Empire and global capitalism. By drawing on the death-of-God and poststructuralist theories of event, plasticity, open rela-tionality, and potentiality, radical theologians and philosophers argue for theologies of immanence. These theologies, therefore, might fit into what Mark L. Taylor calls the post-theological, a theology that does not need a theistic belief in God, but does recognize a kind of agonistic transimma-nence, a world in the making in which agonisms between bodies and social identities burst open possibilities beyond current immanent realities.[26] For these theologians there is no guarantee of a rosy future, but there is a flour-ishing within this tragic uncertainty. As Mark C. Taylor argues in *Confi-dence Games: Money and Markets in a World without Redemption*, the key is not that we are doomed, but rather that it is in the lack of redemption that we find everlasting life.[27]

Finding theology within the immanent world and its creative agonisms returns us to affect, even as emotion goes under-theorized in much of the work of those listed earlier in this chapter. Hence it is my hope that raising the moody ghosts which haunt such theological discourses and asking, with Ahmed and Cvetkovich, what types of creative responses might arise from taking seriously how neoliberal narratives make us feel will help us to reject the redemptive offerings presented to us by such narratives, and in such a rejection make room for alternatives. To encounter such creative responses, we may need to embrace moods that run counter to those expected of us by mainstream culture and the neoliberal economy. We may need to care for what it is to be and how it is to feel irredeemable.

Over the years, my need for greater moodiness has taken shape in embodied encounters with radical theology. Each encounter held moods of great potential and yet left me ill at ease, uncertain of where the moods of gender, race, sexuality, and ability fit within political theology of a supposedly radical bent. Perhaps I existed at the wrong barometric pressure. I had not become acclimated to the scene. I was (or perhaps was in) trouble. I was radical in the wrong ways. Ahmed writes, "How is it that we enter a room and pick up on some feelings and not others? I have implied that one enters not only *in* a mood, but *with* a history, which is how you come to lean this way or that. Attunement might itself be an affective history, of how subjects become attuned to others over and in time."[28] For Ahmed, attunement to the atmosphere can mean learning to not bring up certain topics. What is it about historical and contemporary political theological moods that impede the present moods of race, gender, ability, and sexuality in the current discourse of radical theology? What are the histories to which this theology wants us to attune, and which are being swept into the dustbin of its history?

The question of history *matters*; whose mood gets picked up on and to whose are we coerced to attune were not questions being asked forcefully enough by radical theology. Answers to these questions have largely gone unbegun. I have a feeling that there is something *there* in radical theology, or perhaps more broadly in political theology; there are the beginnings of what might be a truly moody theology, one sensitively attending to the affects of those considered irredeemable or willfully going unredeemed within neoliberal narratives of salvation. Even when I have been out of the mood, I have not given up on the potential for a faith more attuned to a multiplicity of subjects and histories within political theology. But, perhaps it begins with whatever hostility arises when the theories and poetics offered by moody bodies are welcomed in or excluded from these theological rooms.

Scene Three: The Library

During the many years I lived in New York City, when I was lonely, I'd go to Book Culture, an independent bookstore in the Morningside Heights neighborhood of Manhattan, on a side street that if you were to continue down you'd end up right at the foot of the fifth largest Christian church in the world. I often think of that stretch of 112th Street as an extension of St. John the Divine, a kind of hallway on the way to the holy. In Book Culture, on those lonely days, I let my hand slide over spines of books on the shelf. My fingers feel for the smoothness of recent hard covers and the cracks of used paperbacks. I touch for the spaces created by the shifting depth and width of each monograph; I caress embossed titles that texture what otherwise would be smooth spines.

One day my hand was halted by a book that blocked its flow. The book had been put back in such a way that there was no getting from it to the next one without moving my hand away from the shelf. As it turns out the book was that of a colleague at New School University, where I had recently begun teaching. I knew of McKenzie Wark and was hoping to get to know him. That his book, *The Spectacle of Disintegration: Situationist Passages Out of the Twentieth Century* had *found* me, I felt meant I had to buy it. It remained for some weeks, its lime green cover calling to me, from a growing pile of books that sat uncracked on the bedroom chair, which itself had gone mainly unused by any human, as it was perpetually covered with books, clothes, and yesterday's accessories.

When I was a graduate student, a week after I completed my comprehensive exams, I was set to fly to London, where I would spend a month trying to write my dissertation prospectus. I filled a suitcase almost entirely of books. I had my radical theologians and my affect theorists packed together, some transatlantic copulation hoped for. And then that green cover found me again. Frantically looking for my copy of *Depression*, I was halted by *Spectacle of Disintegration*. I tossed it in the suitcase and off I went. Because when you have lots of work you *must* do, you begin to read the stuff you *want* to; I spent part of my first day in London jet-lagged in bed reading with Wark. *Spectacle of Disintegration* led me to Raoul Vaneigem. Maybe there was something to these thinkers of an everyday life that might be free of the social order. I typed Vaneigem's name into the British Library online catalog. At the top of the list was not a book by Vaneigem, but a title so perfect I felt my search fingers itch: *The Soul at Work* by Franco "Bifo" Berardi.

The British library was magical. It was there that I first met Bifo and first ran my eyes over his soul at its work. Here capitalism and depression ran together across the pages. Here, perhaps, was a cipher for what I needed to do. Whereas I had found affect lacking in radical theology, emotion came rushing back to the fore in certain Marxist texts like that of Berardi's.

Hardt and Negri and Berardi write from within the "autonomous Marxist" tradition.[29] According to feminist Marxist Kathi Weeks, this school simultaneously interrogates capitalist production and both capitalist and socialist productivism.[30] A politics of the refusal of work stems from this interrogation. The work of Hardt and Negri, along with other contemporary reimaginings in the feminism of Weeks and the autonomism of Berardi, helps to articulate a counter-capitalist politics does not seek for greater access to work (or better work), but rather demands the right to everyday pleasures and freedom from work. This postwork politics intersects with recent queer, affect, and crip theories and theologies around "negative" feelings and productivism.

Berardi's diagnoses of the affects engendered by neoliberalism (or what he calls SemioCapitalism) as depression, paranoia, and exhaustion stuck with me and the archives of feeling I had already been collecting with Cvetkovich and Ahmed. Sitting for the next month with Berardi's soulful depression and Cvetkovich's political one, my own mad theologies grew. From these texts that stuck with me and that therefore got stuck together, a commitment to an even more forceful engagement with theories of affect, particularly those marked by negative feelings such as depression and madness—and their queer entanglements—took deeper root. It is the combination of these discourses that I argue nurture a deeper attention within political theology to a matrix of threats and opportunities engendered by the affect economy. For instance, a stance of depression might resonate with a postwork politics demanding that ethical attention be paid and worth assigned to the needs, agencies, and bodies of all people regardless of their productivity and mental or physical "ability." Here, a postwork theology takes on its character as a universalist theology—one which holds the inherent worth of all beings, in the beauty of their singularity and the intensity of such singularities coexisting more so than cohering, at the core of its rationale. Being halted by Wark, arrested by Berardi, and in commune with Cvetkovich, the glimpses of what might be holy in all this moody reflecting started to take shape.

Scene Four: The Lunch

It was one of those semesters for which you think, "This time I'll be prepared." You think, "I'll make the scans early, get the course packs printed, and the PDFs available." You think, "I'll read more than one class ahead of my students." You think, "My lecture notes will be perfect and not written at 5 a.m. that morning." You think.

I was already running late to a meeting when I popped into the faculty resource room to see if scans of Michael Snediker's *Queer Optimism* were ready for distribution. When I got there a tall, slender, chicly dressed woman, about my age, was flipping through the book's pages. "Oh sorry," she said, "Is this yours? I love Michael Snediker." Meagan was another adjunct teaching feminist thought in the first-year writing course. The next day we met for lunch. When my new colleague got to the restaurant about fifteen minutes late, she was frazzled. Unsure of new-friendship boundaries, I awkwardly acknowledged that something was clearly awry and asked if she wanted to talk. The dean's office had decided to take away two of her classes at the last minute. This was going to leave her unable to pay her rent. What about the union? I asked. Yes, she was going to appeal to our adjunct union, but she was worried that because she had only been teaching for a few years there was not much standing to get her courses back. I told her the history of unionization of part-time faculty at the New School, which I had witnessed a decade prior when I was there as a student. We discussed the important gains: much more money (and yet still not a living wage); health insurance; retirement contributions; some protections in terms of hiring and firing. And yet, it was clear to us both that we still felt depressed and anxious by the precarity of what it means to be an adjunct; unionized, we had it better than most, but we were not affectually or materially *okay*. Yes, we could get medical checkups, yes we only needed to teach at one or at most two additional schools per semester to make ends meet, but our precarity remained an incessant stress.

Over avocado toast (for twelve dollars) and rosemary lemonades (for five dollars) I told Meagan about the beginnings of this project. I told her about depression as a hermeneutic into how neoliberal economics feel, and I told her that it was from within this state of madness and not in spite of it that I thought we might find different landscapes for becoming. I told her I did not want to be redeemed out of this anxiety and depression, saved from my madness; I wanted to find ways to stop saving the neoliberal machines that had gotten us so depressed in the first place. "You must love

Lynne Huffer," she said. I had no idea who she was talking about. Out of her bag came a tattered, almost falling apart from being lovingly and repeatedly read, copy of *Mad for Foucault: Rethinking the Foundations of Queer Theory*, Huffer's rereading of Foucault's *History of Madness*.

Six months after my lunch with Meagan, I am three thousand miles away and running late to meet another friend for lunch. I cannot yet leave because I cannot stop crying. I am sitting in a 1960s mod style apartment atop a garage in West Hollywood. Across from me sits my host, a friend in his own state of madness from the knowledge that his father, who for years has been battling cancer, will soon be dead. I linger there in the wake of a breakup, and in the hopeful and despairing shadow of a conference set on facing climate disaster. I am crying as I read (with) Foucault. I am haunted by the little foolish ones he surfaces in the pages of *History of Madness*. More than once I am flooded with tears in a way that the voices of the mad, always fully unspeakable, become truly unreadable as my vision becomes wet and blurry. Irrationally, perhaps, I feel as though Foucault has written these words just for me. It is as though I am returning to a long-gone self. It is as though I had been confined and condemned, as though I had let my madness lay dormant in ways that were killing me, but that now my depression, mania, rage, anxiety, and ecstasy might no longer stay buried. In returning me to myself, Foucault and Huffer oddly returned me to God.

Mad for Foucault and my encounters—a bit hysterical—with *History of Madness* changed this book. With Foucault, I began, perhaps ironically, to have confidence in its theological character. Foucault, in allowing me to go unredeemed, helped me reencounter what it might mean to be divine, or encounter divinity. In some ways, despite myself, Foucault helped me to salvage God. Foucault, read through Huffer, and then again through my own affect hermeneutic, brought me back—quite unexpectedly—to Alfred North Whitehead and what it might mean to feel and be felt by a mutable God that feels all of our current becomings, but also all of the past's perishings, including those of the irredeemable mad whom modern progress had hoped would remain buried.

While it was the sense that we might need to feel our way toward the past in order to feel differently in the present and future (a feeling Foucault elicited in me and through my tear ducts) that lured me toward an engagement with Whitehead, there are certainly many other rationales for how process thought might serve as a theological interlocutor for affect theory. Beyond the odd feeling it might come to fruitful engagement with

Foucault (not himself an affect theorist), there are three primary reasons behind process theology's potentiality for this project. First, the fields of affect theory and process theology share similar philosophical forbearers. Some of the theorists that have had primary influence or resonance with affect theory include Baruch Spinoza, Alfred North Whitehead, Gilles Deleuze, and Donna Haraway. These thinkers represent primary and secondary sources for contemporary constructive process discourses, all of which harken back to Whiteheadian philosophy. Second, process thought is centered on concepts that resonate deeply with affect theory: a focus on feeling and affectual interaction between all actual entities in the world (including the inorganic); a deep relationality between creation and God; a mutable God, whose "Consequent Nature" is dependent on others; a complex temporality, which sees the influence of the past and the potentiality of the future interpenetrating the becoming of the present; and an ontology built on becoming and not static being. Finally, despite these critical sympathies, process theology's potential for a queer turn toward the negative, toward more fractured becoming, suspended agency and the productive disintegration or refusal of subjectivity, has barely been tapped. In fact, process theology's own emphasis on harmony and beauty could problematically quell its queer potential. Yet, as I hope to show in Chapter 5, when such concepts are taken in their full meaning, as reflective of the intensity of incompatibility becoming contrast, different *moods* in process become apparent.

There is great potential in a political process theology to offer alternatives to the narratives of redemption on offer by neoliberalism. Perhaps most crucially for political theology, we might have to take seriously God's capacity to feel with us and so to feel and learn from the full spectrum of affects, feelings, and emotions, such that God, too, feels "backward," feels abject, and crucially feels that it is necessary to impede any salvation that is too complete or simplistic. Indeed, in Chapter 5, I argue that one such divinely affecting mood—a mood that helps me to counter neoliberal narratives of salvation—comes through God's "tender care that nothing be lost,"[31] and God's character as Eros of the Universe.[32] As explicated further in the chapter, such erotic care that insists on that which has gone not be lost is divine attention to the significance of what has been, what might have been, and what might be. Perhaps such divine attention is a lure we should follow into alternative archives, ones haunted by those confined and condemned as mad and so unproductive and irredeemable. These are the mad that haunt Foucault's histories, and those with whom this book divinely feels and thinks.

Scene Five: The Class

There are greeting cards you can order off the Internet that are written especially for PhD students. Each card in the series contains drawings of baby animals. The cards are either sympathetic ("Sorry you cried in front of your adviser!") or celebratory ("Congratulations on not crying in front of your adviser!"). Just a few weeks before defending my dissertation I needed one of those cards. I suddenly found myself tearing up in a class I was teaching on affect theory. "Sorry you broke down so unprofessionally," a little bunny with big eyelashes could say to me; or "Congratulations on pulling it together within a minute!" a fawn might say, winking and holding its hoof up for a high five. The day's lesson was on Cvetkovich's *Depression*. We had just completed the memoir section of the book in which Cvetkovich describes the scenes of her depression during times of completing her dissertation, being on the tenure-track job market, and starting her first job at a university hundreds of miles away from everyone she knew. The students were debating the authenticity of voice in the memoir, and then one said, "Also I'm sort of annoyed at Ann." "Cvetkovich," I corrected. "Right sorry, anyway, what does she have to be depressed about? She has so much privilege when you think about it." I burst into tears. It was not that the student was incorrect; Cvetkovich had all kinds of privileges, not least of which that she was and is a highly educated white woman, like myself. Still, for months, if not years, I had been living in what Berardi diagnoses as the "panic-depressive cycle," a cycle nurtured by the neoliberal demand to be ever more productive.[33] The demand to produce, to finish, to have one's ideas arrive right and on time, had me pulsing with nervous energy.

Such energy would often crash into depression, into a feeling of impasse that seemed insurmountable. The dissertation was not going to get done. There was *no* time. I had to pay rent and feed myself and so had been teaching three courses at the New School, one at Marymount Manhattan, while also tutoring fifteen hours a week at Cooper Union. Like Cvetkovich, I had been applying to tenure-track jobs all due at the same time as papers that needed grading, advising appointments that needed conducting, conference presentations that needed polishing, and dissertation chapters that needed writing. It made sense to be exhausted, but why was I so *depressed*? Wasn't I following the career I wanted? Hadn't I chosen this? Hadn't I exercised my own privilege and stopped occupying at Wall Street months prior in favor of taking *my* time to write, think, teach, and do the things that, in spite of the panic and depression, I actually loved? What had gotten me so moody in the midst of such exhaustion? What was happening for

Cvetkovich? For Marie? For Meagan? For me? For us? Was my mood academic? Was it a natural part of academia? Was my teary breakdown just another rite of passage, one on which a whole series of greeting cards could be built?

Perhaps; but I want to surmise that there is a *mood* within our everyday living that has as much to do with the lifeworlds we have been offered, or those we've been told were impossible, as it has to do with any essential nature of who we are and what our momentary particular situations might be. The particulars matter, but each particular mood (a depressed Karen) might also pulse toward a more macro mood (a depressed culture). What was happening that affect had become ambient in academic discourse? What was it about contemporary society that had these different facets of study—feminist literary scholars turned cultural theorists and Italian Marxists—delving into depression? What does the shift in moody slogans from an Obama Hope poster to "Hands Up, Don't Shoot!" say about our societal mood? And what complexity of mood between these two slogans is engendered by "Black Lives Matter"? Do these shifts have anything to do with my own panic and depression? Was there a way to be in the moments of madness other than I had been over those months? Than I was in that classroom? And whose moods was my own mood covering over? For whom was the promise of wholeness or "productive" uplift never on offer? (We return to this question in Chapter 6.) Could something other than a Trump presidency have arisen in the wake of eruptive moods of resentment and disenfranchisement? Could we feel differently about such emotions, both when we can barely get out of bed *and* when we rush into the streets of protest? Could the everyday be inhabited afresh by a hysterical collective ready to break free? Cvetkovich's memoir reminds us that these encounters with our impasses, with our breakdowns, might have something to teach us about how we live and how we might live, not in spite of, but from a critical engagement with our madness.

Scene Six: The Method

This is a book about remaining with the everyday in ways that might change how such a day looks and feels. I argue that such remaining (and here I mean to evoke the Holy Saturday theologies of remaining elucidated by Shelly Rambo in *Spirit and Trauma: A Theology of Remaining*) clears pathways for the possibility of different theological, ontological, political, economic, and affectual becomings. The constellation of texts employed for such caring and clearing are ones that found me as much as I found them.

They are, like affects, sticky; they stuck to me. I am sticky with their matrices of ideas; they are those that got me unstuck from other feelings of being pathologically damaged, not good enough, and feelings of my work being unworthy.[34] Methodologically, this project relies on the intra-actions (to borrow from Karen Barad) of the archive that I weave together from the texts that, to me, cohere. It is an archive of feeling (to borrow from Cvetkovich), time, economy, and worth, but it is also an archive of thinkers that I hope defamiliarize what each of these words might mean.

In many ways I follow Cvetkovich's own instincts in my hope to produce, "what Audre Lorde describes as forms of truth that are felt rather than proven by evidence, the result of 'disciplined attention to the true meaning of "it feels right to me."'"[35] These texts felt right to me. In the disciplined attention I brought to them and they brought to me from the shelves, in bed, in classrooms and conference rooms, in libraries, and in bookstores, the ideas in these texts felt right to put together. However, because these texts are not necessarily or obviously meant to cohere or assemble as a whole, perhaps they are not the perfect fit for all I want to do. I will not dig deep into every recess of philosophical madness, nor will I span the networked breadth of affect theory (and its cousins, queer temporality, critical disability studies, and New Materialism). I will make no definitive declarations on the state of neo-Marxism and relative theological counters to neoliberal economics. I will not dive deeply enough into the moods of blackness that counter my own redemptions. This book will queerly fail at all of that. I will, however, try out what Catherine Keller has called trusty propositions that, while eschewing capital T truth-claims, "[narrate] what has been in order to keep open the democratic space in which the shared future is negotiated."[36] I will pose some tough questions. I will feel for and touch on answers, but I will not give solutions. I will leave too much unbegun.

My propositions will be trusty, if they will not claim truth. I will be following different senses of emotion, feeling, and affect where they lead. With theorists such as Ahmed and Cvetkovich, I will find "happiness," "depression," "mania," "hope," "worry," "rage," and "madness" interesting and not definitive. While some of these terms, particularly madness and depression, will seem interchangeable at times, at other times they will unfold in their fierce particularity. The terms *affect, emotion, feeling,* and *mood* will slip and slide, inhabiting similar and nonsingular meanings. Ultimately, they each refer back to how we come to be and know through the supposedly nonrational, though terms like *emotion* and *mood* more readily bring to mind the cultural production and policing of feeling than any preconscious sensory experience that affect occasionally implies.

For the purposes of the following project, the meaning of "depression" and "madness" in general and as hermeneutic lenses come primarily from the affect, crip, and neo-Marxist theories listed earlier, as well as my own felt experiences of the world. Following Cvetkovich, I argue that depression or madness must be depathologized and deindividualized. She argues that we can only deal with what we traditionally think of as "clinical" depression if we confront political depression; the one is never inconsequential to the other. Cvetkovich sees this endeavor as an opening to a different kind of utopia: "[a] utopia that doesn't make a simple distinction between good and bad feelings or assume that good politics can only emerge from good feelings; feeling bad might, in fact, be the ground of transformation."[37] In support of this suggestion, madness in these pages is a mode of approaching alternate utopian visions, those with counter-salvific and counter-redemptive sensibilities, and therefore carries theological weight; it can most concretely be defined as a state of being that refuses digestibility by the neoliberal machine and so marks its subjects as irredeemable and unprofitable. Madness is the mood of those ransomed for the construction of the good citizen and productive member of society. Additionally, depression and madness serve as my entree into a larger discourse within affect theory around "negative" feelings, or what I come to call mad feelings, and cannot be read as significantly unique or separate from theoretical engagements with boredom, disgust, melancholy, shame, and anxiety.

Taking a cue from McRuer and Mollow, who argue that compulsory heteronormativity is also compulsory able-bodiedness, I further suggest that heteronormativity is compulsory able-mindedness, and I argue that "madness" can become a kind of queer site of insight, desire, and resistance. Following such theorists, we might view madness temporally as a depressive impetus for a slowing down and deeper paying of attention as well as the manic hope that we might feel otherwise. Though sometimes tragically so, mad feelings, like depression, often manifest as extreme sensitivity to the world. Furthermore, even times of extreme de-sensitivity might provide key insights that help us to look critically at the often deadening or suppressing space of the affect economy. In short, moods of madness and maddening moods function here as diagnoses of how capitalism can feel on social and individual levels, counter visions of collectivity and utopia, sites of alternate desires and affectual flow, and embodiments of an agonistic politics and theology, all of which are formed through our poros-ity to one another and the rest of the becoming world.

Given madness's (and most prominently depression's) function in this project as an insight into how capitalism feels and as an embodiment of a politics and theology that refuses to "go with the flow" of society, it is important at this point to mark both my understanding of what that capi-talist flow is and which problems I hope to diagnose through my deploy-ment of such feelings. First, I understand these problems to significantly stem from capitalism's theological proposals. For instance, Joerg Rieger details the ways in which the neoliberal economic proposal that a rising tide will lift all boats is in fact a theological assertion. This rising-tide theology carries with it bold faith claims: that economic deregulations promote growth, that tax cuts for powerful corporations and the wealthy spur the economy, and that wealth gathered at the top eventually trickles down.[38] Assumptions about value and worth also stem from these claims. The equation of wealth with worth and a fundamentalist belief in a rising tide result in both the material and emotional marginalization of a major-ity of the world's people. Materially the prioritization of the accumulation of wealth at the top, along with the false conclusion that wealth at the top will provide for those at the bottom, has resulted in the economic and social disenfranchisement of whole communities. Emotionally, that one's worth is defined by neoliberal capitalism as proven through one's material gain, profitability, and socioeconomic prestige means that when the wealth does not trickle down, people not only are forced to struggle to meet their most basic needs, but also are assumed to be ontologically less than those at the top. Viewed from the perspective of an affect hermeneutic, one can explore not only how this marginalization feels, but also how it might be a source of resistance and transformation.

Further, the unwavering belief that neoliberal capitalism, if only we would learn to successfully play the game, will set us free nurtures both emotional and material oppression and depression. To reengage one's depression in resistant modes would be to sit with our feelings and ask where they came from and what insights they bring. Such an attention to this depression, one loosed from an anxious need to be cured, might help us to resist the neoliberal demand that we get over what has got us so down and open up alternatives for how we might live in counter-relation to hege-monic systems.

In finding each of these affects interesting and following where they may lead when we explore some of their entanglements with political theology and neoliberal economics, I hope to begin to shape both a hermeneutical approach and a theo-ethical response to such encounters. Such a hermeneutics would be an affect hermeneutics. It would be an approach to reading of text and world that would look for moments of emotional rupture, dissonance, and overflow within spaces overtly and subtly marked as emotional. For the purposes of this project, my affect hermeneutic will be particularly attuned to those affects we consider maddening or pathological and to the moody relations between those redeemed as good subjects and those ransomed for such redemption. I want to read for, listen to, and touch on those moments in which the given or expected mood of a text or situation is challenged by the mood of those who can neither accept what has been given nor rise to expectations.

In reading for such moodiness—the moodiness of not being in the mood—I am also seeking out and offering up a theo-ethical response to such moods. I name such a response *grave attending*. Grave attending is a caring for the gravity, the pulling down to the material world, the listening and feeling for what all its myriad emotions have to tell us and where they have to lead us. It is also a witnessing to those identities, collectivities, and possibilities assumed to be buried over and gone, the ghosts that haunt us and so gift us a sense of what we might have been and an imagination of what we might become. Acts of grave attention refuse to efface the material mattering of others on the way to our own redemption. Such a grave attending is an attention to the lamenting cries (those released in word and affect) of those who have been crucified by neoliberalism and its concomitant heteropatriarchal, ableist, and white supremacist ethics. As such, theologically speaking, grave attending is what happens on Holy Saturday, on the day between crucifixion and resurrection. It is a style of life that does not look or wait for resurrection as much as it tries to remain with a difference on the day after damage and death. It does not and cannot rush toward redemption out of the gravity of such damage, because it is attendant to the damage of those who, in the wake of our resurrective impulse, we have let drown. To not resurrect might be to fail to overcome our damage. And yet a theo-ethic of grave attending affirms that in resistance to such a successful raising up, we are brought down to be together with all the others who have failed to be redeemed. There is hope, and even joy, in the remaining in that there is a thirst for all of life.

Each chapter functions as a thought experiment or scene of interpretation, not a linear narrative. While the chapters are, of course, consequent to one another they can also be read independently as vignettes of how an affect hermeneutic and a political theology of grave attention might feel and what it might do. Most particularly, I surmise that in looking for the

pains inflicted by problematic pulses in these discourses we might feel for
critical alternatives not in spite of feeling bad, but creatively through such
sensitive attunement and attending. This book does not glorify suffering,
nor is it convinced that rehabilitation out of our damage is salvific. It seeks
to attend to what might come when we feel our way around, through, and
beside myriad pain and pleasure.

Thus, each chapter brings together thinkers of affect (broadly conceived)
with political, radical, and postmodern theologians to see what might happen when we read for the mood and modes of such encounters. Chapter 2,
"Unsaved Time," explores the temporal structures nurtured by the eschatological and counter-eschatological orientations within orthodox and
democratic radical theologies. It then places such temporalities into dialogue with: Shelly Rambo's Holy Saturday theology; the queer temporalities of Heather Love, José Muñoz, and Elizabeth Freeman; and Robin
James's feminist critique of resilience. From this dialogue I construct the
concept of bipolar time as a Saturday and mad resistance to neoliberal
time. Chapter 3, "Unproductive Worth," reads with the autonomism of
Berardi, the political and quotidian depression of Cvetkovich, and a disability poetics in order to challenge both neoliberal and more progressive
(the latter represented in this chapter by Hardt and Negri and their theological deployment by Joerg Rieger and Kwok Pui Lan) productivist theologies that tie our worth to our work. Chapter 4, "Unwilling Feeling,"
reads John D. Caputo's material theology and his conception of the insistence of God alongside Sara Ahmed's work on affect alienation and willfulness to offer biblical scenes of affect alien prophets. Jonah and Martha
embody such moody prophecy in this scene. The chapter applies and constructs an affect hermeneutic to and with biblical texts and reads for what
might happen when we follow moodiness to unexpected theological conclusions. Chapter 5, "Unreasoned Care," returns us to God through a
sojourn with Foucault's archives. This chapter takes on an alternate mood
to the previous ones. Instead of staging scenes of encounter between a
hermeneutic of affect and political theology, Chapter 5 begins a theological construction attendant to the moods of madness raised by the affect
alien prophets that populate previous chapters. Hence, Chapter 5 attends
to how the Process God as Eros of the Universe might open us to a nonre-
demptive or counter-salvific and yet ethically attentive theology that sticks
with the mad we've condemned, confined, and left unredeemed. Chapter
6, "Unattended Affects," concludes by asking to which affects and archives
my own political theology has not yet trustily attended. Engaging Black
studies and Black political theology, most particularly in the work of Fred

Moten, Christina Sharpe, and Kelly Brown Douglas, the concluding chapter draws a picture of how a political theology of the unredeemed might take shape when it gravely attends to the spaces of blackness unwilling to participate in the making proper on offer by white supremacy. The conclusion acts as a scene of lament against white redemption and offers a grave attention to the bad credit earned by political theologies and theologians too narrowly grounded in Anglo-American and European thinkers and definitions of the human, the holy, and wholeness. Ultimately, it asks what it would mean to put the proposals in the chapters into action at the sites of today's most violent practices of redemption and its most promising spaces of unredemption. Following the work of Moten and Sharpe, I argue that it is in the unattended affects, those left open by the unpaid debt of whiteness to blackness, where a political theology of and for the unredeemed might take its most forceful shape. Surmising that our inability to sit with individual and collective guilt over these debts is, in part, what stands in the way of societal transformation, I offer in this conclusion grave attending as witness and resistance to these sites of cheap and violent redemption. Ultimately, grave attending requires an accounting by the redeemed while refusing an erasure of difference. The concluding chapter asks us to remain willfully unredeemed as long as our redemption is bought through the effacement of others.

At their heart, these scenes are of moody lament, demanding our attention, gifting us different theological moods and modes.

CHAPTER 2

Unsaved Time

In *The Theology of Money*, Phillip Goodchild warns of the "eschatological judgment of money." Money defines value and, through its promissory nature (as in the promise that "*One day* I will have enough money," or in other words, "*One day* I will finally be enough,"), money holds us in suspense of achieving worth. The sovereignty of money fortifies an eschatological hope akin to what Lauren Berlant has diagnosed as cruel optimism: "A relation of cruel optimism exists when something you desire is actually an obstacle to your flourishing."[1] We desire to be happier through our wealth, so we work as hard as possible, leaving little time for moments of flourishing in the present. Or, horrifically, we work ourselves to death before any happy goal could ever be reached. The question of the *moneyed eschaton* leads us to apocalyptic ponderings. Is there an end to capitalism? Does capitalism have an end time, an eschatological climax—the apex of which we might be nearing? Does capitalism have an end goal, a telos toward which it strives? Or, on the contrary, does it presume endless progress, no end in sight, the Kingdom always deferred? Further, what does it mean to live in the *time* of twenty-first century neoliberal economics? What are the "signs" (mores, theologies, moods) of our time? *And*, under what constructs of temporality do we labor? Questions of ends, times, and end-times have been at the forefront of contemporary political theology.

According to Goodchild, under neoliberalism, *spending time is subordinated to saving it*,[2] for, if as the saying goes, "time is money," then we have to "use our time wisely" by saving as much of it as possible. Hours need to be spent productively, meaning profitably. We wear Bluetooth headsets to the playground so that family time is also work time. We never saunter errands; we run them. No one ever says "You wouldn't believe what a great uni-tasker Becky is!" Conversely, spending time—to play, to make love, to just be—places us into debt. To spend time unproductively, neoliberalism tells us, is to have "wasted our time." Hence, even as we are held in suspense of the moneyed eschaton—held captive to the promise that one day we will be saved from our wretched state and transformed into one of financial worth—we must be ever more efficient producers of promised wealth. By promising its fulfillment in a nearly unattainable state of future wealth, the eschatological judgment of money holds our flourishing at bay.

Political theologians have sought to counter this eschatalogy.[3] Radical orthodox (RO) theologians propose a return to the Christian Kingdom. Others, known as radical theologians (RT), propose the eventiveness of the multitude, or an in-breaking of democratic potentiality.[4] Yet it remains for theology to address how post-Fordist temporalities *feel*, by which I mean how the material weight of such a temporal structure rests cruelly on some bodies and psyches more than others. To take the material affects and effects of such a time seriously might open up possibilities for embodying a different *sense* of time. While this project is not ethnographic in nature— it does not rely on observations of particular communities and their engagement with neoliberalism—it is my contention that queer theories of affect and temporality, those written by and attuned to the bodies and subjectivities out of joint and bent down by the *time* of neoliberal economics, can help us to take seriously what such material effects have meant. As touched on briefly in the introduction, contemporary queer theory has moved well beyond an exclusive focus on sex, gender, and sexuality. Current discourses on queer temporality seek to examine the ways in which heteronormativity and white supremacy fortify the neoliberal political economy. Many queer theorists uncover the resonance between the demand to be a productive member of society and the manipulated desire to be a reproductive member of the heteronormative family. Such demands nurture in us an optimistic belief that the straighter and whiter we become, the happier we will be. This cruelly optimistic promise (to borrow from Berlant) impedes alternate desires of community, family, and self.

The effects of such cruelly optimistic demands must be of critical importance to theologians who take seriously the question of how we might ethically spend time instead of obsessively saving it. Although I affirm Goodchild's diagnosis of the moneyed eschaton, there is still more to ask of political theologians and the alternatives they offer to the hold on us that this eschatological promise has. Hence, I trace the following framing contentions throughout this chapter. First, I propose that the field of political theology, in its radical orthodox and radical theological forms, while addressing neoliberal structures of value, still contains problematic universal claims *and* anemic concepts that seem to elide the effects neoliberalism has on marginalized subjects, psyches, and collectivities. Hence, although certain theologies in this field, particularly those in the RT camp, provide fertile ground from which to ask these questions, more seeds need to be sowed. Second, I surmise that both the fertile potential within and the more barren grounds of political theology can be brought to light in an examination of the different approaches to temporality undertaken by radical orthodox and radical theologians. Third, I suggest that although queer theory sometimes mirrors some of the same contentious issues found in political theological debates, queer approaches to temporality and affect offer invaluable resources for a political theology that takes seriously embodied consequences of neoliberalism. In particular, we might learn from subjects whose temporal and affectual orientations impede productivity and efficiency. This suggestion is further elaborated in Chapter 3. Finally, through an engagement with queer theories of temporality and affect, as well as theologies of Holy Saturday, I propose the concept of bipolar time as a temporal reorientation that resists the eschatological demands of neoliberalism.

It is my hope that bipolar time will reorient us toward different modes of feeling and living. These modes (the thinking of which is begun here and continued in subsequent chapters) do not offer resurrection out of the pain of neoliberalism from which we might come to be its productive agents once more: happy customers and efficient laborers. Nor does bipolar time offer a nihilistic acceptance of the pains endured in the quotidian crucifixions perpetrated in service of neoliberalism's cruelly optimistic promise. Depression is not crucifixion. Mania is not resurrection. The *bi*furcation of bipolarity cannot be viewed as separable states of being or linear modes of becoming. *Bipolar temporality* is disordered temporality. Manic stages are haunted by depressive ones. In depressive stages one might feel the pressure of what mania has done and can do. There is no clear linear narrative from one to the next. Further, bipolarity, as embodied by states of extreme feeling—extreme dullness, despair, rapidity, and creativity—impedes demands to get over it, to move on, to save time. In disordering time, bipolar sensibilities disrupt a crucifixion/resurrection binary because they reveal how states of both self-shattering and of self-inflating interpenetrate one another. Ultimately, this chapter begins the ongoing question of the book: How might embracing our moods of disorder challenge the econo-political and theological orders of the day?

Perhaps it is in the complex and affectual interplay of past, present, and future, as found in the work of Heather Love, Robin James, Elizabeth Freeman, and José Esteban Muñoz, that we might encounter a counter-capitalist hope more attentive to the experiences of those marked as irredeemable by neoliberal salvation narratives. This queer supplement takes on its theological weight in this chapter's constructive comparison between queer temporalities and the temporality of Holy Saturday, as explicated in Shelly Rambo's *Spirit and Trauma: A Theology of Remaining*. From the theological ground cleared by a reading of queer time as Holy Saturday time, I propose bipolar temporality as a sensibility that helps us to live into the day after crucifixion, taking seriously what form (temporal, spatial, and sensorial) hope might take when we accept that a resurrection may not be needed, wanted, or coming. Bipolar time, as a time that hovers between the depression of a crucified world and a manic belief that the world as it stands need not be all there is, is offered in resistance to teleologies that rely on stable Christian origins and certain eschatological ends *and* as a corrective to theologies that often imply an active temporal pull toward the future while regularly eliding the material hold the past and present have in the midst of such a pull.

Radical Theologies of Our Time

For both radical orthodox and radical theologians, the temporality of the event is key for political and theological questions of sovereignty. According to RO's standard-bearer John Milbank, "The Church is the most fundamental of events, interpreting all other events."[5] For Milbank, the seemingly uniform Christian Church becomes the standard by which all other historical events must be judged. Here Milbank is proposing a very particular concept of time. He critiques an eventive temporality, one which instead of moving forward toward a certain end goal, is animated by and structured through the often eruptive, fractured, and discontinuous movement of the immanent world. Such a discontinuous temporality is one, for example, embraced by radical theologians such as Clayton Crockett and

Jeffrey W. Robbins and their interlocutors, Gilles Deleuze and Antonio
Negri, in *Radical Political Theology: Religion and Politics after Liberalism* and
Radical Democracy and Political Theology, respectively. In his critique of what
he refers to as the *philosophers of nihilism*, Milbank writes:

> What matters is the objective surface presence of a teleological order-
> ing where intention of a goal shows up in visible structure. . . . Of
> course one can still see phenomenal drag of effect upon causes as infi-
> nitely wild and interminable, rather than properly teleological. This is
> Deleuze's path, which a Christian ontology must clearly refuse.[6]

For Milbank this Deleuzian time is a "directionless time" and, as such,
cannot be accepted by a truly Christian ontology, one necessarily predicated on a sense of the particular good of Christianity as transcendent and
universal.

For RO more broadly, a teleological ordering modeled by the event of
the Church implies a temporal pull toward a historical given or providential plan. Milbank's understanding of the all-interpreting-event of the
church is a statement against both an open-ended future and an uncontain-
able past. In other words, instead of modeling its sociology after its theology, liberal Christianity names the sociopolitical as theology and begins to
model its theology after its sociology. Further, for Milbank, without reference to the supernatural, society fails to speak concretely of the human
because it fails to grasp the human's "most fundamental aspect, which is
precisely [our] relation to a transcendent, final cause."[7] The transcendent,
final cause allows us to understand the human being in its concreteness in
that we come to understand the purpose of our lives. Locating salvation in
the Ecclesia becomes the rationale for viewing the Church as that event
which interprets all other events. If salvation must be thought of as concrete and particular and can only happen through the Church, which is
oriented to a certain Christian past and a promised Christian future, then
the event of the church dictates a spatiotemporal reality in which you
either make it on time and at the right stop or you miss the train altogether.
No salvation for you, not there, not then, not now.[8]

Additionally, any reading of RO as a theology that resists this totalizing
narrative occludes Milbank's more exclusionary instincts. He writes:
"Against difference, by contrast, I do not bring forward dialectics, nor even
virtue in general, but rather Christian virtue in particular, which means
that *I can claim to be the more serious advocate of the conjunction of the univer-
sally objective with a particular social option.*"[9] To be a more serious advocate
is crucial in the formation of Milbank's ideology. If one is to make the

universal Good concrete, one cannot choose a multiplicity of paths toward this Good; this would not be to take seriously what it is to be properly theological or sociological. To take the message of the incarnation seriously is to see that the path toward the universal Good comes only through the particular incarnation of God in Christ.

Hence, the anti-democratic implications in Milbank's thinking and its internal inconsistencies nurture the need for a different type of radical theology, one suited to a world full of more multiplicity than for which Milbank makes room. Although Milbank spends pages on particularity and the need to turn back to the particular relations created by the incarnation, his is a concept of the particular (one particular particular) as the universal. Milbank's reading of the Church as the event that dictates the shape of human history, and so of time, is essentially and unapologetically exclusivist. His "event" excludes those outside or not welcomed into the church, but so too does it exclude the potential in-breaking of temporal and affectual possibilities yet unimagined in *this* universal/particular Christian narrative.

Democratic Events as Temporal Alternatives

A more democratic theology must resist turning one particular particular into the universal. Indeed, for Crockett and Robbins, in contrast to Milbank, the event is that which precisely cannot be interpreted by uniform and imperial structures demanding obedience. For instance, in his reading of Negri, Robbins argues:

> The political potency that is key to radical democracy's resistance to all forms of hegemony comes not by a way of transcendent authority— by an appeal to some power outside ourselves—but by way of an exodus emanating from within: "In Postmodernity," Negri writes, "the eminent form of rebellion is the exodus from obedience, that is to say, from participation in measure, i.e. as the opening to the immeasurable."[10]

We can understand this reading of exodus as an example of democratic temporality. To move from "participation in measure" to the opening of the immeasurable is the movement from a providential time—one that can be measured by proper eschatalogical ends radiating from certain Christological beginnings—to an open-ended future, one beyond measure and therefore beyond absolute consciousness, control, or conformity. Here, contra Milbank, Robbins illuminates how the temporality of a more radically open concept of event changes the mode of sovereignty implied in the political theology that follows. For Robbins, an opening to the immeasurable is a refutation of Milbank's understanding that the all-interpreting event is that of the Church. This exodus is a "creative event," and so an exodus that does not flee toward a particular salvific end. It is a rewriting of teleology and so temporality.

In *Radical Political Theology*, Clayton Crockett proposes a similar reimagining of sovereignty, one found in a theology written in the wake of the death-of-God. Crockett employs Deleuze's concept of the event as that which goes beyond the law and which the law cannot predict to propose a political theology written from a space and time of responsiveness as opposed to one of Providence.[11] It is precisely in the infinitely wild and indeterminate character of Deleuze's event worried over by Milbank that Crockett finds democratic potential. For Crockett, the event is a rupture into a world that can no longer be viewed as stable, particularly in the wake of the death of the kind of transcendental ontotheological God invoked by RO theologians.

This democratic turn toward the event in terms of temporality is further explored in Crockett's constructive applications of Deleuze's conception of time in *Cinema II: The Time Image*. According to Crockett:

> Deleuze is not interested in developing a metaphysical understanding of time as unchanging eternity; he is interested in building a brain. Building a brain involves producing the event as time-image, a pure image of time that cuts entities away from their automatic sensory-motor linkages and reconstitutes them in another series or another order.[12]

To build a brain is to reconstruct a concept of time as responsive, such that time finds cracks in history that break open new possibilities. Deleuze is not interested in a teleologically ordered and predetermined history. Rather, he is interested in what happens when we realize that this progressive History is no longer a viable way to view time in the world.[13] Deleuze finds these cracks or cuts that serve as temporal openings exemplified in forms of political cinema in which "the cinematographic image becomes a direct presentation of time, according to noncommensurable relations and irrational cuts. . . . [T]his time-image puts thought into contact with an unthought, the unsummonable, the inexplicable, the undecideable, the incommensurable."[14] This image of time in which one can no longer trace a universal line or procession from old to new opens up a politics in which one can ask whether the story, as it stands now, and its end were inevitable.

Asking this question might spark others including: Whose stories have gone and go untold when one universal narrative is assumed to be natural, virtuous, or given?

For Deleuze, cinema which exposes the inconsistencies found when moving away from a relation of direct association to one of cuts and fissures, which results in an incommensurability revealed when old and new are juxtaposed, "makes up an absurdity," which is also the "form of aberration."[15] This aberration, or absurdity, is what calls into question the progressive temporality that has worked to disappear from history those who refuse to or cannot toe the line. Hence, modern political cinema is a politics of "putting into crisis,"[16] but it is this crisis that reminds us that time need not be what we think it is; time itself contains more potential. The march of History is not inevitable; there can be new twists in the tale, or new chances to become differently.

If History is not inevitable, if it is loosed from the stable teleology on offer by RO, then options for our becoming that had been silenced and effaced in the past might resurface and haunt both our present and future. Indeed, for Crockett, via Deleuze, the possibility of the event is the opening in time for the radicalization of democracy. Such a radicalization would take, Crockett proposes, an impossible future that is not a clear temporal extension of the present, but rather exists in the shadow of an "unforeseen event."[17] This possibility radicalizes democracy by reminding us that there must always be more democracy to come.[18] Crockett, following Deleuze, suggests that a time-image puts us into contact with the unthought and so contributes to the invention not only of a people, but also of new ways of thinking time and democracy.[19] For instance, in locating this type of eventive time in Haitian social movements, Crockett argues that when Haiti's first Democratically elected president, Jean-Betrand Aristide, spoke of democratizing Democracy, he was tapping into the potential of the Deleuzian time-image: "Democracy is not based upon a present arrangement or explicit state of affairs, but is predicated on justice and freedom, which are technically incalculable and exceed any and all determinate horizons."[20] To extend all determinate horizons is to challenge the certainty of orthodox Christian origins and ends; it is to ask us to live in such a way that the unforeseen of the future allows for new visions of the present.

It is clear that the event as the unforeseen that allows for an impossible future and an exodus from obedience is a radically different event from that of the Church and its future as proposed by Milbank. This difference revolves not only around the very constructs of time, but also around the definition of freedom.

Free from or Free for Capitalism?

Although their methods and conclusions greatly diverge both RO and RT,
theologians seek to challenge neoliberal constructs of value. I find the manner of challenge undertaken and the conclusions drawn by RTs more
convincing and in greater sympathy with the values purported here. And
yet I am left wondering, in terms of each school's concept of temporality,
whether there remain problematic resonances with capitalistic structures of
time. How might the structure of indebtedness to Christ, upheld by RO
theologians, resonate with, if unintentionally so, indebtedness to the Market? How might concepts of plasticity, exodus, and event, while helpfully
resisting oppressive teleologies, risk falling prey to neoliberal values of
flexibility, resilience, and rehabilitative change? These questions frame the
following sections and are helpfully supplemented and challenged through
an engagement with queer theory.

According to most RO theologians, liberal theologies too easily lend
themselves to the free-play of desire viewed as characteristic of capitalism.
For instance, William T. Cavanaugh has argued that true freedom is not
found in the free-floating desire-without-ends of capitalism, but rather in
the freedom to choose obedience to Christ over the Market.[21] His critique
of an untethered desire is emblematic of the issue of desire found in RO
writings. In a chapter on negative and positive freedom, in his *Being Consumed: Economics and Christian Desire*, Cavanaugh argues that the key
theological question for a free market system is: What makes an exchange
free? Deploying a very particular reading of Augustine, Cavanaugh suggests that, unlike the assertion of neoliberal economics that sees freedom
as freedom from interference by others (most prominently the State), true
freedom comes in the freedom to choose one's *proper* desires. Here *proper*
means orthodox Christian desires. Therefore, to ask if an exchange is free
is to ask if the exchange represents an end that is commensurate with the
values of RO's particularized universal Christian God/Good. For Cavanaugh, most desires in the free market are restless desires with indeterminate
ends, and hence sinful.

But is there really no determination to capitalist desire? In other words,
is there no goal, no "good" toward which a faith in the Market is oriented?
Is capitalistic freedom free of the regulations of progressive History and
imperial demands? Let us return to the opening questions of this chapter.
What is the time of neoliberal capitalism? Or rather what is the arc of its
time? What does it mean to be held in suspense of the moneyed eschaton?

Looking again to Berlant, we can note how a focus on a particular end goal or grounding value assumption, which we are told is given, inevitable, and righteous, can cause not only cruelty, but also psychological and physical death. The cruelty of the promissory structure of the closed-telos goes unquestioned by Milbank and his fellows. Berlant, therefore, is an instructive interlocutor. In her chapter on "slow death," Berlant analyzes how bodies are worn down by the optimistic promises that fortify demands to work for a living, or in other words, the tying together of work, wealth, and worth. The producers of such demands rely on the goals of work being nearly, if always, unattainable. Slow death "refers to the physical wearing out of a population that points to its deterioration as a defining condition of its experience and historical existence."[22] This wearing out happens at the confluence of a matrix of oppressions in which one's racial, economic, gendered, and sexual histories and identities are shaped by and reflected in: the availability of jobs, the reliability of schedules, the mobility of wages, the nurturing of diets, and significantly the flexibility of time. For example, the demand to be healthy, while faced with systematized obstacles, most particularly the lack of *freedom of time* and access to mechanisms of health (nutritious food, clean air), makes health a problematically normativizing concept.[23] Radical theologians of all bents have fallen short of analyzing how it is not just what the goal is—wealth, happiness, whiteness, heterosexuality, able-bodiedness—but also the exclusive character of particular goals made into universals that cause a cruel limiting of options for our present flourishing. This does not mean we seek out a valueless society, but rather one that admits to its own occlusions, and looks out for those it has deemed invaluable.

Our orientation to a promised telos—of the moneyed, healthy, and "Good" life—can prevent our flourishing in ways that impede the possibilities sought for by Crockett's sense of a time lived in the shadow of an unforeseen event. Additionally, this structure of death from within the temporal flow of neoliberal capitalism is not always slow. Here we might recall the August 2014 tragic death of Maria Fernandes. Fernandes worked four jobs. One afternoon, likely exhausted, she pulled over to take a nap in her car in between shifts. The combination of a spilled gas container (which she kept in her car) and fumes from the running car killed the sleeping thirty-two-year-old. This moment of rapid death, one brought on by Fernandes's attempt not necessarily at the good life, but at *any* life—the attempt to make ends meet—began before that August afternoon. The eschatological judgment of money was already in the process of claiming another life.

In this way the problem of capitalistic desire may not be its free-floating nature, but rather its very particular, yet unreachable, telos. To be sure, one might argue that if we would just reorient to the right end, the right future, we would not be working, eating, and fighting each other to death. But as Berlant has noted, it is not just what we are oriented toward that does violence to our present and future selves, but the ways in which the processes of orientation imply value judgments in terms of what types of bodies and modes of living are worthy of orientation.

For instance, looking to RO theologies of the Eucharist, Steven Shakespeare argues:

> The attempt to save the world ends up by condemning the world outside a few Christian enclaves to darkness. But even within those enclaves, the desire for God is so identified and fueled by a desire for immediate connection provided by the Eucharist that it turns into a desperate parody of capitalistic desire. The Eucharist becomes the object to end all objects, the ultimate commodity to satisfy our lack. It becomes an addiction.[24]

The optimistic objects offered up by the "good life"—a big house, a flush back account, a spouse of the "opposite" gender, two able-bodied children, and a profession—mirror this Eucharistic addiction. Instead of living, we consume in a manner that closes off alternate possibilities of life in favor of the certainty of our orientations. Hence, even while they refuse a capitalist structure of value, RO cannot get out of its own parodic way. The fact that its method resonates so deeply with that of the system it claims to be countering unravels the proposal that it is only through the enslavement to proper ends that we might break the chains of propertied ones. Additionally, as Steven Shakespeare further notes, RO's forceful projection of *one* truth has enchained all other concepts of truth into warfare with it.[25] The imperialistic tendencies of RO reflect those of global capitalism in ways that prevent it from fully countering such neoliberal systems of belief.

Evidence of the commonality of effects of such a temporal orientation (one structured around Predestination and Providence) between that of an orthodox Christian Kingdom and that of the Neoliberal Market are not inconsequential. We can see similar commonalities in William Connolly's concept of the Evangelical-Capitalistic Resonance Machine (ECRM). The ECRM is bound together by shared fundamentalist faiths: The belief in an omnipotent God resonates with that of an omnipotent Market. As this relation is amplified, the machine becomes increasingly invested in the stabilizing force of the Christian-family-erotic assemblage:

> The radical Christian right *compensates* a series of class resentments and injustices produced by the collision between cowboy capitalism and critical social movements by promising solace in the church and the family; it then cements (male) capitalist creativity to the creativity of God himself, fomenting an *aspirational politics* of identification by workers with men of prowess and privilege; these self-identifications and compensatory entitlements then encourage those sweltering in the pressure cooker to demonize selected minorities as nomadic enemies of capitalism, God, morality, and civilizational discipline.[26]

Although Milbank might refuse an association with the sort of Evangelical Christian who practices this unwavering faith in the Market, and although he would sharply critique Evangelicalism for its lack of sacramental unifying practice, the results of such a faith mimic the exclusions proffered by Radical Orthodoxy. Milbank takes aim at nomadic enemies of *his* definition of the Christian Good. One can take solace in Milbank's church, which proclaims to be a solution to the ills suffered under neoliberalism, but which perpetuates violent exclusions of some of the same minorities that Evangelical Christian resentment vilifies.

Besides its exclusionary nature, the return to orthodoxy sought by RO theology feeds into what Connolly has diagnosed as an impossible dream: "Both religious and economic fundamentalists dream an impossible dream of a world of simplicity in which complete redemption is possible, overseen by a rational and dependable God."[27] This possible redemption is, in part, an impossible dream because of the very exclusionary practices set forth by both RO Christianity and Market Fundamentalism. Neoliberalism relies on keeping the majority of the population in states of precarity in order for those at the top to maximize their share of the market. What Naomi Klein has named "disaster capitalism," functions in this exclusionary way. In order for investors in disaster capitalism (the architects of subprime mortgage lending for example) to reach their promised wealth others must be put into crisis.[28] For certain people to rise to the top, others must fall. Further, capitalism's handmaidens—heteronormativity and white supremacy—rely on the making of exclusions of people of color and queer folk (an issue to which we return in a moment). Capitalism's elect rely on those who cannot rise through the ranks of wealth to keep producing wealth for those at the top without redistributing it. Heteronormativity's power relies on the exclusion of those who do not hold the nuclear family as the arbiter of value. White supremacy relies on dehumanizing people of color and placing boundaries around who can "overcome" their race.

Therefore, we are in need of a different dream, of a different structure of temporality—one resistant to a closed and determinate telos. Reading Robbins, we might say that we need a time of exodus from such cruelly optimistic systems. But just how free are we each able to get? How might we recognize how this sense of the immeasurable and of exodus are radically felt and experienced differently, particularly by those in the process of fleeing? Indeed, to better understand the consequences of such a democratic time we will need to investigate how this immeasurability *feels* for those choosing to or forced to flee, *and* we will need to problematize the linearity that an act of fleeing might imply. To do so, we must turn to theories undertaken by those who were never supposed to count in the first place—those on whose effacement Western philosophical concepts of freedom were built. Here such theories will come from queer and feminist work on affect and time (in Chapter 6 we look to Black studies for insights into such questions of capture and flight). Although the event as radical exodus may embrace a future without ends, can it also sensitively contain a past-without-measure? Further, will we be able to or wish to fully flee such a past? In other words, can we embrace the potential in an immeasurable exodus without eclipsing the mattering of our often measured, material lives?

While exodus as a concept does not necessarily preclude sensitive attention to the past, a focus on the flight of the immeasurable as though everyday matters can be eclipsed in favor of what comes next might prevent us from attending to the conditions that allow some more than others a greater chance of flight, and which dictate the options of to where we might be fleeing. Further, although it resists the programmatic nature of time as illuminated by Milbank, does radical theology's sense of freedom also lend itself to an ungrounded desire that might hinder a sensitive engagement with the strictures of captivity and those of resistance found not in the productivity of the event, the action of exodus, but in the refusal of the productivity of a time-in-action? This is a question that will be more forcefully engaged in the chapters that follow, but for now perhaps we can begin a search for structures of temporality that waver between action and passivity. Left in the shadow of the moneyed eschaton and the wake of the uniform Church, we can look to temporal sensibilities that find their potential in the equivocacy between capture and flight, obedience and openness. This equivocacy can be found and provoked in theological constructions of Holy Saturday and those in queer engagement with temporality, to which we now turn.

Queer Time: No Day but Today?

Queerness is also a performative because it is not simply a being but a doing for and toward a future. Queerness is essentially about the rejection of a here and now and an insistence on potentiality or concrete possibility for another world.

José Esteban Muñoz,
Cruising Utopia: The Then and There of Queer Futurity

Despite my concern that the radical democratic concept of the immeasurable, even in its best intention, might elide issues of history and everyday embodiment, it does help us to destabilize false universals. RT temporality, in its lack of measure, might make room for those, like the queer Christian, who do not fit into neatly measured categories. Indeed, if we were to replace the word "queerness" in this section's epigraph from Muñoz[29] with "event" such that it became "the event is essentially about the rejection of a here and now and an insistence on potentiality or concrete possibility for another world," we would strike at the heart of radical democratic temporality. Drawing on the work of Ernst Bloch, Muñoz locates concrete utopian performance in queer subcultures. Such queer collectivities provide an alternative vision of how one could (harkening back to Goodchild) spend time over saving it.

Counter to queer thinkers of the so-called antisocial turn, or queer negativity, Muñoz proposed the concrete performance of hope from within queer sociality. He saw the future as integral to the queer imaginary: "Queerness is a structuring and educated mode of desiring that allows us to see and feel beyond the quagmire of the present."[30] For Muñoz, queerness—as not only a sexual identity, but more so a marker of non-normate desires and a critical stance toward normative society—is "that thing that lets us feel that this world is not enough, that indeed something is missing."[31] The very utopian thinking that allowed Muñoz to imagine something beyond the quagmire of the present might be proof for thinkers of queer negativity that we find it impossible to think politics without what Lee Edelman finds to be an oppressive future promissory. Yet temporality in *Cruising Utopia* is more complicated. Drawing on Bloch, Muñoz asserts that "in our everyday life abstract utopias are akin to banal optimism. . . . Concrete utopias are the realm of educated hope."[32] For a utopia to be concrete, it must not merely be one of future vision—one that might trap you not only in banal optimism, but, worse, in cruel optimism. Rather, concrete utopias must be performed in the present. It is in this sense of presentist performance that we begin to see an alternate way between theological elisions of persisting pasts, or open futures.

The concreteness of hope in Muñoz's work keeps the importance of everyday embodiments at the fore of political thought. Hence, placing Muñoz into dialogue with radical theology, we might insist on the potency of quotidian queerness (its fleshy attention to past, present, and future) as a key supplement to concepts of event, immeasurability, and exodus that would benefit from attention to myriad affecting histories that shape our orientations to such narratives of flight. For instance, although I find it hard to *touch* on how exactly an exodus from obedience and an opening to the immeasurable looks and feels, I can imagine getting physically lost and loosed from my chains on the dance floors where Muñoz wishes to take ecstasy with me. I can vibrate with the screams of Vaginal Crème Davis in the drag punk bar as she helps undo any sense of stable separation between my pleasure and my pain.[33] As discussed further below, with Ann Cvetkovich I might caress the crocheted sides of artist Alison Mitchell's "Hungry Purse" and slip into a sense of being together with others gathered in the art piece and with the material threads that encompass us.[34] And with Elizabeth Freeman I might tremble with expectation—time finally slowing down to the point where it is pleasurably unproductive—as I wait to be dominated in the S/M club.[35] From within these performances—ones in which one is still both here in the present and feeling their way through a dream of a different past, which might have been, and in a different future, which might still be—binaries between past and future, crucifixion and resurrection, and pain and pleasure begin to crack under the weight of both the immeasurable and the particular affects of our time. Further, the concrete utopias found in the work of Muñoz, because they are enacted by collectives of people in the present, are textured with histories and bodies that confront and are confronted by moments of inscriptional violence. Hence, these utopias contain the undeniable potency of *feeling* that comes from being out of joint with the temporal and emotional demands of neoliberalism.

Although I am uncertain of the ability for radical theology's conceptions of event to sensitively attend to particular moody histories, the utopic time proposed by Muñoz is reflective of Crockett's understanding of the present allowed for by a Deleuzian event. Constituted from within the shadow of an unforeseen event, this present escapes a sense of inevitability dictated by a containable past and a predestined future. The shadow of the unforeseen event might be, in Muñoz's terms, the queerness that lets us know this is not all there is; the unforeseen event provides space for a different dream of the present—a democratizing of democracy. Although it may not be obvious how the punk rock drag show or the singing of cover songs inside a feminist art installation is a democratizing of democracy (if we are to take seriously the utopic sensibility of Muñoz's concrete performances of community), we see how the creation of lifeworlds and dreamscapes within quotidian expressions of our entangled yet singular selves democratizes the availability of flourishing for myriad desires and embodiments in the present. This is not a grand political program, but rather the performance of how life under a democracy-to-come might look and feel. It is a democratizing of the options of spending time over saving it, and the explosion of possibilities of which feelings might be welcomed and nurtured in such acts of spending.

Might there be a theological grounding that helps us to spend this time? Where are the acts of theological attention that counter the cruelly optimistic promise on offer by neoliberal redemption narratives? Can we theologically witness the damage done by such a narrative without nihilistically giving in to such damage—a time between our quotidian crucifixions and seeming impossible resurrections?

The time of Holy Saturday, as proposed by Shelly Rambo in *Spirit and Trauma*, can help us to touch a persisting past. Exploring a Saturday temporality can bring us back to queer theory through a new theological lens, one which looks not only to what might come next, but more particularly to what remains in the wake of traumatized pasts and uncertain futures. This strain of queer and feminist theory, represented here in the work of Heather Love, Robin James, and Elizabeth Freeman, clears pathways toward what I come to call bipolar temporality.

Holy Presence of Past and Future

According to Shelly Rambo, "In the aftermath of trauma, death and life no longer stand in opposition. Instead death haunts life."[36] Rambo looks to what remains in the time between crucifixion and resurrection, the experience of witnessing to what remains of life, which is an encounter with what is not recognizable. This encounter involves the interplay of the senses in an attempt to find one's way.[37] Following Rambo, we can ask: What if the temporality of the post-Fordist moment is one of Holy Saturday—a day lived in the wake of crucifixion and the shadow of an uncertain resurrection? The wake of a failed American dream and the shadow of fractured revolutions? Indeed, might we be living in a moment reflective of a life haunted by death? And if so, how does this Holy Saturday *feel?* Or rather, where within our own lives might we locate a sense of Holy Saturday? Might Holy Saturday be a more apt descriptor of how most of us remain in the face of our quotidian crucifixions, when flight is either not on offer or not desired? For instance, in such states, even as we are beckoned forward, held cruelly captive to the promise that Sunday is coming, we feel ourselves pushed back, pulled asunder.

In constructing a Holy Saturday pneumatology, Rambo looks to the writings of Hans Urs von Balthasar, who was deeply influenced by his partner Adrienne von Speyr's mystical experiences with Jesus' descent into hell. Agreeing with Rambo that although Balthasar and Speyr construct a Holy Saturday that still relies too heavily on Sunday's redemption, I suggest there is great potential for the rethinking of temporality found in this work. For instance, Balthasar argued that the time of Holy Saturday describes an indecipherable time that resists a sense of mere waiting for the event of resurrection.[38] The time of Holy Saturday is a time out of joint or, reading with Deleuze, a crack in history. We might find similar Deleuzian resonances between political cinema's revelation that the people have been missing[39] and what Rambo describes as "The middle-day [as] the site of witness to the truths that are in danger of being covered over and buried."[40] As explored further in this chapter and in subsequent chapters, this refusal to be covered over is similarly demanded by paying greater attention—what I call grave attending—to bipolar time and disordered affect; bipolar time and disordered affect ask us to feel what it is to be that which neoliberalism has worked so hard to suppress.

Holy Saturday, as described in Speyr's mystical experiences, marks not a faith in redemption, but rather one of endurance. This is a persistence found in the space not of God's victory, but rather of God's abandonment.[41] The sense of what it is to live in the wake of crucifixion and the face of uncertain resurrection saturates Holy Saturday. The temporality of Rambo's "middle spirit" marks a crucial alternative to the binary between being locked in the narrative of the past and being held captive to a cruelly optimistic belief in a fully unchained new life. It resists both an overemphasis on an *active* exodus from the dead God and an unwavering faith in the new life promised but rarely, beyond the saved elite, provided by Milbank and Market orthodoxies. Holy Saturday time, as theorized by Rambo, favors instead a focus on the moodiness of a present where the binary between death and life no longer holds.

Lives lived under such a structuring of time and feeling may often be unproductive. Balthasar, recounting the experiences of Speyr, narrates the temporality of Holy Saturday as such:

It is a beginning without parallel, as if Life were arising from Death, as if weariness (already such weariness as no amount of sleep could ever dispel) and the uttermost decay of power were melting at creation's outer edge, were beginning to flow, because flowing is perhaps a sign and a likeness of weariness which can no longer contain itself, because everything that is strong and solid must in the end dissolve into water. But hadn't it—in the beginning—also been born from water? And is this wellspring in the chaos, this trickling weariness, not the beginning of a new creation?[42]

This is a present-future less evocative of the eruptive event of the multitude or that of the resurrection than with the quotidian process of feeling one's way through the weariness of a life penetrated by the past. It is a finding of flow from within the stuckness of those worn down to such a point that not even sleep is redemptive. It is a time not of stable beginnings and ends, but of watery wellsprings (manic life flows) and a trickling weariness (depressive attention to mortality). As Rambo notes, "This residue of love [that found between Father and Son even in utter abandonment] is not powerful but weary and impotent."[43] It is in this sense of Holy Saturday in which temporality shifts such that we no longer see utter despair in such impotence, but rather what remains of love. This sense of time is a particularly apt theological referent for queer temporalities, because these theories, like Holy Saturday, can throw our senses of success, productivity, and redemption into crisis.[44] In doing so, they demand that it is not we unproductive, disordered, deviant wasters of time that need to be rehabilitated and redeemed, but rather the system that devalued us that must be resisted. This sense of the weary love that remains in the face of that which is trying to either kill us or resurrect us back into its system of exploitation may actually provide hope.

Queer Saturdays

Feelings of being witness to our traumatized past, of waiting, and attempting another way similarly reflect the reading of queer time found in Heather Love's *Feeling Backward: Loss and the Politics of Queer History*. Love frames the temporal problem in queer studies as such:

> Insofar as the losses of the past motivate us and give meaning to our current experience, we are bound to memorialize them ("We will never forget"). But we are equally bound to overcome the past, to escape its legacy ("We will never go back"). For groups constituted by historical injury, the challenge is to engage with the past without being destroyed by it.[45]

The tension between never forgetting and never returning frames Love's question of how best queer life in the present might deal with its past *and* its future. Making reference to the queer utopias on offer by thinkers like Muñoz and influenced by the antisocial thesis, Love notes that while uto-pian desires have been primary in the project of queer studies, the future vision on which they build has too often impeded the act of facing the past from which that vision is trying to escape.

Here we might remember the problematic sense of a time of exodus, and the worry that it has not yet fully addressed that from which it flees. Love reminds us that neither the present nor the future is ever fully free of the past. This is in part due to the affectual legacy the past holds on the future. Often faced with the choice to either move on to happier times or cling to the past, even as they are beckoned forward, queers, Love argues, cannot help but feel "backward."

Feelings not only persist, they also have critical work to do; these "back-ward feelings," are "all about action: about how and why it is blocked, and about how to locate motives for political action when none is visible."[46] Moreover, "backward" feelings arise through the experience of being marked as "backward." Whether one is "backward" because one is queer, disabled, indigenous, black, woman, impoverished, or mad, the feeling of being so arises through plays of power that have allowed certain bodies to flow easily into societal space and others to be impeded. In this way, "back-ward" feelings can interrogate the eventive flow of time proposed by radi-cal theologians *and* the providential time, which has historically served as an imperial rationale for marking certain people divergent, proposed by the radical orthodoxy. Hence, one need not overcome these feelings as much as learn from them, feel them in order to feel a different kind of future, what Love calls a "backward future," one "apart from the reproduc-tive imperative, optimism, and the promise of redemption."[47] Rather than a project invested in voiding the future, we might say that Love seeks to unvoid the past by refusing to avoid it and therefore to feel our way toward more viable lives beyond reproductive futurism. Hence, a backward future might be another name for the time of Holy Saturday. Holy Saturday the-ologies can view the day between crucifixion and resurrection not merely as a time of reflection on our way to happier futures, but rather as *the* place and *the* time from which we can find alternate ways of living and structures of feeling that better enflesh a democratic temporality.

Love's work is representative of a queer canon of reflections on loss, mourning, and melancholy that begs us to rethink linear narratives of tem-poral progress. Perhaps the most famous engagement with these negative affects is found in the work of Judith Butler, most particularly in *The Psychic Life of Power: Theories in Subjection*. In her book, Butler deconstructs the binary between mourning and melancholia on offer from Freud, and she ties such moods to sexuality and gender. For instance, in *Psychic Life of Power* Butler suggests that heterosexual identity is

> Purchased through a melancholic incorporation of the love that it disavows: the man who insists upon the coherence of his heterosexuality will claim that he never loved another man, and hence never lost another man. That love, that attachment becomes subject to a double disavowal, a never having loved, and a never having lost. This "never-never" thus founds the heterosexual subject, as it were; it is an identity based upon the refusal to avow an attachment and, hence, the refusal to grieve.[48]

For Butler, subjection is stitched in loss. Further, as abjected attachment, queerness becomes the effaced object in the melancholic subjection process of heterosexuality. Loss and the inability to grieve ground the redemption of heternonormative subjects and the ransoming of queer ones. This foundational work of Butler haunts and frames many of the essays in the volume *Loss: The Politics of Mourning*, edited by David L. Eng and David Kazanjian. This volume "insists that the dawn of the twenty-first century is a moment when the pervasive losses of the twentieth century need to be engaged from the perspective of what remains. Such a perspective, these essays suggest, animates history through the creation of bodies and subjects, spaces and representations, ideals and knowledges. This attention to remains generates a politics of mourning that might be active rather than reactive, prescient rather than nostalgic, abundant rather than lacking, social rather than solipsistic, militant rather than reactionary."[49] In attending to what remains, the essays in *Loss* are imbued with racial, gendered, decolonial, and queer politics that refuse to avoid the past, and so unvoid it, and ask what it might say to the present: "By engaging in 'countless separate struggles' with loss, melancholia might be said to constitute, as Benjamin would describe it, an ongoing and open relationship with the past—bringing its ghosts and specters, its flaring and fleeting images, into the present."[50] Hence, queer work on such backward and melancholic feelings serves as the kind of Holy Saturday hauntings that will return as a motif throughout this book. This project is indebted to the clearing of ground constructed in such queer work on affect—in particular, its focus on melancholia for the structuring of subjectivity.

Approaching melancholy less from psychoanalytic or queer registers and more so from within a cultural studies frame, particularly the study of

affective registers in pop music, Robin James constructs her own feminist—
and, we might add, Holy Saturday—mood. In *Resilience and Melancholy: Pop
Music, Feminism, Neoliberalism,* James offers melancholy as a feminist counter to neoliberal narratives of resilience. Such narratives, read theologically
as contemporary redemption stories, teach us we must be redeemed out of
our damage (perhaps our quotidian crucifixions) if we are to become healthy
subjects. According to James, neoliberal subjectivization processes no longer assume a modernist subject, the self as originally whole and stable.
Rather, they assume *and* rely on damage:

> Resilience is the hegemonic or "common sense" ideology that every-
> thing is to be measured, not by its overall systematicity (coherence) or
> its critical, revolutionary potential (deconstruction), but by its *health.*
> This "health" is maintained by bouncing back from injury and crisis in
> a way that capitalizes on deficits so that you end up ahead of where you
> initially started. . . . If resilience is the new means of production, this
> means that crisis and trauma are actually necessary, desirable phenom-
> ena—you can't bounce back without first falling.[51]

You cannot resurrect without first being crucified. In other (theological)
words, neoliberalism relies on crucifixions (crisis, trauma) in order to
establish meaningful and profitable selves. A saturated globalized economy,
with few new terrains to exploit and on which to grow, needs the damage
and resilience cycle because it provides surplus value and new zones of
profit maximization. Here we might think (and James does) of Klein's concept of "disaster capital," in which industries grow by gambling on and
profiting off of crises.[52] Disaster capitalism includes the subprime mortgage and predatory payday lenders as businesses models that profit on
crisis and trauma, but importantly, too, on the command that we bounce
back from the crises nurtured by neoliberalism through our individual
resilience. The command to be resilient is the command to become healthy
subjects; once debilitated, we are redeemed into model citizens, "free" to
adapt to whatever of us the Market demands.

To counter this societal exploitation/individual resilience/societal
exploitation cycle, James offers melancholy as a mode of short-circuiting
the neoliberal machine. To short-circuit neoliberalism would be to resist
the command to overcome (be resilient) that profits off the renewed human
energy (our surplus value) produced through rehabilitating damage. This
short-circuiting, according to James, can come from making "bad investments" in those the Market views as waste—those unable to be "rehabilitated," or theologically speaking, "redeemed."

James traces these resilient (resurrection/redemption) narratives and their possible melancholic counter through contemporary pop music. For instance, she finds in Lady Gaga's Goth style not the rejection of neoliberalism, but the turning of an aesthetic of damage into a narrative James names as "Look I Overcame" (LIO). The LIO narrative makes Gaga recognizable to society. It subjectivizes her through the narrative of overcoming, such that she might profit on societal damage, but also such that we need not investigate the neoliberal exploitation that persists despite individual resistance: "If she can overcome, maybe I can too!" There's no need to worry why we were asked to overcome in the first place.

To achieve her LIO identity, Gaga adjusts the location of pleasure within Goth damage. Historically, Goth subcultures have found pleasure within the damage itself; Gaga's version finds pleasure at the site of one's overcoming of the damage: "[W]hereas traditional goth practices use an identification with monstrosity as a way to achieve a critical distance from mainstream culture . . . Gaga's performances of monstrosity are not identifications with, but incitements of the damage that she ultimately overcomes."[53] Gaga's fans, for instance are known as "Little Monsters," but Gaga makes the monster lovable, not as monstrous, but because the monster is revealed to be natural (born this way) and perhaps more importantly, resilient (able to resist gender norms). In other words, her monstrous fans "grow up into resilient citizens."[54] They do so not through systemic changes, but through individually (if with a reference to a Gaga collectivity) overcoming.

James further suggests that much of the anarchic performance in contemporary pop music supports, instead of subverts, neoliberal logic. Under neoliberalism not stability, but flexibility is the prize:

> Noisy an-arche sounds [are] queer and illogical only to ears tempered by a *logos* that privileges development, teleology, euphony, virtuosity, and rationality. Neoliberalism, however, doesn't care about linear progress, teleology, or euphony; in fact . . . neoliberalism courts and incites damage, glitch, and imperfection. Neoliberalism co-opts classically queer negation and critical black aesthetics, redistributing their negative, critical force and putting it in service of privileged groups.[55]

This key temporal shift diagnoses neoliberal constructions of value. Such a diagnosis might reflect those on offer by both radical orthodoxy and radical theology. Perhaps if noise out of measure is part of the neoliberal plan, then an exodus to the immeasurable is not the resistant tactic for which we are in search.

However, as I have argued—and as James seems to imply despite saying otherwise in the previous citation—neoliberal economics, while claiming to be flexible and free, are actually teleological and restricted. For instance, James (following Jodi Dean) suggests that "'the market as a site of truth' is the main thing that distinguishes neoliberalism from its predecessors and alternatives. . . . Market logic is a site of truth because that's the instrument we use to evaluate and assess everything, to tell us, for example, whether society is healthy or whether an artwork is any good."[56] In other words, the Market is the ground of all interpretive events. Under the "truth" of neo-liberalism, everything is measured and accounted for. Freedom is in service to the Market as its master. Indeed, James notes that this is why we mark some consumer choices, like those of people on welfare who spend their money on luxury goods or high-end foodstuffs, as stupid.[57] Because adherents of the Truth of the market (Market fundamentalists) have to act as though there is "free choice," they must also mark those who make choices that deviate from certain systemic rules—those that wander away from the teleological path toward the moneyed eschaton—as unhealthy. This "free" actor must be making such a choice because she is not of her right mind. So perhaps it is the radical theological flight to the immeasurable that will release us from such a caged freedom. And yet, as James further makes clear, such a flight risks becoming the resilient (adaptable) flexibility that creates surplus value out of damage. This is value that now can be reworked into a neoliberal market.

Additionally, reading with James, we might view this flight as increasingly difficult for those made most precarious by neoliberalism to actually partake in. Those who cannot bounce back are not considered resilient, but rather toxic. Those who cannot flee their damaged situations have no worth. Analyses of neoliberalism's treatment of race, gender, sexuality, and ability uncover disparities in terms of one's access to a "healthy" resilience. Neoliberalism makes, of certain subjects, exceptions to overcoming through performances of race, gender, and sexual *inclusions*. James rewrites the white supremacy of neoliberalism as *multiracial white supremacist patriarchy*, or MRWaSP. MRWaSP includes certain "good" (meaning healthy and resilient) women, people of color, and gay people in its structures of power: "*This inclusion is always conditional and always instrumental.*"[58] Inclusion is conditioned on exercising the right kind of resilience: making the right kind of choices out of one's damage. It is instrumental in that it serves to show that MRWaSP, this time, truly does believe in equality for all.

According to James women are also the most important instruments in the resilience labor that works to show that MRWaSP "good guys" are good. "Just look at the good girls that have been able to rise through our ranks" MRWaSP says. Look I overcame. This type of instrumental inclusion pathologizes those that cannot or refuse to be resilient; it marks them as irredeemable: "*MRWaSP uses resilience* to cut the color line—and the gender binary, the line between homonormative and queer, and to differentiate between mainstreamable and non-mainstreamable people with disabilities."[59]

So what is to be done? Follow a resurrection event that moves us out of time or return to a time of values other than that of neoliberal flexibility and resilience? James offers us a third way. The third way between—or better, beside—the MRWaSP (and, I argue, RO) exclusionary through inclusion cage and the MRWaSP (and perhaps RT) embrace of the value of flight out of the situation of damage comes through a close reading of the feeling of what it is to remain with the damage, or to invest in those who MRWaSP makes exceptions to resilience/resurrection: the feeling of melancholy. To invest in the exceptions and to stay melancholically with the damage is to act as an entropic force on the MRWaSP machine, a machine always looking for more surplus value on which to run.

To better understand such "bad investing," let us return to James's analysis of Lady Gaga and, in particular, the difference she finds between on the one hand Gaga and Beyoncé (models of the labor of resilience) and on the other hand Rihanna (the model of melancholic care for the exceptions). Analyzing Beyoncé's video "Video Phone" and Gaga's "Telephone," James suggests that while each claims a kind of place of damage, which is inflicted on them by patriarchy, their resilience (their LIO narrative) is built on making urban black men the exception to overcoming.[60] Beyoncé and Gaga—feminist and queer icons *and* profitable investments thanks to having overcome the damage inflicted on them by patriarchy—are resilient in such a way that turns their damage into their surplus human capital (literally their profitability in the market). In order for their music videos to properly tell this narrative, they need a representative villain—he who has damaged them—to overcome. In both videos this "villain" is the urban black man that portrays an ex-lover. Non-bourgeois blackness is the price paid for "good girl" inclusion in MRWaSP.

The videos suggest that "black men were singularly responsible for patriarchy's monstrous excesses, and overcoming patriarchy was simply a matter of punishing or eliminating black men."[61] Indeed, MRWaSP inclusions function only because there are still exceptions. Some are included and others are excluded to show that it is up to the individual to prove her health; the (sick) system remains unchallenged: "*Neoliberalism needs privileged folk to individually 'go gaga' so that society (relations of privilege and oppression) can stay the same.*"[62] While its structuring logics remain the same, MRWaSP claims a difference because it supposedly has become more inclusive. Holding up individual resilient people of color ("Just look at Beyoncé!"), MRWaSP mimics change while ensuring that certain exclusions remain. These exclusions are those defined as irredeemable in the face of MRWaSP functionality: "[Urban black masculinity] can't be recycled because it is toxic to the system."[63] Resilience (redemption/resurrection) is healthy; being unwilling or unable to be "redeemed" is sick.

Counter to this type of "healthy resilience," James offers melancholy, which, as

> misfired resilience, insufficiently profitable overcoming—is an alternative to biopolitical discourses of resilience and acceleration. Instead of resiliently recycling damage into human capital, melancholy goes into the death, investing in damage without properly overcoming it.[64]

Going into the death need not mean accepting crucifixion, but rather attempting to kill off MRWaSP power by making "bad investments," by which James means investments that impede the machine from turning damage into profitable human capital. Melancholy, by making space for damage, remains in a darkness that is inefficient, and yet in being inefficient or irredeemable it is a darkness that shows care for those that have been damaged by MRWaSP. Melancholic bad investments are refusals to overcome on the backs of those nonresilient exceptions (urban black folks) that serve as our ransom for the price of inclusion. This is a kind of weary remaining that embodies a Holy Saturday sensibility and temporality. This is an act of care that might be a middle way between democratic exodus and orthodox return.

James finds the performance of this middle way, of melancholy, in the tracks and videos of Rihanna's album *Unapologetic*. Her music

> doesn't overcome, but *invests in* gothy damage and stereotypically urban black men (namely Chris Brown). Rihanna's work is not resilient, but *melancholic*. This melancholy isn't the failure to get over a loss (as Freud understands it); rather, Rihanna's melancholy is a way of actively investing in the biopolitical, MRWaSP death that blackness represents. Melancholy is a feminist method of going *into the death*. Rather than investing in damage, melancholy invests in MRWaSP *exceptions*.[65]

This is not to say that Rihanna chooses death or to remain in physically abusive situations (Chris Brown famously assaulted Rihanna at the 2009

Grammy Awards), but rather that her affect and her melancholic rhythms, images, and performance refuse to stop witnessing to the crucifixion of blackness on offer by MRWaSP. While I am not completely convinced that James does enough to address the abusiveness of Brown, I am convinced that Rihanna's music acts as a witness to modes of being that have been marked as irredeemable. Rihanna short-circuits the narrative by investing in what MRWaSP finds toxic.

One such melancholic image takes place at the end of the music video for Rihanna's hit but critically panned (for not "going anywhere") song "Diamonds." At the end of the video Rihanna's character is "floating—not even swimming or treading water, just floating face-up—in the water. Drifting directionlessly atop tiny ripples of water, there are no crises for her to overcome—no storm, no tsunami."[66] The ripples hold Rihanna; there is no sense that she needs to escape or be rescued out of the watery depths, or that she will be pulled under by them; she remains carried by, and feeling, the watery rhythm. This is an unproductive end to the video; there is no narrative punch, no radical stance or uplift as in "Video Phone" and "Telephone." "Diamonds" leaves the viewer and listener to do their own affectual labor in the face of damage. Not granting us the satisfactory end (the rush to Sunday out of Saturday) may be Rihanna's request to remain with her in the melancholic places. This is not a request to drown, but rather to block up a flight from that which needs our attending.

Rihanna's refusal to give us a happy ending can be read as an act of attentive care work. She is caring for the damage by being unwilling to redeem it as human capital. Ultimately this is the work of melancholy: "At bottom, this strategy of making 'bad investments' [is] really an argument for a more even distribution of care work. . . . Caring, I understand it, is investing in others without expecting or receiving a return, in the form of human capital, to the people making the investments."[67] Rihanna remains with non-bourgeois blackness. She cares for what it has been to be marked as damaged. To remain with the damage, to witness to the crucifixion without resiliently resurrecting on the backs of the toxic "exceptions," and to do so without expecting a return, is a kind of grace. In attending to her own weary remaining, refusing a narrative of her individual resilience, Rihanna gifts us the opportunity to attend to her mood. In not overcoming, she demands our care for her melancholy; this demand turns self-care into communal attention. To attend is holy; it is to take care for the processes of inclusion and exclusion such redemptive narratives come to mean within MRWaSP.

This care is often missed in contemporary political theology. Indeed, in terms of radical theology, James can be read as offering a warning about narratives of change that might eclipse the material experience of those that either do not have the surplus energy to flee, or those for whom such a narrative might slip too quickly into "healthy" resilience at the expense of marking others as toxic remainders. For instance, drawing on the work of Steven Shaviro, James argues that "deregulated worlds can be 'entirely incoherent, yet immediately legible to anyone' (Shaviro *PC* 80) because *the superficial chaos is intentionally produced and controlled for by the work's immanent structure.* If regulation limits and prohibits irrationality and incoherence, deregulated visualization leverages and exploits it."[68] This is not to say that radical theologians intend to produce superficial chaos. Rather it is to argue that if we are to ensure that concepts of "immeasurability" and "event" not easily be leveraged by neoliberal economics, we may need to practice some ecstatic *and* melancholic attention to Muñoz's concreteness and James's bad investments.

Melancholic care refuses to be captured. It floats on the damaged water, short-circuiting the productive programs on offer by MRWaSP. This bad investing might be a kind of careful remaining, or "grave attending." Grave attending is a caring for the gravity, the pulling down to the material world, listening for what all its myriad emotions have to tell us, and where they have to lead us. It is also a witnessing to those subjectivities, collectivities, and possibilities assumed to be buried over and gone—the ghosts that haunt us and so gift us a sense of what we might have been and an imagination of what we might become. Acts of grave attention refuse to efface the material mattering of others on the way to our own redemption. Hence, remaining with the damage is, perhaps, a Saturday mood, a way between crucifixion and resurrection.

We can find a similar sense of grave attending in Elizabeth Freeman's discussion of S/M and her reading of Isaac Julien's short film "The Attendant" in *Time Binds: Queer Temporalities, Queer Histories.* Freeman offers us another scene of Holy Saturday time, one in sympathy with the kind of melancholic refusal to overcome on offer by James. Freeman's analysis of sadomasochistic practices can be understood as an erotic of queer ritual enactments of time. She "treat[s] S/M as a deployment of bodily sensations through which the individual subject's normative timing is disaggregated and denaturalized."[69] Through her analysis of "The Attendant," Freeman argues that this disorganization is collective and that "sadomasochistic sex performs a dialectic of a rapid-temporal 'modernity' and a slower 'premodernity'; the latter indexed by any number of historical periods and, crucially, by forms of labor and affiliation that do not accede to capitalist imperatives."[70] The particular visceral practices of S/M might be refusals to give in to the coming of the moneyed or Christian eschaton. Further, to denaturalize bodily time such that demands for efficiency are thrown into disorder by our most intimate plays of desire is to feel a backward future.

In this subcultural practice we might find modes of feeling and becoming that sensitively attend to both the desire to flee toward a different possible world and the one to intensely witness to each micro-sensation of what it is to live in this present. Quoting Carla Freccero, Freeman locates in S/M a "'Passivity—which is also a form of patience and passion—[that] is not quite the same thing as quietism. Rather it is a suspension, a waiting, an attending to the world's arrivals (through, in part, its returns)."[71] This is the Attendant's attendance, but this might also be the witness of Holy Saturday, of the love that remains instead of redeeming. Freeman's reading of "The Attendant" reminds us that since the pleasures and pains of histories infuse temporality, any counter-capitalist theology, including a radical democratic one, must address how moments of time are felt and embodied differently by different people. Hence, relations to revolt, exodus, and infinity will be received and undertaken in variant ways from within historically constructed subjectivities.[72]

"The Attendant" is set in Wilberforce House, a British museum of the history of slavery. The primary plot of the film centers on either the sexual fantasy of a black museum guard/attendant about a young white visitor or the actual S/M encounter between the two (the line between reality and fantasy is left ambiguous in the film). When the museum closes, a large painting by Francois-Auguste Biard depicting a white master bending over a dying black slave comes to life as it is reimagined as a leather S/M scene. According to Freeman, various reimaginings and reenactments of the Biard painting "intimate that sadomasochism overtly engages with the dialectic between an era's dominant temporal modality and other historical moments and their temporal fields. And [the film] gestures toward the possibility of encountering specific historical moments viscerally, thereby refusing these moments the closure of pastness."[73] For instance, Julien creates a triptych of the black attendant about to be whipped by the white visitor, the white visitor about to be whipped by the black attendant, and the two standing side by side. This triptych reengages the past both to reimagine it, but also to attend to its material reality in the present.

Freeman finds important temporal and material insight not only through viscerally entering such historical moments, but also through the structure of the pause created by the "about to be whipped." For Freeman, drawing on Benjamin, "the pause does not signal an interval between one thing and another; it is itself a thing, analytically and experientially available, that reveals the ligaments binding the past and the present."[74] Might the pause of the whip in S/M be the middle spirit in Shelly Rambo's pneumatology where in the wake of trauma, death haunts life and yet love still remains; Rihanna floating at the end of "Diamonds"; and Love's feeling backward? The pause, or remaining, does not give into the past as though the past were static and its results inevitable, nor does it flee the past. In the pause of the whip, and in Julien's play between painting and film that, for Freeman, represents "flow and freeze,"[75] there is a kind of melancholic attending, a caring for what was, is, and might have been.

In S/M's material attending to the past through its destabilization of linear time, and in the nonlinear rhythms (what she calls a "proliferation of visual and tactile rhymes") of Julien's film, Freeman locates "a kind of *short-circuiting*, circuiting, a jolt seen or felt, a profane illumination or kinetic leap into history otherwise. If S/M in its sensory elements encodes and transmits the bodily knowledge of personal and collective trauma, Julien seems to argue, it can also release this knowledge for new bodily experiences in the present."[76] Might this short-circuiting be similar to the short-circuiting James finds in making melancholic bad investments? Both short-circuit a linear or uncomplicatedly finished narrative of crucifixion and resurrection, but they do so without giving up hope that the past might not foreclose a different present.

For James, short-circuiting is also "going into the death" instead of investing in life. To go "into the death" for James means making investments that kill off the surplus value that MRWaSP needs to live. To go into the death, to remain with damage, is not to die, but to rest in the pause that keeps different possibilities (for instance not sacrificing blackness as toxic) open for the present. Hence the attendance in "The Attendant" might recall the redistribution of care work imagined by James's melancholy. James hopes to short-circuit future overcoming, while Freeman sees S/M as short-circuiting the dualistic reading of time in which one must either go back into stable damage (crucifixion/slavery) or forward into fated utopia (resurrection/obligatory forgetting). Both inhabit a space that refuses narratives on offer without overcoming (and so rehabilitating and making available for profit) the past.

This sort of Holy Saturday labor of attending and care might be what Foucault had in mind when in his *Hermeneutics of the Subject: Lectures at the Collège de France 1981–1982* he spoke of the care of the self that would permit us to "become *again* what we *never were*."[77] This ethic of care will be the focus of the Chapter 5, for now we might note here that to become again what we never were is to feel backward, to remain tied to the past, while allowing for the past/present/future to remain open. This Holy Saturday labor might be the "kinetic leap into history otherwise." These queer Saturdays do not call for an exodus toward resurrective novelty, nor do they call for a "radical" return to an imperial history of crucifixion (of exception making). Rather, they call for a creative equivocacy between the two. This might be a call for an attendant pause that invests in the bad investment rather than in individual overcoming.

The need to attend better, to witness, returns us to the work of Clayton Crockett. In *Deleuze beyond Badiou: Ontology, Multiplicity, and Event*, Crockett asks, "So what is to be done? Do we militantly wait for another event and hope that it happens before we die or become extinct? Or do we create an event of thinking?"[78] He continues, "As Paola Marrati suggests, Deleuze believes that concepts like History, God, and Self are too big to function for any effective political action, and that, in fact, politics based on action runs into serious problems because the movements become programmed in advance and then reduced to clichés, or else captured by state and capitalist apparatuses."[79] Here we recall the programmatic nature of Milbank's event of the Church. The universal Good of the Church has, of course, been used to justify the neocolonialism of global capitalism and earlier forms of "civilizing" colonial projects. In Freeman's pause and James's melancholy we find not only events of thinking, but also of feeling—of felt events that resist a programmatic politics of action without falling into apathy. Crucially such events, do not break in from without, but rather pulsate within the pause, from within our attendance to the everyday.

I want to pause in the everyday as much as, if not more so than, any revolutionary moment or change. I desire to inhabit refusals and bad investments that arise in our most quotidian of embodiments. I propose we might find such sensibilities by pausing in and attending to temporal shifts within so-called mental illness, most particularly bipolar disorder.

Disordered Time

What would it mean to view the "disorder" we name bipolar as a site from which to question the value of neoliberal civil order? Following Cvetkovich's work on depression, I suggest that we can deindividualize and depathologize bipolarity and affirm that good politics need not only come from good feelings.[80] I propose bipolar time—that disordering of a linear movement from crucifixion to resurrection—as a protest and potency from within the eschatological shadows of capitalism.

Following crip theorist Robert McRruer, we can name the indictment to save time as a heteronormative insistence on able-bodiedness.[81] Bipolar time argues that this indictment is also an insistence on able-mindedness. Viewing bipolarity as a crip sensibility disrupts its pathologization in order to reveal, while acknowledging its pain, its pleasurable potential.[82] Embracing the crip reformulation of disability as not that which should be fixed, but rather as a site from which we might learn to resist society's demands for profitability and efficiency (an issue to which we return in Chapter 3), bipolarity can question the thrust of normativization inherent in neoliberal temporality and sociality. Further, bipolar disorder opens up questions of redemption or cure similar to those brought to the fore by crip theory. Hence, bipolar time returns us to Holy Saturday time, taken now not from the point of view of divine abandonment, which in Balthasar's reading will be redeemed, but rather from a stance that says resurrection may not only be unattainable, but also unnecessary. Bipolar time is not rehabilitated out of its damage as much as it cares for what happens within the damage. Bipolar time is a kind of queering of Holy Saturday theologies because it serves, in Balthasar's words, not only as a "radically disorienting space of death and hell,"[83] but also as a radical reorientation of the meanings of life and of (present care-full) heaven.

Like the time of S/M, which according to Freeman can serve as "a dialectic between the will to speed up and annihilate and the will to slow down and dilate,"[84] bipolar time illuminates the ties and tensions between the soul-deadening effects of capitalism and the mad feeling that things might be otherwise. Further, bipolar temporality marks the inseparability of time and feeling. Bipolar time, a time saturated by unnerving feelings, can offer ways in which we might better learn to touch and feel a counter-capitalist hope in mania, depression, and their interpenetration. Hence, bipolar temporality refuses the cruel optimism and happy efficiency of neoliberalism and affirms a different sense, one that is enacted through microtactics of the self: collapsing into bed, embracing one's feelings of overwhelming exhaustion; or living into one's porosity to the world, collectivizing connections and so insisting that we need not be alone in facing that which has got us so tired. Bipolar time does not seek to construct, reveal, or capture subjects of depression and mania. Rather, bipolar time attempts to clear space for different modes of becoming, those dependent on paying greater attention to where moodiness takes us. Bipolar time asks us to attend to what our moods reveal about the world and to what feelings will us to do. Hence, while the rupturing of a certain temporality is key for a bipolar sensibility, bipolar time might not cohere to queer pessimism (let alone optimism) as much as to queer attentiveness.

To gravely attend to our moods is to find both manic joy and deadening depression ethically interesting. To find moods ethically interesting is not to sublate one into the other, but rather to follow moods where they will and to practice a multiplicity of moody responses, a following to which we will biblically return in Chapter 4. In practicing both the fall into the bed *and* the flight into the world, bipolar time seeks not a final end to its penetrative flows of despair and desire (a Sunday for its Friday), but rather questions the very nature of resurrection. It cares for what has been, what might have been, and what might be.

Bipolar time is a dream of a temporally reordered world, one where worth is divorced from waged work, value from efficiency, and the raison d'être from redemption. In many ways it is reflective of the temporal eventiveness proposed by radical theologians and resistant to the providential time advocated by the radical orthodoxy. Yet because bipolar time is a nonlinear penetrative time in which there is also a slowdown with every speed up, it can interrogate excessive foci on rapidity, newness, and action implied by the radical theological concept of the event. Within a time of bipolarity, mania is always haunted by depression and depression by mania. Hence, a life lived in bipolar time might resist a sense of an ultimate freedom-to-come, in favor of what we come to name, with Fred Moten, in Chapter 6, an improvisational rupture that questions the terms of freedom on offer. In this way bipolar temporality questions both a radical theological narrative of exodus and a radical orthodox narrative of salvation. Further, to political theologies of all stripes, bipolar time adds the acknowledgment that each moment of past, present, and future is deeply felt and therefore carries affectual resonances that matter for how we imagine and presently live out our political, theological, and social lives.

Bipolar time also shakes any sense of clear agency. One does not choose to be chained to depression or to take off in flights of manic exodus. Yet there is a partial agency of response. This partial agency of response cannot be simply individual. To be sure, there are micro responses we might attempt as individuals in pleasure and in pain. One might choose to cry in public or in private. One might choose to call in sick or go to work. One might choose to live or to die. However, I want to propose that our greatest agential and ethical hope lies not as much in how we each individually feel (or separately respond to such feelings) as in how we come to be ever more sensitively oriented toward one another. In other words, we might have an agency of response even if that agency is simply to better attend to how both the world and we feel. We all can respond ever more sensitively. We can attend to what choices are actually on offer for which people. We can look to what remains of love in a mania haunted by depression and a depression haunted by mania. We can respond to the anxiety produced by demands for efficiency and productivity by feeling these alternate emotional states in such a way that we refuse to subordinate spending time to saving it, and we refuse to stop attending as long the option to spend time over saving it is only available to the few.

The depressive side to bipolar temporality is a reminder that inaction is also a way of faithfully remaining. It attends to how the love that remains in the wake of the collectivizing trauma of neoliberalism feels often weary and impotent. Therefore, the inaction implied in microtactics, like the fall into the bed, confronts demands for action implied in the politics of event, exodus, and utopia. And yet, we can still find a sense of performativity in our attempts to feel ourselves through bipolar time, reorienting us to each other in ways that reorient our macro senses of value.

This reorientation is one that might be philosophically traced in the thought of mad thinkers and thinkers of madness. For instance, in *The Rebellious No: Variations on a Secular Theology of Language*, Noëlle Vahanian, drawing on discussions of madness in the works of Foucault, Nietzsche, and Derrida, surmises that "simply put, . . . what is called reason is a form of blindness, a suspension of thought which produces sanity—the ability to desist from willing, a 'being caught up and carried along.' She's hyper-aware of the saliva in her mouth or the ticking of her heart; hyper self-conscious to the point of self-alienation, unable to let be and let go; he's a model citizen, an average consumer, a good soldier, a man of the crowd, a cog in a wheel."[85] The hyper-awareness that madness nurtures is the kind of resistance to dulling orders of civility found within a life lived in bipolar time. Characteristic of both phases of depression and mania is an "over-sensitive" orientation toward the world. Whether it comes in the form of a manic reading and feeling of the world or the depression that comes when the world feels like too much to bear, living in a bipolar time means being the woman who cannot let be and let go. It is to be unable to become the model citizen and average consumer. Through the madness of living in a bipolar temporality, we can resist becoming cogs in the wheel.

Additionally, while one might understand depression as the very shutting down of the will, Vahanian, quoting Louis A. Sass, counters: "'What prevents the [insane] from returning to a more normal existence is no simple failure of will, but, in a sense, an inability to desist from willing—an inability to let themselves be caught up in and carried along by the ongoing flow of practical activity in which normal existence is grounded.'"[86] Refusing to be carried along by the temporal pull of productive activity, when productive activity has become monetized and often cruelly optimistic, is at the heart of performing bipolar temporality. Hence, bipolar time is resistant to the flows of productivism and captivity demanded by the eschatalogical judgment of money.

Further, the madness of the mad, like the backwardness of the queer, brings to the fore power-relations that have shaped the history of the model citizen known as "rational man." Reading with Foucault's *History of Madness*, Lynne Huffer notes that "Madness is the 'ransom' paid by the 'other' for the historical rise of the rational moral subject."[87] This should conjure up the urban black man made to be the exception on whose exclusion good girl inclusion is built. Further, as Huffer artfully argues, the ransomed mad cannot be disentangled from the ransomed queer:

> At stake in Foucault's tracing of these figures in their historical appearance and disappearance are ethical questions about subjectivity and alterity within a modern rationalist moral order. Faced with an objectifying language of reason for the telling of history, *History of Madness* refigures those sexual subjects transformed by science into objects of intelligibility—as homosexuals, onanists, perverts, and so on—by allowing them to hover as "fantastical" ghosts. They haunt our present but we can't quite grasp them.[88]

The sensibilities of those that are mad not only serve to diagnose how the post-Fordist moment feels, but they also pose ethical questions about the historical sacrifice of certain people—queers, perverts, the impoverished, the differently abled, the differently minded—for the construction of Modern *Man*, an issue to which we will return throughout the following pages.

Like the hauntings of trauma felt within Holy Saturday, the mad of the past haunt our present, asking not for resurrection but for a reorientation of feeling and attending, or what Huffer names "an archival listening: the creation of a pathway for a different hearing."[89] This different hearing is an ethical call responded to more fully in Chapters 5 and 6. For now, what such a request for hearing might do is ask us how our current structures of time either make room for such a hearing (a pausing and an attending) or impede practices of attention required to hear. Bipolar time offers time to hear in that it resists the demands to stop attending, to get back in time with the order of the day. Whether one is too hot (manic) or too cold (depressed), one's disordered mood disrupts the atmosphere, and as such moodiness becomes a personal failing that must be fixed in time to save time.

For all its resistance to the ordering rods of the world, bipolar time as a crip time is not necessarily a queering of the symbolic order, but rather an attempt to short-circuit contemporary neoliberal orders that shape the symbolic as such. As Vahanian has offered in her response to my concept of bipolar time:

> [It] offers a different resistance, one beyond a psychic disordering of drives failing "normal" accession to the symbolic where such so-called failed accession would be a resistance, a subject-less resistance to this symbolic. Why? Because bipolar time is not a production of linear time. It is not a response to capitalistic time, and in that sense it does not develop as a resistance to it. But yet, it resists.[90]

Bipolar time does not develop in direct reaction to neoliberalism; neo-liberalism cannot be traced as its origin or as its ultimate target, as though if once neoliberalism was destroyed we would no longer need processes of feeling and responding differently to whatever norms arose in its place. Rather the styles of life allowed breath under bipolar time are those that will continue to wound *and* wonder.

Bipolar time is a dream of a time in which we can spend time depressingly critical of any new norm that a revolution against neoliberalism might bring, and we can spend time manically joyful about such newness. Key for a nonlinear penetrative time such as that of bipolarity is the chance that when one is made depressed by society (even a revolutionary new one of our own making), one might be haunted by the crazy belief that things could be otherwise *and* that a possible despair in the novel might continue to persist through any complacent joy in the new. This is neither a linear nor particularly revolutionary state of being. Bipolar resistance does not come from the programmatic politics worried over by Deleuze and found in Milbank; rather, it wells up from the ways in which we are always already "disordered."

Bipolar time, as representative of disordered time, is not interested in being "saved." It will not be saved by an ordering cure, nor will it need to save time over spending it. Indeed, bipolarity makes saving in either sense nearly impossible. It is this impossibility that returns us to the appropriateness of Rambo's reading of trauma as a time of Holy Saturday. Bipolarity asks us how we should better remain and therefore live when we are unsure whether we really want a resurrection that may not be coming. Crucial to bipolar time's sense of disorder is that those with alternate mental orientations to the world often cannot live temporally in the constant demand for efficiency. The "dis-ordered" may experience times of rapid creativity and production, but also times in which the slow-down of depression means saving time is no longer an option. Hence, bipolar time can throw our sense of self into a spiral of worth. This spiral might force us to divorce who we are from what we produce. This is not an easy feat in light of a societal ethos that, as McRuer and Mollow remind us, affirms Joseph Conrad's assertion, "'A man is a worker. If he is not then he is nothing.'"[91] Not easy, but crucial, as growing wealth disparities are throwing more of us out of work and into our beds or worse (a worse that might include being made to produce and serve at a life-threatening pace and for an unattainable future).

So what might happen if we viewed this ever increasing collective "disorder" not as something that needs to be overcome, but rather as a site from which we might question the demand to be productive and efficient? And if in doing so we concede that we need to spend time instead of saving it, just how might we enact such a need?

Bipolar Practices, Concrete Hopes

Although bipolar time helps us to resist even a radical democratic overemphasis on the future, and although it is a sensibility resistant to neoliberal resilience narratives, I suggest if we are to practice spending time over saving it we may still need utopian dreaming—a dreaming performed within the smallest quotidian moments as well as in the social utopias described by Muñoz. Concrete utopias are a doing for and toward the future; they are an enactment of what might be. The becoming rather than the telos is of utmost importance. For instance, Muñoz viewed the queer punk scene as a collective space in which identity and acceptability—even that of acceptable queer identity—were challenged, and in which this challenge was communal. Cvetkovich describes a similar utopian moment when she writes of the collective singing of cover songs performed by Feel Tank participants.[92] During a gathering in Toronto the line "My loneliness is killing me" from Britney Spears's "Baby One More Time" embodied the loneliness felt by Cvetkovich while also helping her to feel a little less lonely because it was sung collectively.[93] This is the performance of a utopia in which the love that remains in loneliness, while not curing loneliness, feels like concrete hope.

In his concluding chapter, "Take Ecstasy with Me," Muñoz writes, "Knowing ecstasy is having a sense of timeliness's motion, comprehending a temporal unity, which includes the past (having-been), the future (the not-yet), and the present (the making-present)."[94] Drawing on the etymological meaning of *ekstasis* as to stand or be outside of oneself, Muñoz conceives ecstasy as a moment in which one is brought not only beyond oneself spatially, but also temporally. Perhaps to join Muñoz on the dance floor, or Cvetkovich in "The Hungry Purse," is to attend to the other, to take care of those we've made other, or in James's words, the exception. The temporal shift of Muñoz's ecstatic encounters embodies a Holy Saturday mood. We may not know what kind of Sunday will come in this movement from within our closure to the present utopian openness that comes from ecstatic entanglement; we may not need a Sunday. And yet, in being together in material difference from past, present, and future as they have been offered to us, Muñoz's ecstasy is a moment of presentist hope.

This temporal movement is an invitation to, as Muñoz puts it, "desire differently, to desire more, to desire better."[95] This call to desire differently, more, and better is also a call made by radical theologians of both camps. However, in their assertion that this desiring must direct itself toward the Church and nowhere else, orthodox theologians miss the very heart of desire. Hence, Muñoz's invitation to take ecstasy with him might be the open communion rejected by radical orthodoxy, but demanded when we take seriously the inexhaustibility of divine desire.

Indeed, might concrete utopias be more pause than eschaton? They may be performances of attending more than ending. Concrete utopian hope is an attending performed (sometimes melancholically) in the present at the punk bar and through the collective singing of cover songs, but also in quotidian moments of the weary love that remains but does not redeem pain in order to persist. It is in these spaces that I hope to spend some bipolar time. Perhaps I will spend it in the hours of teaching that remind me that moods and modes of collective thinking matter; perhaps I will spend it in the moment of sharing both a weariness from and a mad hope for the world, a moment that reminds me that collective feeling matters; or perhaps I will spend it in the hours of *not* getting out of bed, which remind me that impotency is also a way of witnessing to how this world feels. Perhaps, taking a note from Cvetkovich, I will spend it at the karaoke bar, singing "St. Dolly's" great lament against saving time: "9 to 5, what a way to make a livin', barely gettin' by, it's all takin' and no givin', they just use your mind and you never get the credit, it's enough to *drive you crazy* if you let it."[96] There, spending time surrounded by the collective out-of-tuneness of my fellow patrons, this disordered space might become a reminder of our attunement, or perhaps better our attend-ment to one another—an attendance that reminds us that we need not let the *rich man's game* take our time and use our mind, but also that we need not be on pitch in order to sing out. We do not need to flee toward certain redemption—an all-curing salve in the Church or the Market—to avoid becoming a slave to the cubicle, the commodity, or consumption. After all, this life of faith, one in which none of us needs to find our pitch in order to know our (im)potency, is the embodiment of bipolar Saturday time because it concretely refuses the eschatological judgment of money.

CHAPTER 3

Unproductive Worth

What definitions of value might need rethinking if we are to imagine alternative modes and moods of spending our time? In other words, might a closer investigation into the *affects* of the value-system that demands we save time help us to offer up alternate ways of structuring worth beyond that of work? Continuing to read political theology anew through the hermeneutic of affect clears space and time for attending to the potential for a political theology that takes seriously the emotional mattering of both neoliberal value-systems and the counter embodiments that rise up from within, alongside, and in rejection to such systems. This chapter sustains an engagement with political theology to open a discussion on the neoliberal value of (in particular, monetized) productivity and efficiency in order to reveal its material violence, but also in hopes of encountering different sources of value and so generating alternatives. I read counter-redemption theories of affect and disability in order to clear ground in the realm of political theology for a radical refutation of the assumption that our work defines our worth. Perhaps we might find pleasure and resistance from within what the social body has deemed our brokenness (emotional and physical); perhaps we might live imaginatively by living without the need to be redeemed as a resiliently productive part of the social whole.

Questioning Productive Redemption

In *Multitude: War and Democracy in the Age of Empire* Michael Hardt and Antonio Negri argue that today "No social line divides productive from unproductive workers . . . these distinctions . . . have often been used to exclude women, the unemployed, and the poor from central political roles, entrusting the revolutionary project to the men (with calloused hands from the factories) who were thought to be the primary producers."[1] This troubling of the productive/unproductive divide appears to be a radical rejection of a neoliberal politics of efficiency and exclusionary productivism. And yet, in their continued emphasis on the *productivity* of the multitude, might Hardt and Negri undermine the radicality of this rupture? Or put otherwise, what goes missing in their turn toward what the multitude can *do*, rather than how we might differently become? If the line no longer stands, why not look afresh at the multitude's unproductivity? What types of inscriptional violence does embracing the value of productivity commit? What does productivity as the site of the collectivization of subjectivity for the empowerment of the multitude say to those subjects who refuse their productive capacities? In other words, if the power of and commonality among the multitude come from the very value held so dear by the Empire—that of productivity—can the multitude (in its productivity) effectively counter neoliberalism? Through a reengagement with *Multitude* and its theological deployment in Joerg Rieger and Kwok Pui-lan's *Occupy Religion: Theology of the Multitude*, this chapter offers alternate affectual orientations toward work and productivity. I do so alongside the postwork imaginaries of Franco "Bifo" Berardi and Kathi Weeks, and in conjunction with the affect theory of Ann Cvetkovich and a theopoetic engagement with crip theory.[2] If in the previous chapter we began an analysis of what neoliberal economics does to our time, in this chapter we will expand on the feeling of such demands. By attending to those with "bad timing" we can reencounter political theology from the space of an affecting everyday. In doing so, we begin to not only divorce our worth from our waged work, but also encounter new structures of value beside and beyond neoliberal and liberal productivisms.

Continued philosophical and theological emphases on the productivity of the multitude resonate with a salvific narrative embedded in both a

Fordist and a post-Fordist understanding of work as redemptive. Rereading Max Weber's *Protestant Ethic and the "Spirit" of Capitalism*, Kathi Weeks
reminds us that "The Protestant work ethic hailed the individual as a moral
agent, responsible for achieving the certainty of his or her own salvation
(see Weber 1958, 115)."[3] Work was a reflection of one's state of election
and one's capacity to be saved. In Weber's formulation, under industrial
capitalism, "This orientation to work was . . . less the result of one's faith
in the afterlife than constitutive of it; hard work and success are not a
means to salvation, but at most signs of it."[4] However, within a post-Fordist
value-system, "[the work ethic] serves a more directly productive function
today: where attitudes themselves are productive, a strong work ethic
guarantees the necessary level of willing commitment and subjective
investment."[5] Whereas under Fordism one's productive labor was a reflection of God's election (and so was used, according to Weber, to turn productive work into a calling), today the call to be productive is a call to be
productive "with a smile." To be productive with a smile is to make what
Weeks refers to as one's hands, head, and heart essential for the ethic of
work. This, in turn, means that to become a good subject, to be redeemed
out of any subjective lack, is to become a happy and efficient worker.

If being saved by God *or* redeemed as a proper social subject takes place
through one's physical and emotional labor, would rethinking work—not
simply in order to reorient where we place our resources and assign our
social and monetary values, but also to nurture a refusal of neoliberal
"happy" productivity—better disentangle our acts of resistance from narratives of individual resilience/redemption? In response to this question I
offer a political theology of unproductivity. Such a theology takes shape
through an engagement with autonomist and feminist Marxist critiques of
the salvific structure of work.[6] Here both Weeks's reading of the Protestant work ethic in *The Problem with Work: Feminism, Marxism, Antiwork
Politics, and Postwork Imaginaries* and Berardi's examination of the affectual
effects of what he calls SemioCapitalism in *The Soul at Work* along with his
post-futurist proposals in *After the Future* will be key.[7] Berardi's reading of
how neoliberal structures of worth and time impact the production of
affects serve as an alternate to a eulogistic reading of productivity. Ultimately, however, it is Hardt and Negri's turn to the monstrosity of the
multitude, read anew through crip and affect theories, which opens us to
how this unproductive stance might be embodied in a theology of worth
divorced from efficient production. Through reading Hardt and Negri's
affirmatively monstrous multitude with a crip sensibility, I seek out a theology that resists both neoliberal and uncritical liberal productivity as a

method of salvation and so troubles the concepts of worth on offer by neoliberalism and by certain productivist political theologies hoping to counter its deleterious effects.

The Productivity of the Multitude

In *Occupy Religion* Rieger and Kwok draw on Paul's epistles to discuss the importance of the multitude's common productivity: "The eye cannot say to the hand, 'I have no need of you,' nor again the head to the feet, 'I have no need of you.' On the contrary, the members of the body that seem to be weaker are indispensable, and those members of the body that we think less honorable we cloth with greater honor, and our less respectable members are treated with greater respect (1 Cor. 12:21–24)."[8] For Rieger and Kwok, the productivity of the multitude honors the contributions to the social body made by those considered inferior. For Hardt and Negri, the very fact that even those who we normally assume to be outside the traditional labor economy are part of social production is what ensures that the multitude can resist the capitalist empire. That all classes *produce* in common allows them to resist in common: common productivity as bond. And yet, might this sense of common productivity rely too heavily on one's ability to produce and hence contribute *productively* to the common? Indeed, what might a theology built on the way in which each part of the body matters for the whole have to say to a body missing some parts? What of the blind woman who does not need the eye or the amputee who does not need the hand? What of those cut off or breaking away from the community that is the social body? What of those who reject a traditionally productive path to subjectivization? Is the focus on common productivity too eerily resonant with soteriological and anthropological structures embedded in neoliberalism that tie our worth and election to our work—who we *are* to what we can *do* (and how happy we are to do it) for one another? In other words, does a theology that reasserts our productive worth to the function of the social body affirm the current principles of the social, those that marked us as disposable in the first place? Does it recycle us as surplus value back into MRWaSP?[9]

Rieger and Kwok continue:

> The multitude picks up the concerns of working people, the so-called working class, because it values the notion of production. While the multitude is forced to endure the pressures of the system, it does not remain passive. Working people make substantial contributions to society, which are often overlooked and underappreciated. Hardt and

Negri extend the multitude to the unemployed, unpaid domestic laborers, and the poor, who also make substantial contributions to society. We agree with their idea that "the multitude gives the concept of the proletariat its fullest definition as all those who labor and produce under the rule of capital." (10)[10]

While, as Rieger and Kwok make clear, Hardt and Negri include the unemployed and underpaid in their definition of the productive multitude, I am arguing that the fact that political emphasis remains on production and societal contribution is problematic. To be sure, the dismantling of what we can recognize as the "We Built This" notion, made famous by Mitt Romney's 2012 presidential bid, is key for the work of solidarity sought for by Rieger and Kwok. Members of the 1 percent (and allies that perhaps believe one day they, too, will rise to the upper echelons) rallied behind the notion that those in the lower classes owed their livelihoods to those at the top, to the wealth the rich claimed to have built and then benevolently shared with the rest of us. An emphasis on the productivity of the multitude resists this narrative, helpfully bringing to the fore the ways in which wealth relies on the work and exploitation of the impoverished. Yet, the ways in which the productivity of the multitude not only built the wealth of the 1 percent, but also sustains that wealth is obscured by Rieger and Kwok's productivism. Hence, the attempt to regain the worthiness of the multitude through what we have done for an economic system, and the social cohesion it engenders, that continues to betray us, is at best rash and at worst a tightening of the chains that bind us to an exploitative market. If we are to regain power through a reassertion of our worth in productive capacity, then we have not unbound ourselves from the tragic narrative that it is what we can do for the system rather than who we are—our singular embodied desires and becomings—that defines our worth.[11] Indeed, a focus on labor allows the terms of worth to remain within a theological system fortified by (and which strengthens) the idea that our work is a sign of our Divine election. The addition of the unemployed and underpaid domestic worker to the definition of the multitude does not adequately refute the work ethic; rather it affirms that regardless of our employment status, we all are indeed workers.

Instead of a more radical refutation of the need to be a worker in order to be of worth, a productivist theology in the form proposed by Rieger and Kwok borders on apologetics—a theology begging for the *recognition* of the impoverished as societal contributors. The terms of value may remain intact. Rieger and Kwok continue, "Hardt and Negri focus on economic class, in part because this concept has not received enough attention in recent debates, but also because the multitude needs to be understood in terms of economic production. It is both the 'common subject of labor, that is, the real flesh of postmodern production' and 'the object from which collective capital tries to make the body of its global development.'"[12] The focus on class can indeed help us to raise issues of fair wages and just labor practices (it has done so to great effect, as generations of labor movements have shown). And yet from a theological point of view Rieger and Kwok's proposals obscure the problem of where we place ultimate value, focusing instead on how that value gets measured and compensated (an issue to which we return later in this chapter).

Rieger and Kwok insist that if one is going to follow the teachings of Jesus, one cannot "serve two masters" and so cannot serve both God and wealth.[13] Yet, in using the gospels to theologically valorize agency and productivity (which may not be able to escape the fact that contemporary demands to be productive are injunctions to worship the promise of money), their theology begs for further interrogation. They note that "Jesus' healings tend to encourage agency and productivity as well. He responds to a man who has been waiting for help for thirty-eight years with these words: 'Stand up, take your mat and walk' (John 5:8)."[14] And they continue, "[Jesus spent time healing] the paralyzed, whose agency had been shattered, and the possessed whose personalities had been destroyed. He combated religious neuroses by proclaiming the forgiveness of God and put people back on the road: 'Stand up and take your bed and walk' (Mark 2:9) and 'Get up!' (Mark 5:41)."[15] Theirs is a theology in which, "In short, discipleship means becoming a productive agent in relationship with other productive agents."[16] Does not the demand to take your mat and walk overlap with a neoliberal demand to get to work? Might the demand to "Get up!" reflect a demand resonant with "Stop being so lazy!"? What about the agency of the paralyzed as paralyzed? Or that of the shattered as shattered and the neurotic as neurotic? What of those too sick to work? Too tired to participate? Too isolated to contribute? Too willful to attune to the demands of other productive agents?[17] What of those considered exceptions in the sense Robin James means, as in those who are considered toxic to the social body and therefore cannot overcome or be redeemed back into the system? What of those who, while not valorizing sickness or suffering, choose not to rehabilitate their brokenness into productive energy for the social body that marked them as broken in the first place? Must *we* adjust to the call for productivity, or might we learn from unproductivity? Might we make "bad investments" by attending to what we can learn from those who do not work in the time frame demanded by neoliberal economics? In other words, how might political theologians better counter neoliberal constructions of value?

The Redemption vs. the Refusal of Work

In *The Problem with Work: Feminism, Marxism, Antiwork Politics, and Postwork Imaginaries* Kathi Weeks maps how Weber's diagnosis of the Protestant work ethic has developed in the transition from Fordist to post-Fordist economic systems. This mapping reveals the persistence of the work ethic within post-Fordist value structures. Productive work continues to be fundamental to how we define individual and social worth. Within feminist and Marxist struggles against capitalist labor relations, Weeks finds a similar persistence of productivism along the lines detailed earlier in this chapter in the theology of Rieger and Kwok. Weeks does affirm the gains made by feminist struggles which demanded access to work and the recognition of "women's work" as work. However, she makes clear its limitations: "But all of these demands for inclusion serve at the same time to expand the scope of the work ethic to new groups and new forms of labor; and to reaffirm its power. Thus the laborist ethic may have helped in the struggle to win Fordist concessions, but it did so by affirming the ideal as a lifetime of 'dignified' work (see also Rodgers 1978, 181)."[18] To affirm care work as work might be to affirm that it is within work that we find our worth.

For Weeks, this does not break open the moral order in which "the individual's economic achievement or lack of achievement depends on and is reflective of his or her character."[19] This not only means that the collective need no longer take care for those who do not or cannot work, but also that those who work need not care for time outside of work. The fight for inclusion in the work ethic is a fight for our worth, but it will always necessitate sacrifices, whether they be the "undignified" who do not work, or the sacrifice of our own time and sense of self outside that of waged labor.

Like the need for exceptions diagnosed by James in her concept of MRWaSP, Weeks suggests that "[the exclusion of some] from the dignity and worth conferred by the work ethic can serve to render its prescriptions more attractive to others."[20] When work is tied to (Divine) election (and so worth), one becomes more able to sacrifice as exceptions those who remain unelectable in order to be affirmed in one's own redemption into the labor system. In order to discuss the way in which a productivist ethos can inhabit social movements critical of political economy, Weeks draws on Baudrillard's observation that "The 'class of laborers . . . is thus confirmed in its idealized status as a productive force even by its revolutionary ideal' (1975, 156)."[21] It is worth quoting Weeks's analysis of Baudrillard's insight at length as she here best illuminates how the work ethic continues to function within leftist struggles, including those that may inspire theologies like Rieger and Kwok's:

> Although opposed to the work society's hierarchies, such tactics were complicit with its ethics. This is a potential problem with both of the long-standing feminist strategies regarding work and its dominant values: the demand for inclusion in the form of "real" (that is, waged) work for women and the demand to expand the category of work to include what has been mischaracterized either as idleness and leisure, or as private, intimate, and spontaneous acts of love—but in any case, as nonwork. Each of the approaches risks contesting the gendered organization of capitalist work society by reproducing fundamental values. Claiming one's place as a productive citizen and one's value in relation to the legitimating ethic of work, whether or not the original ethic is thereby altered, remains in this specific sense a mode of rebellion susceptible to co-optation.[22]

The lingering problems with the legitimatization of the work ethic (even as it resulted in important material gains for women and the impoverished) are a mirror we might hold to Rieger and Kwok's (and to a lesser degree, Hardt and Negri's) "redemption" of the multitude by illuminating its productive contribution to society. More people become dignified and worthy (more are redeemed), but the terms of redemption and value remain intact.

The post-Fordist economy's fractured boundaries between the public and private sphere crumble even further when the pervasiveness of this work ethic becomes increasingly and intimately engaged with definitions of personal worth. Whereas the inclusion of women in "real" work and the recognition of women's work (care work) *as* work were necessary steps for the material well-being of women, they were also harbingers for the way in which the Market, and its demand that we be productive workers, would come to define every aspect of our lives. The work ethic persists even as work and workers become more precarious. Particularly in the service sector, workers must give not only their labor but also their intellectual and affectual capital in the service of their jobs. Service workers have never produced tangible commodities, but with the service sector taking on an ever increasing role in the U.S. economy, the stakes of what Hardt and Negri name "immaterial labor" and the affects it requires are raised.[23] Hardt and Negri call such an economy the "affect economy."[24] According to Hardt and Negri, "When our ideas and our affects, our emotions, are put to work, for instance, and when they thus become subject in a new way to the command of the boss, we often experience new and intense forms of violation or alienation."[25] One's ability to provide comfort, affection, and joy becomes the product she must sell.

Additionally, when it becomes harder to identify individual contributions to the collective production processes, the surveillance of workers increases. In particular, observations of a worker's commitment to her job become all the more important for the proper functioning of the business. Hence, "A worker's devotion serves as a sign of his or her capacities just as it once served as a sign of his or her status among the elect. Strong work values are thus increasingly highlighted in management discourses as significant remedy to the new problems of surveillance simply because they render it less necessary."[26] Whereas under Fordism workers were disciplined by a belief that their work ethic was a sign of their election, under post-Fordism a work ethic (which includes a positive attitude) is a sign not only of self-worth and employability, but also social value.

Dave Eggers's recent dystopian novel *The Circle* exposes this *happy* work ethic. *The Circle* tells the tale of a kind of Google/Facebook/Amazon/Apple conglomeration; Silicon Valley's best, but on steroids. In the novel Mae Holland gets a job at *The Circle*, a tech company that provides social networking, online shopping, digital pay services, search engines, and "wearable" technologies. Mae's first job is in "Customer Experience," which is the Circle's customer service department. After each interaction with Mae the customers rate their experience. If Mae gets less than a 100 percent satisfaction rating, then she must reach back out to the customer asking what she could have done better. Customers often write back, upping their satisfaction scores to 100 percent. When Mae's ratings fall, she gets worried e-mails from the head of her team. When she does not show up to the myriad social offerings on the Circle's campus (concerts, cookouts, talks by famous inventors), more worried e-mails and texts fill Mae's inbox. The ethic at the Circle is not "Get your work done," it's "Be happy about getting your work done," or perhaps "Be your work." Even while couched as social, being happy to participate becomes part of the job.[27]

The demand to be happy and social, to give of personal time and energy to one's work, is a phenomena detailed by affect theorist Melissa Gregg in her essay, "On Friday Night Drinks: Workplace Affect in the Age of the Cubicle." Gregg, reads scenes from the television series *Six Feet Under* for what they have to say about an affect economy. She focuses on what happens when Claire, the artsy daughter of the show's central family, drops out

of art school and must start an office temp job. Whether it's the requirement to join for after-work drinks, or sign a birthday card for someone
she's never met, Claire (as well as the viewer) quickly comes to understand
"that in this situation friendship isn't much of a choice. You don't even
need to know the person, you just have to participate."[28]

In *The Circle* such demands lead to all sorts of disastrous ends; it is clearly
a dystopian read. It is also a realistic one. Companies like Facebook and
Google have massive campuses with an array of social and leisure offerings, napping pods, and hotel rooms. When one works for these companies
there is never any reason to go home. Work and leisure converge. These
companies are lauded for such services; they make work fun, as long as one
is fun at work. Recently, Facebook and Apple were praised by some for
offering to pay for female employees to freeze and store their eggs. This
was seen as recognition of the various demands placed on women of child-
bearing age, as well as representative of the companies' commitment to
diversity and inclusion.[29] And yet, we should read such a "perk" as a demand
that one continue working for Facebook or Apple during one's most productive *and* reproductive years.[30] The message is clear: "Wait to have those
distractions from work when you are past your laboring prime." The work
ethic demands hands, heart, head, and ovaries.

While couched in a less friendly package, recent articles on the culture
of the Amazon workplace also illuminate the realism in Eggers's fictional
account of contemporary work culture. An August 15, 2015, *New York
Times* article, "Inside Amazon: Wrestling Big Ideas in a Bruising Workplace" (which subsequently went viral), examined the harsh reality of the
work ethic employed by Jeff Bezos and the managerial teams at Amazon.[31]
The article detailed systems of peer surveillance and impossible performance standards: "At Amazon, workers are encouraged to tear apart one
another's ideas in meetings, toil long and late (e-mails arrive past midnight,
followed by text messages asking why they were not answered), and held to
standards that the company boasts are 'unreasonably high.' The internal
phone directory instructs colleagues on how to send secret feedback to one
another's bosses. Employees say it is frequently used to sabotage others.
(The tool offers sample texts, including this: 'I felt concerned about his
inflexibility and openly complaining about minor tasks.')"[32] The culture in
which such demands on performance and acts of surveillance become
naturalized operates under Bezos's fourteen principles of what the *Times*
reporters call his, "Philosophy of Work."[33] Bezos's principles (his articles
of faith perhaps) include: No. 2 *Ownership*, which encourages employees to
take responsibility for every element of the Amazon business and brand;

and No. 8 *A Bias for Action*, which affirms that "speed matters for business," and that calculated risks are better than slowing down to get more information.[34] In the *Times* article, current and former employees described various levels of burnout: seeing at least one person cry at their desks every day; being bullied about taking time off to treat cancer; and being pushed out after having miscarried twins, even though the person in question left for a business trip the next day, because being at a place in life where she was trying to start a family would be too much of a distraction from what needed to get done at work.[35]

So why stay? Why put oneself through this? Here is where Weeks's understanding of the strength of the work ethic within post-Fordism is most apparent. According to several current and former employees interviewed for the *Times* article, it was precisely the impossibility of achieving what Amazon demanded of their employees that became definitional for an employee's sense of worth. Only the strong survive at Amazon, so if one has survived she has become one of the chosen, the few, the worthy. According to the article, even those that had left realized they had been intoxicated with the Amazon work ethic. Dina Vaccari (who worked at Amazon from 2008 to 2014) noted, "'I was so addicted to wanting to be successful there. For those of us who went to work there, it was like a drug that we could get self-worth from.'"[36] The article continues, reporting that "Company veterans often say the genius of Amazon is the way it drives [employees] to drive themselves. 'If you're a good Amazonian, you become an Amabot,' said one employee, using a term that means you have become at one with the system."[37] This is the Protestant work ethic on digital steroids. To become good is to become one with the system. To be deemed of worth, one must become fuel for one's workplace. While we might understand Amazon to be extreme and unique, according to trends discussed by the *Times* they are "in the vanguard of where technology wants to take the modern office: more nimble and more productive, but harsher and less forgiving."[38] Productivity trumps humaneness. Flexibility trumps grace. The Amazon articles of faith resonate with the neoliberal narratives of resilience critiqued by Robin James and explored in the previous chapter. Amazon's ethos relies on its workers overcoming damage, including the damage Amazon has itself inflicted on them. What's more is it requires they overcome (resurrect) with speed and perhaps a smile. Here to overcome damage is to make damage profitable and digestible by the neoliberal machine. This runs counter to the kind of persistence we might find in remaining with the damage, in doing the melancholic care work that refuses to ransom others on the way to our redemption. To overcome, then, is to continue to avoid the past, whereas to persist in spite of damage, does not redeem a damaged past, but rather relates to it differently. Persistence refuses to let our crucifixions have the last word, nor does it cling to a cruelly optimistic hope that we are not irrevocably haunted and changed by past damage—the damage done to us or that which we've done to others in the construction of our own narratives of overcoming.

Further, the ritual formation of self-worth within the workplace (a workplace that spills into leisure space) is not only the territory of high-tech jobs. According to Weeks, during Fordism the label of "professional" was reserved for those whose careers acted more like a calling, a spilling over into the zone of the personal and most particularly described doctors, lawyers, and the clergy. However, today the term "professional," and the command to "act professionally" are democratized such that they serve as disciplinary techniques for the control of workers across economic strata. One's job becomes one's career, which becomes one's life. According to Weeks:

> Because, like the high-priced man, the professional "wears a badge of prestige" (C. Mills 1951, 138), the practice of hailing a wide range of workers as professionals also serves to cash in on the term's cachet and encourage employees to identify with jobs further up the labor hierarchy. To recall Weber's description of the Protestant work ethic, according to which all waged workers are expected to approach their work industriously as if it were a calling, those in low-waged service-sector jobs under post-Fordism are asked to approach their work professionally as if it were a "career."[39]

When labor becomes career and, in consequence, work becomes the center of one's prestige and worth, one is more susceptible to demands to sacrifice material well-being (including the wealth of time to do non-work activity or to just rest). One gives up freedoms for the prestige of being deemed a good worker or a productive member of society.

I witnessed such rationale for exploitation when in 2004 the adjunct faculty at New School University, including a majority of the faculty at the Parsons School of Design, embarked on a campaign to unionize with the United Automobile Workers (UAW). During the campaign and before the certification vote, the university administration posted signs that read, "Are you an artist or an autoworker?" This classist slogan tapped into the prestige adjuncts and artists gain by being "professionals," and not merely workers. No matter that adjuncts at the time made far less than minimum wage and few had health benefits. Might management have been using this democratization of prestige in hopes of retaining a separation of laboring classes through rejecting the alignment of artist with autoworkers? The desire to be recognized as either a prestigious career person and/or a productive laborer only affirms that it is through our employment and our happy productivity at such a job that we must find our worth. I hope here that we see glimpses of the dangers of a theology that tells the invalid to take his mat and walk or understands discipleship to be in action and productivity. Whether we are disciples of Bezos, the Customer Experience, or Jesus, if we are told our worth lies in our productive capacity to serve our God, how much harder does it become to pause, stop working, and question the terms of work on offer? I wish to both conflate those we would never want to conflate (Jesus and Jeff Bezos) *and* acknowledge that faithful action writ large need not be problematic. There are ways to read discipleship that honors holy action *and* inaction, but if we do not sensitively attend to the moments in which the conflation between Market productivism and theological productivity seems all too easy, we are in danger of fortifying those systems we hope to resist. An examination of the affectual effects of such a system of worth provided by Franco "Bifo" Berardi helps us to attend to these questions, and to trace possible alternatives to such productivism.

Soulfully Unproductive

Similarly to Rieger, Kwok, and Weeks, Berardi draws on (both to embrace and supplement) the work of Antonio Negri, and the radical thought of others in the 1960s and "70s Italian Workerist (*Operaismo*), Autonomist, and Compositionist movements. In these engagements Berardi resists productivist rhetoric and questions the political potency of the concept of the multitude. In *Soul at Work* and *After the Future*, Berardi explores the affectual effects of post-Fordist modes of production and communication (SemioCapitalism) on our individual and social psyches. He not only diagnoses the toxic effects of neoliberalism, but also elaborates a politics and poetics of the refusal of work. The unproductivity on offer by Berardi exposes the affectual and ethical issues raised when we remain within the logic of productivism, even that which claims a revolutionary and counterimperial stance. According to Berardi, SemioCapitalism "takes the mind, language and creativity as its primary tools for the production of value."[40] Under SemioCapitalism the soul is not left out of work, but rather becomes the very mode of production and therefore the tool of its own estrangement. Hence, whereas the resistance to alienation through the reassertion of the importance of one's mind and soul was at the heart of organizing workers on the factory floor, acts of resistance must take on a different character under post-Fordism.

The goal of autonomy, or what Berardi rewrites as out-onomy, becomes not how to overcome alienation—as in how to bounce back from damage in ways that would return one to profitability within a neoliberal system— but rather how to increase the estrangement between the soul and capitalist labor relations. As Berardi notes:

> The working class is no longer conceived as a passive object of alienation, but instead as the active subject of a refusal capable of building a community starting out from its estrangement from the interests of capitalistic society. . . . Alienation is then considered not as the loss of human authenticity, but as estrangement from capitalistic interest, and therefore as a necessary condition for the construction—in a space estranged from and hostile to labor relations—of an ultimately human relationship.[41]

To become increasingly estranged from labor relations involves, for Berardi, a multistep process. First, we must understand the way in which SemioCapitalism has redefined value. Second, we must identify the affectual effects of SemioCapitalism on our individual and social psyches (effects which Berardi names as exhaustion and depression in *After the Future* and the panic-depression cycle in *Soul at Work*). And third, we must engage Deleuze and Guattari's schizoanalysis as a political therapy which helps us to reorient the field of desire and so reframes the concept of wealth, reengaging us in authentic human relationships. Each step happens not through reasserting our productive capacity, but rather through refusing to participate in the systems of production on offer by SemioCapitalism's labor relations.

Under SemioCapitalism, value has been divorced from all material referent points. When Richard Nixon canceled the direct convertibility of the U.S. dollar to gold, the referential logic of value was discarded in favor of what Berardi calls "generalized indeterminacy."[42] From a radical theological point of view, a sense of generalized indeterminacy may sound appealing because it denies a determinate telos. It might resonate, for instance, with Jeffrey Robbins's call for resistance to all forms of hegemony that will come by way of an immanent exodus from the measurable. Or it might reflect the indefinite or infinite eschatology proposed by Clayton Crockett.[43] Yet as Berardi notes, the indeterminacy of value and the process of economic deregulation brought on by SemioCapitalism did not result in anarchic freedom. It remains tamed and obedient to the judgment of money: "Deregulation does not mean that society is freed from all rules, not at all: it is instead the imposition of monetary rule on all domains of human action. And monetary rules are in fact the sign of a relationship based on power, violence and military abuse."[44] Following Berardi's analysis of how deregulation has fortified the violent power of money in its encroachment on all zones of life, we might be brought back to Philip Goodchild's assertion that neoliberal deregulation has trapped us in the eschatological shadow of money. Money without a material referent is all about the promise of future wealth, to which every realm of our lives is held cruelly captive. That the referent has become deregulated does not free us from this captivity, but rather insists we must be ever more flexible in how we play the game or, in other words, how we become obedient actors under deregulated neoliberal regimes of power and the cruel promises they make.

Although this eschatological promise may be indeterminate because money no longer refers to a stable referent, it serves not as a source of freedom, but rather as one of entrapment. To counter this mode of violent entrapment Berardi, similarly to Goodchild, redefines wealth as "time for pleasure and enjoyment," which includes time to travel, learn, create, and make love.[45] This wealthy time is not a time that asks "What have you done for me lately?" Rather it is unproductive time, it is a time to be lazy, to be pleasured, to play, and to just be. It is not discipleship in action; it is not worth in productivity; it is not a man who is a worker or nothing at all; rather it is a soul who is wealthy because she is much more (and perhaps much less) than her labor. To break free of neoliberal time and feeling might be to say that we need not overcome our unproductive sensibilities or inefficient embodiments to be of worth. To be sure, there is political work to be done in order to democratize the availability of this wealth of time, but by reorienting wealth and worth away from work, indeed in finding it in the refusal of work, Berardi rejects hegemonic structures of value.

Both SemioCapitalism's rejection of wealth as time and its degradation of unproductive time lead to a mental and soulful breakdown in individual and social psyches. Berardi diagnoses this breakdown as a panic-depressive cycle (158) and exhaustion and depression (Berardi, *After the Future*, 135–38). Acknowledging Baudrillard's prescience, Berardi further notes that "The dominant pathology of the future will not be produced by repression, but instead by the injunction to express, which will become a generalized obligation."[46] The constant demands to be expressive and productive, combined with the overwhelming flow of information and signs without stable referents, leads to panic, which eventually leads to depression. Elsewhere, Berardi marks the panic-depression cycle with Baudrillard's concept of exhaustion.[47] Exhaustion sets in because "in semiocapitalist hyperreality, the brain is the market. And the brain is not limitless, the brain cannot accelerate indefinitely."[48] Rather than (or perhaps as both counter and supplement to) an emphasis on the plasticity of the brain (an emphasis embraced by followers of Catherine Malabou, including Robbins and Crockett), Berardi asks us to look to the limits of the brain—to our exhaustion—for the rethinking of how we might come to *become* differently.[49] This rethinking should remind us of Robin James's resistance to resilience, which produces surplus value out of exhausted material (including our brains).

The depression and exhaustion—the markers of the limit of the brain (or perhaps better, the "bodymind")—that follow the panic induced by our overstimulation can be traced back to the demands for the brain to accelerate indefinitely (a bias toward action).[50] In other words, "the constant mobilization of attention is essential to the productive function: the energies engaged by the productive system are essentially creative, affective and communicational."[51] Instead of rejecting the need for creative and affective communication, or for action *tout court*, Berardi—through his diagnosis of the overstimulation of the brain—illuminates how *the demand to be* productive and expressive pushes the individual and collective psyche to their breaking points. He writes, "Not silence, but uninterrupted noise, not [Antonioni's] *red desert*, but a cognitive space overloaded with nervous incentives to act: this is the alienation of our times."[52] We might say that "our times" takes on a double meaning in this case, since it is the very demand for more of our *time* that defines the nature of the *Time* of Neoliberalism or, in Berardi's terms, SemioCapitalism.

This is not to uphold all manner of dulling the mind, but rather is an injunction to seek out new ways of thinking and feeling ourselves through the affectual experiences of the bodymind under such temporal and evaluative demands. For instance, the chaotic hyperactivity of indeterminate signs that often engenders depression can also contain a sense of creative ecstasy (what I might call a manic sensibility, which calls to mind bipolar temporality or a sensory-temporality that refuses to disentangle mania from depression, as discussed in Chapter 2): "The world-chaos that Guattari talks about in his last book is not only depression, fog, and miasma. Chaos is much more than this. It's also the infinity of colors, dazzling lights, hyperspeed intuitions, and breathtaking emotions (Deleuze and Guattari 1994, 203)."[53] In this way, a turn toward our exhaustion or depression need not be the silencing of the sounds of indeterminacy and chaos, but rather a slowing down to the point where we take pleasure in the cacophony of singularities; when exhausted, we would grant ourselves permission to fall back into bed and just listen.

No longer trying to harmonize sounds that will not or will *to* not come together, we might clear a path to see what can happen on the other side of exhaustion when we are no longer fueled by the panicked desire to numb our depression. This fall into bed, the being exhausted, need not be a passive nihilism. Rather, feeling ourselves to be backward in a society that says we must move forward recalls the backward feelings of being queer explored in the previous chapter, and as explicated by Heather Love. If, as a reminder, backward feelings are "all about action: about how and why it is blocked, and about how to locate motives for political action when none is visible,"[54] then perhaps witnessing to our depression and exhaustion might actually be a way of asking how we might feel, become, and even act differently. In other words, a turn not toward the productivity of the multitude but rather toward its depressing exhaustion uncovers invisible political possibilities, including at times a depressing and at times a manic chaotic creativity.

The slowness and quotidian nature of depressing passive acts, like the fall into bed or the listening for the sounds of chaotic miasma and those of the infinity of colors, further troubles a productivist politics within contemporary political theology. We can locate within these theological fields (or within theologies and philosophies arising in the wake of the death-of-God) a discomforting emphasis on eventive action. Whether it takes the form of multitudinous productivism, event, exodus, messianism, or revolution, none of these concepts (no matter how immanent their theological constructions may be) seems to sensitively attend to the slow, often banal and backward feeling of the everyday. Indeed, they often come burdened with forward momentum won at the expense of the receptive/nonproductive/bipolar times of those not able or unwilling to participate in rapid change or forceful action.[55]

This sort of revolving and revolting (a sort that risks its own version of a teleological fantasy) is reflected in leftist movements nostalgic for the time of labor *up*risings.[56] As Steven Shaviro has noted:

> Given the failure of economism, many Marxists have instead gone to the opposite extreme: they have embraced a kind of voluntarism. Capitalism can be abolished by sheer force of will—as long as this is supplemented by proper methods of organization and mobilization. We

see this sort of approach in the Leninist doctrine of the vanguard party, and also, I think, in the ultra-leftism of such contemporary thinkers as Slavoj Žižek and Alain Badiou.[57]

Shaviro continues, "We cannot wait for capitalism to transform on its own, but we also cannot hope to progress by appealing to some radical Outside or by fashioning ourselves as militants faithful to some 'event' that (as Badiou has it) would mark a radical and complete break with the given 'situation' of capitalism."[58] Berardi counters the Badiouian/Žižekian event with radical passivity. Instead of viewing exhaustion as the inability to escape capitalism, the position of radial passivity acknowledges exhaustion's capability to clear a way toward an autonomous collectivity.[59] Might the slowdown of exhaustion serve as a radical opening for radical thought? In other words, can political theology embrace its own times of exhaustion and depression?

To counter (or perhaps reencounter, but with a difference) the radicalism of the event, we may need to look to the radicalism of the everyday. We may need to seek out a slowness performed in quotidian acts of refusal. For instance, instead of waiting for *or* forcing the revolution, we might wander toward ways of slow living proposed by Lauren Berlant in her counter to "slow death" (a concept touched on briefly in the previous chapter). Slow death might come in the form of the panic-depressive cycle, a crash from the over stimulation of the brain—or, as Berlant traces it, in the wearing down of bodies through excessive food consumption, which she ties not only to exploitative food and labor policies, but also to the exhaustion of work and the search for momentary pleasure in food.[60] To counter slow death, Berlant offers the possibility of counter-exploitative activities, those that are anarchist, cooperative, and radically antiwork.[61] Examples of such activities can be found in the European "slow food" movement briefly touched on by Berlant. Slow food marks a movement in which practices of food cultivation, preparation, and consumption "[recalibrate] the pacing of the day into a collective program for deliberative being in the world in a way opposed to the immediatist productive one of anxious capital."[62] Berardi similarly offers counter-exploitative practices through the slow life of a "relaxed soul":[63] "Rather than a swift change in the social landscape, we should expect the slow surfacing of new trends: communities abandoning the field of the crumbling economies, more and more individuals giving up their search for a job and creating their own networks of services."[64] These quotidian microtactics will take *time*, but if time is wealth, then perhaps slowing time down is a way of honoring the worth of life. A relaxed soul might let us honor and attend to our depressions and manias without anxiously trying to overcome them, as in perform as though we had been cured and our troubles no longer haunted us.

This slowdown will not be easy. Berardi offers a mode in which politics and therapy are no longer separate. He asks us to learn to better take care of those made depressed and anxious by what he names as the "post-growth" economy.[65] This might be in sympathy with the redistribution of care work on offer by James's concept of "bad investing," or by the care work implied in the Foucauldian erotic ethics that I draw on in Chapter 5, or the "wake work" proposed by Christina Sharpe that animates this book's conclusion, or the grave attending I further elaborate in forthcoming pages. But who will lead the way? Who are we that are too anxious, and on whom are we placing the therapeutic responsibility? Who gets to decide which type of depression is being exhibited—the exhaustion that leads to a slow movement toward a new civilization, or that of those made hopeless by the coming of such a civilization? Berardi suggests—playing on a post-Fordist adjustment from the proletariat to the cognitariat—that "Poetry and therapy (thera-poetry) will be the forces leading to the creation of a cognitarian self-consciousness: not a political party, not the organization of interests, but the reactivation of the cognitarian sensibility."[66] This cognitarian sensibility, that which Berardi hopes to reactivate, might be best understood through affirmations proffered in his "Post-futurist" manifesto: "Poetry is a bridge cast over the abyss of nothingness to allow the sharing of different imaginations and to free singularities," and "We sing of the rebellious cognitariat who are in touch with their bodies. We sing to the infinity of the present and abandon the illusion of a future."[67] Perhaps this is the cognitariat who refuses a bias toward action, who is in touch with the body that needs to remain seated and not get up and walk, but also who is the adjunct who *actively* or, through strategies of the refusal of work, "passively" demands her right to paid vacation and sick leave: the right (to the time) to rest and make love.

For the productivism Berardi, Weeks, and I hope to counter, we may need to look to some poetic bodies, to bodies rebelling from an ethic of work that defines our worth through our efficient labor. Indeed, whose poetics might help lead the way, such that our political therapy does not reaffirm a redemptive individualistic resilience? Perhaps, moving into the realm of the embodied sensibilities of those already living slowly—already refusing productivity and efficiency; those living in the interstices between flesh and body; those we have marked as monstrous—will help us to seek out such rebellious theopoetic possibilities.

Cripping Cure

What would it mean to embody an unproductive monstrosity (one in which little monsters do not grow up to be resilient citizens)? Rereading the productivity of the multitude through a crip sensibility helps us to unpack this question. Crip theory is a version of disability theory that rejects assimilationist politics and apologetics. To be crip is to be unwilling to come back together as part of a productive whole, when coming back together strengthens the system that abjected you in the first place. It is to refuse to wear the prosthesis so that the non-crip need not rethink the wholeness of her body. It is to refuse the cochlear implant such that mainstream society might rethink how communication looks and sounds. It is to learn to live differently from within exhaustion and depression and not only to medicate them. According to crip theorists Anna Mollow and Robert McRuer, a crip politics says "Fuck employability: I'm too sick to work."[68] To embrace the stigma of sickness is not to chain oneself to suffering, but rather to question the demands of productive labor on offer by society. To embrace one's own stigma is to turn the gaze back on the sickness of the society that stigmatized one. Hence a similar crip politics, one that tells the Empire it is too sick to work and that it is too depressed to produce, might loose the multitude from its redeployment in the very technologies of power that it hopes to resist. To say "fuck employability" is also to say "fuck productivity," as long as productivity too easily slips into commodified resilience or neoliberal redemption.

As McRuer and Mollow note, many disability studies projects "often [emphasize] the project of securing places for disabled people within what Deborah A. Stone calls the 'work-based system' (21), rather than challenging the structure of that system itself."[69] Hence, similar to the productivist ethos risked by Rieger and Kwok's reading of the multitude, access-based disability studies often seek to return a sense of productivity to the disabled. Cripness, on the other hand, refuses assimilation and rejects recognition by the systems that have betrayed us.

For instance, in *Crip Theory: Cultural Signs of Queerness and Disability* McRuer exegetes *Gary in Your Pocket: Stories and Notebooks of Gary Fisher*, the collection of Gary Fisher's work published by his former teacher Eve Kosofsky Sedgwick three years after his death from HIV/AIDS. Fisher identified himself as a "black, queer, sociopath."[70] In this work Fisher's identities as queer, sociopathic, and black destabilize one another as well as compulsory heterosexuality and able-bodiedness. According to McRuer, "as Fisher himself well knew, almost thirty years of collective action had made available (through various machineries of publication) understandings of black identity that specifically resisted white conflations of 'blackness' with anything 'sociopathic' or 'queer' (broadly and negatively understood)."[71] We might think here of James's understanding of non-bourgeois blackness as the exception. Queer blackness and sociopathic blackness are not options; they are forms of blackness that cannot be recycled into a rehabilitated narrative of blackness as goodness. Fisher resists this rehabilitation, living instead into the parts of him that are "bad investments."

This destabilization is further intensified in what McRuer names as Fisher's noncompliance with demands for "healthy" rehabilitation and redemption. Fisher's acts of noncompliance included sadomasochistic, often anonymous sex, which involved fantasies of racial degradation and his frequent refusal to take his medication. In rejecting secur(e)ity and salvific health, Fisher refused the system that had always already marked him as crip: as an untouchable monster. These acts of refusal performed a political stance of autonomy within Fisher's everyday life. They are not eventive revolutionary acts, but rather the wealthy embodiments of time by a man rejecting the pressures to be sane, straight, and healthy.

McRuer ties Fisher's noncompliance to the work of seminal disability thinker Henri-Jacques Stiker, who writes, "'rehabilitation marks the appearance of a culture that attempts to complete the act of identification, of making identical. This act will cause the disabled to disappear and with them all that is lacking, in order to assimilate them, drown them, dissolve them in the greater and single social whole' (128)."[72] McRuer continues quoting Stiker: "The practice of rehabilitation 'succeeded in making alterity disappear' and founded a world where 'identicalness reigns, at least a rough identity, a socially constructed identity, an identity of which citizens can be convinced' (131–132)."[73] Becoming identical to nonmarginal identities supposedly redeems marginal ones. And yet this redemption is never complete. As Robin James reminds us, it is always conditional and instrumental. To be rehabilitated as one of the good queers, the good disabled, the good blacks, is not to achieve social and material equality, but rather to fortify the system that marked one as bad in the first place. Fisher's quotidian resistance to such rehabilitation keeps the question of such marking open. He does not become part of the productive whole; he questions the terms of wholeness and worth on offer. In other words, Fisher's crip sensibility, while bringing on death more quickly, honored the time of life through his "bad investing" and refusal to be redeemed as surplus value.

Such bad investing might also be a kind of hypersocial or relational investing—a caring for all those made exceptions by MRWaSP, a going into the death, in order to attend to those that might short-circuit that which is killing us. The call to short-circuit what might be killing us can be read constructively through Fisher's desire for a "big big room." In commenting on what McRuer reads as Fisher's "Whitmanian (or perhaps Whit*manic*) efforts to think and write differently, expansively,"[74] McRuer surfaces Fisher's desire to inhabit the "impossible space he imagined five months before he died . . . '40 million people will have it by the end of the decade,' Fisher writes, 'I'm in good company. I'm in plenty of company. I'm less afraid. It's a big big room and it's full of everybody's hope I'm sure' (272)."[75] According to McRuer, such a big room, full of *everybody's* hope, cannot be achieved through rehabilitated identities that are made to become identical, but not equal. Fisher's noncompliance keeps questions of subjectivity and worth (and so the hopes of everybody) alive within discourses on queer and disabled identity. By refusing productive identities on offer, by refusing to take his mat and walk, or to become a good investment, Fisher refused to limit the size of the room or curtail whose hope inhabits it. In this way, Fisher's noncompliance might have been the care work on offer by James's melancholy, and the queer attention on offer by my grave attending—an attending which takes place when there is *time* to feel both depressed about and manic for the world. Fisher's cripness, in this way, is an insistence on worth outside productivist ethics.

From within this big big room, we can encounter and attend to the work of Janet Miles. Miles, who Susan Schweik names as a poet writing in part from the lens of disability, engaged similar acts of noncompliance, including noncompliance with the mark of "disabled" in her work. In a discussion of Miles's life and work in the edited volume *Beauty Is a Verb: The New Poetry of Disability*, Schweik draws on Stiker's 1999 *A History of Disability* to illuminate the importance of such acts of refusal:

> The "thing" has been designated, defined, framed. Now it has to be scrutinized, pinpointed, dealt with. People with "it" make up a marked group, a social entity. . . . The disabled, henceforth of all kinds, are established as a category to be reintegrated and thus to be rehabilitated. Paradoxically, they are designated in order to be made to disappear, they are spoken in order to be silenced.[76]

Like (and as one of) the "mad" figures traced by Michel Foucault in *History of Madness* (which we return to in Chapter 5), the disabled are named in order to be either saved out of disability (like the worker recognized as productive) or confined and silenced. Stiker's call in response to such confinement is to refuse the category of disability.

Fisher's noncompliance is similar. However, instead of refusing to be marked, he embraces the stigma carried by the mark sociopathic. By refusing to be named as redeemable, Fisher willfully goes unredeemed. This is the sensibility of the crip who embraces "the cripple" and so cannot be made straight. The term "disabled" (the term as deployed by disability projects critiqued by McRuer, Mollow, Stiker, and Schweik) marks those who we work to fix and, in fixing, reassemble back into an efficient economy of production. But what of she who chooses to stay bent? Like the mad bipolar, or hysterical, woman who plagues society and so needs to be tamed, the willfully bent and so unproductive take on a monstrous character.

The Monstrous Multitude

It would be crucial to critique the issue of productivity within a theology of "the multitude" regardless of the term's deployment by Hardt and Negri. However, in turning back to the original we are better able to uncover some crip complexities. Hardt and Negri highlight the autonomy of the multitude from the Empire. If the Empire relies on the multitude to produce its wealth, then to refuse to be productive is to refuse to contribute to the wealth of the Empire. As Hardt and Negri note, "Capital, in other words, must exploit the labor of workers but it cannot oppress, repress, or exclude them. It cannot do without their productivity."[77] They continue: "[The multitude] are, in fact, extremely powerful, because they are the source of wealth."[78] In other words, while the multitude could do without the Empire, the Imperial machine runs on the energy of the multitude. This emphasis on the productivity of the multitude opens pathways for the radical passivity proposed by Berardi. Instead of asserting that our faith traditions have been built on action and honoring the demand that the "invalid" in John 5:8 stand up, take his mat and walk, to locate the potency of the multitude in its unproductivity is to ask why the man was sitting in the first place and for whom and what would he be walking.

It is this power that is recognized by Hardt and Negri when they write:

> If sovereign power were an autonomous substance, then the refusal, subtraction, or exodus of the subordinated would only be an aid to the sovereign: they cannot cause problems who are not present. Since sovereign power is not autonomous, since sovereignty is a relationship, then such acts of refusal are indeed a real threat. Without the active participation of the subordinated, sovereignty crumbles.[79]

Given the multitude's ability to make sovereignty crumble, why not focus on the unproductive side of the line that has been dismantled between productivity and unproductivity? Perhaps we worry that such a focus will lead the multitude into inertia and despair. Perhaps this is why Slavoj Žižek's own politics of refusal quickly move to a call for a Badiouian event and the *revolutionary* power of those in the urban slums.[80] And yet, this multitudinous refusal need not be that of eventive action. Rather, we might find a poetics of refusal within the bodies of the monstrous crip who in her everyday incapacities to productively come together with the whole declares along with Berardi "that the splendor of the world has been enriched by a new beauty: the beauty of autonomy. Each to her own rhythm; nobody should be constrained to march at a uniform pace."[81] This new beauty should not be read as a wild individualism in which how we are sensitively entangled goes eclipsed; just the opposite. The splendor of the world that allows for disuniformed pace is the splendor of relation that is only relation when one can recognize the importance of difference, a difference that is never a separation.

This type of entangled relation, one that honors the beauty of the singularity, is a demand for a fairer distribution of care work as it is the demand that we attend to our differences instead of trying to attune them to one rhythm. Another name for attending to, or caring for, our singularities might be reflective of Weeks's attention to the demand to "get a life" on offer by the "Postwork Manifesto," edited by Stanley Aronowitz and Jonathan Cutler:

> It is not *the* life that we are encouraged to get, not life as essential common denominator, but *a* life . . . to draw on Deleuze's description, it is a life of singularities rather than individualities (1997, 4) a life that is common to and shared with others without being the same as theirs." Weeks continues, "Finally, the injunction is not to get *this* life or *that* life; there is an assumption, by my reading of the phrase that there will be different lives to get. To borrow another formulation from Deleuze, the indefinite article serves here as 'the index of multiplicity' (5); to say that we should get a life is not to say what its contents might be."[82]

This is not the life on offer by rehabilitated identities of those who overcome damage to be productive in the market, or of the Amabot worker whose life must become one with the system. To get *a* life would be to find *a* space in *a* big big room. To affirm the hope of this big bigness, we will have to make *room* for those unwilling to come back together as part of the whole. This is not common productivity as bond, but rather multiplicity of life as relation.

Can we find the beauty of *a* disunified pace, *a* life, in Hardt and Negri's multitude? Perhaps one is there when they name the multitude a flesh that is not a body.[83] Whereas Rieger and Kwok seem to focus on the potential unity of the social body, Hardt and Negri are concerned with the uncontainability of the social flesh. As not-a-body, they argue, the flesh can often appear monstrous.[84] In an essay in *In Praise of the Common: A Conversation on Philosophy and Politics* that follows the published conversation between Cesare Casarino and Negri, Negri traces how Power (which Negri uses with a capital P to differentiate the Power of the Empire from the potential force of the multitude) has historically been tied to eugenics, the establishment of those who are "beautiful and good" over and above those who threaten that good, those whom we name as monstrous.[85] According to Negri, "*[labor] becomes class by recognizing itself as monster*. A monstrous subject that produces monstrous resistances. The existence of class is no longer spectral but monstrous—even better, such is its essence, which carries the inscription of the force that refuses capital's productive labor."[86] The monster is monstrous in its refusal of capitalist productivity.

Negri develops the monster further as the "autonomy of the multitude," as that which "shattered the eugenic teleology," and that which "produces the common," but also that which might be captured once again, either in its return to its historic function in a eugenic economy as the site of alterity from which the "beautiful and good" are birthed, or through the techniques of the biopolitical which monstrously "improves" the monster's functioning, saving him and so returning him to the productive labor of capitalism.[87] Yes! The possibility of an autonomous monster who refuses productivity and capture! I'm even willing to abide, undisturbed, by the return of the language of the event when Negri writes:

Therefore, today is the moment to verify whether dialectics has truly ended; whether, consequently, the monster (as hegemon, through resistance of the class of those who work and are exploited) can triumph; whether the proletarian class can oppose, really, as monster, the masters' eugenic Power, *kaloi kai agatoi*. We say: long live the monster! Long live his capacity to dissolve any idea or project of capitalist development and of order (both old and new) that organizes it! . . . Today the monster is *the event waited for* . . . neither miscarriage nor wreckage . . . even though it could be such . . . but it's not![88]

Indeed, it is this sense of the multitude's monstrosity, its ability to disorder the Empire, that might be reclaimed and reread through a crip sensibility. And yet, uneasiness for me remains; something doesn't *feel* right.

In *Multitude* Hardt and Negri locate the monstrosity of the multitude in the figure of the vampire. The vampire is unruly; its desire for flesh (of all genders) is insatiable. It produces outside of the heteronormative family and outside of sexual reproduction altogether. It creates new forms of family and sociability. The vampire marks how we must all come to recognize our monstrosity, our monstrous capabilities for imagining new forms of being assembled. And yet, I argue, the vampire's desire turns the subjects of its desires into other vampires; it is the making of one, an atonement-sameness over difference. Does the becoming-same of vampiric reproduction return us to a redemptive narrative too evocative of neoliberal rehabilitation? Have we managed to get out of a resilience narrative that teaches us that it is not in the monster's damage where pleasure might be found, but rather in its ability to overcome such monstrous markings? The vampire as the monstrous figure of the multitude might be disabled but resurrecting!

I seek not to reject commonality out of hand, but rather to push Hardt and Negri to be ever more monstrous. Indeed, we might wonder just how monstrous one can be if one's monstrosity begins to mimic, without ironic difference, the monstrosity of all the other monsters. For vampires (re) productivity is replication. What if instead we looked to Frankenstein's Monster who disappears into a frozen wasteland to the North, embodying a monstrous impediment to social cohesion? Or to the disembodied hands from a slew of horror movies, hands that, counter to Paul, do not need eyes to see? This monstrous handness creeps away from demands for productivity and wholeness. This sort of crip monstrosity, a monstrosity unable or unwilling to cohere, might enflesh an alternate political theology, one in which we need not be redeemed through our common productivity. We need not overcome our brokenness (our existence as flesh and not whole body) in order to be considered valuable.

The vampire produces through over desiring. Conversely, Frankenstein's Monster and the horrific hand turn out to be unproductive. They are impediments to cohesion and communication. They say "Fuck reproductivity I'm just a hand!" and "Fuck employability I'm too monstrous to work!" To reclaim that level of monstrosity within the multitude would perhaps better serve Hardt and Negri's assertion that "We need to use the monstrous expressions of the multitude to challenge the mutations of artificial life transformed into commodities, the capitalist power to put up for sale the metamorphoses of nature, the new eugenics that support the ruling power. The new world of monsters is where humanity has to grasp its future."[89] But what if Berardi is right when he declares in his post-futurist manifesto that the future is an illusion we must abandon in order to live in the infinity of the present?[90] What if the promise of the monster as humanity's future robs the monster of its melancholic complexities today?

What types of monsters can help us to resist an overemphasis in both SemioCapitalism and political theology on movement, productivity, and revolutionary change? Who might be lurking in the shadows waiting for us, hoping we might finally come to recognize their singularity and through them possibilities for our own monstrously unproductive lives?

The Monster That Therefore I Am Follows Me

In her "Dramatic Monologue in the Speaker's Own Voice," poet Vassar Miller, who spent her life in a wheelchair (a result of cerebral palsy) writes:

> I'm either a monster
> or else I'm a brain floating within a body
> whose sides I must gingerly touch while you glance
> discreetly away . . .
> I wish you'd learn better before we all totter
> into our coffins where there's no straight way to lie crooked.[91]

Might *It Follows*, written and directed by David Robert Mitchell and released in 2015, be the horror film which Miller was in search of? Can we read the *it* that does the following in *It Follows* as that figure of the monstrosity of the multitude that might both embody a radical slowness *and* diagnose the anxiety nurtured by a eugenic economy?

In the film the blond, thin, cisgendered, able-bodied teenage protagonist Jay Height "contracts" a "following *it*" through sexual intercourse with her boyfriend Hugh. The *it* that follows is singular, only following one person at a time (although others who have been followed can still recognize *it*). *It* appears in human form and can look like anyone, including one's loved ones. In order to make sure Jay understands that she is now being followed by *it*, Hugh drugs Jay and ties her into a wheelchair from where she will have to face *it*; incapacitation seems to be the only way one will fully grasp that *it* is coming for her. Or, perhaps we do not see the incapacitation that hovers all around us until we feel the limitation of our mobility.

Hugh goes on to tell Jay that she should never be anywhere without at least two exits because *it* is slow, but not dumb. Indeed, the viewer quickly realizes that, because of how slowly *it* moves, we can spot *it* even within a crowd. Like the "cripple" who cannot rush up the subway steps, whose slowness blocks paths on crowded city streets, *it* is identifiable through its speed (or lack there of). And yet even though *it* is slow, one cannot escape. *It* is always following Jay. The *it* in *It Follows* behaves like our collective fear of disability and unproductivity, the specter that follows us around and is amplified in a culture bent on escaping from such a haunting.

This desire to escape remains palpable even as it/*it* follows us home. Home and homey places are the key staging ground for most of the action in the film. Jay is trapped in her bedroom by her fear even after she has passed *it* on to her friend Greg (whom, believing he will not be infected/affected by *it*, sleeps with Jay). When *it* does eventually follow and then kill Greg, *it* appears as his mother and does so at his bedroom door. Additionally, the climactic battle with *it* takes place at the site of Jay's first kiss (a space of innocence in contrast to the wildness of the woods, the site of Jay's infection [through sleeping with Hugh]). Perhaps *it*—depression, exhaustion, panic, and incapacitation—follows us home because the pressures of SemioCapitalism and neoliberalism do. Everyday depression (and the many worldly worries which nurture it and which it nurtures) follows one home, breaking down the duality between domestic and public life. Hence, in these scenes of hominess we find not only depression, but also our anxious attachments to relations that might infect us. Despite Greg's assumptions of untouchability, his handsome masculinity and youth do not protect him from the attack of mortality we might see represented in the appearance of his mother, an appearance *it* takes on at the moment of Greg's death.

Further, the sexual nature of contagion in *It Follows* begs for a crip reading. Panic over sexually transmitted infections (STIs)—the designation of sexual Others as a plague on the "normal" and healthy, which enlivened decades of homophobia and queer politics—resonates with the disgust and panic induced by the creep of the slowness of disability. Disability as contagion. Before Miller voices her search for a horror movie, "Dramatic Monologue in the Speaker's Own Voice" reads:

> I walk naked under my clothes like anyone else,
> And I'm not a bomb to explode in your hands.
> of course, you are not (I would not accuse you of)
> Thinking of holding me down, but of holding me up.
> Yet sometimes I'd love to be eased from the envelope of sleep,
> Stroked gently open (although it would take some doing—

on my part, that is). My lost virginity
would hurt me the way ghosts of their limbs
make amputees shriek, my womanhood
too seldom used. Have you ever viewed me this way?
No, none of you ever have. . . . [92]

We have made of those with disability, like those with STIs, untouchables. Either too sexed or too desexed, the disabled are no longer or never were for stroking gently open. The crip may not be held down, but being held up may still not be being desired for all one feels oneself to be. If ever viewed as desirable, and for Miller that seems to be a big if, she is now a bomb ready to explode in our hands. Careful, *it* might catch you, or worse you might catch *it*. Tick tick . . . boom. We panic, we flee, we fear to the point of depression that we will be caught by the bomb of undesirability, unproductivity, and so unmeaning, in essence, inexistence.

Attempts to flee this fate pervade *It Follows* (what would a horror movie be without a young girl running for her life?). Through modes of speedy mobility, like a car, Jay can get away for a brief time, but eventually *it* will always find her/us. Is this not the function of disability in a society that demands ever more adaptability and rapidity? Like the driver of a car that cannot escape a breakdown in a crash, our bodyminds pushed to the breaking point crash into depression—into disability. Indeed, like the depressive crash that comes from the demands on the bodymind to be ever more expressive, when Jay flees a place where *it* has attacked, she crashes her car and ends up in the hospital with a broken arm. Becoming herself broken, she is slowed down and driven mad by her desperate attempts to escape what follows.

The slowness and immobility is that which always follows, what always haunts at the edge of our performances of able-bodiedness. The disabled are often the ones too precarious and inefficient to be recycled back into MRWaSP. Therefore, the true horror embodied by *it* might just be its slowness. We run, panic, crash just so as not to be caught by an infecting immobility, one which will mean the death of our capable, productive, and efficient selves. Fittingly, in the film, if one is caught by *it* one dies. And at least in the opening death, it is a death that is also a cripping. The film begins with a young beautiful girl frantically running. The audience does not see what she runs from; we only experience her visceral panic. Then the screen jumps to the image of her dead body: Her leg is broken and bent at a forty-five-degree angle; it hangs over her in a seemingly impossible position, her kneecap directly over her stomach, the point of her shoe over her chest, the heel reaching up toward the sky. *It* has caught up with her; no longer mobile, no longer beautiful, she is bent. *I wish you'd learn better before we all totter/into our coffins where there's no straight way to lie crooked.* The death of the straightness of youth births the crip.

What if we had learned better? What if, in addition to being haunted, we were halted by what follows? What if, besides being spooked, we let what follows spoil us, making us toxic with *it* such that we cared not to escape *it*, but rather to attend to *it*. Can we see that which haunts as also that which halts? That which spooks as that which spoils? Halts and spoils the flow of neoliberal economics? When one reads a "Dramatic Monologue in the Speaker's Own Voice," who exactly is in search of a horror movie? Whose "womanhood" (read desirability) haunts like an amputated leg? Who has gone untouched? From whom have others glanced away? Is it not the "I" reading such a monologue now in my own voice? The *it* that follows me, even in its singularity, is also, of course, the me that is afraid of being followed. Running counter to the eugenics of neoliberalism, a wealth that is time and a beauty that comes in true singularity encourage the touching and desirous care of all, regardless of how bent we might—or might feel ourselves to—be, regardless of how long it might take to stroke us gently open. In this wealthy crip time, there is a listening to the cacophony, not merely a frantic taming of the noise. In attending to the monster that therefore I am follows me, we might clear room for a slow living that would represent a different kind of assembly than that birthed by the eventive productivity of the multitude.[93] We might find an unproductive value and hence a release of worth from the chains of our work.

(Un)commonly Unredeemed

If the horror of disability spreads like that of an STI, then perhaps there is something we can learn from a return to noncompliant and counter-redemptive quotidian acts, like those embodied by the mark of the sociopath (the mad) as represented in *Gary in Your Pocket*. For instance, a similar counter-redemption can be found in the queer and feminist work of Ann Cvetkovich. Berardi's use of depression resonates with that of Cvetkovich. Like Cvetkovich's proposition that individual depression cannot be divorced from political depression, Berardi argues that since depression is so intimately entangled with affectual demands of the economy, one cannot divorce the individual pathology from the social one. Berardi sees a certain kind of potency in the depressive mood. For instance, he notes:

> There is a truth within depression. And in fact, as we have read, "it is as if the *struggle against chaos* did not take place without an affinity with the enemy." Depression is the vision of the abyss represented by

the absence of meaning. Poetic and conceptual creativity, like political
creativity, are the ways of chaosmotic creation, the construction of
bridges over the absence of meaning. Friendship makes the existence
of bridges possible: friendship, love, sharing, and revolt.[94]

And yet what Berardi finds interesting in depression falls short of that which
Cvetkovich does.

For Berardi, depression is the lament over the loss of meaning, whereas
for Cvetkovich one can find meaning from within depression. For Berardi,
depression marks a lack of desire, the absence of the libidinal energy
needed to make meaning, and the space of incommunicability. For Cvetkovich, depression can mark the refusal to give up on one's desire for a
different kind of world; "[she] asks how it might be possible to tarry with
the negative as part of daily practice, cultural production, and political
activism."[95] Instead of negative feelings getting in the way of politics, and
a proper politic as in need of more action than depression can provide,
Cvetkovich's work "attends to felt experience as not only already political
but as transforming our understandings of what counts as political."[96] This
is the bad investment of melancholy that serves as a care for those made
exceptions by MRWaSP. This is the Holy Saturday that may not need or
seek the certainty of resurrection, but also does not succumb to the hope-
lessness of crucifixion.

Both Cvetkovich and Berardi find in depression a diagnosis of how neoliberalism and SemioCapitalism feel. However, whereas Berardi finds depression useful as a way into a political plan for healing depression and so
redeeming the soul through a refusal of work, Cvetkovich, I argue, finds
depression itself to be a part of living estranged from labor relations. She
writes of "the utopia of ordinary habit" in which one might learn to live
into the impasse and so does not force oneself to be productive and expressive in times of blockage.[97] Rather, Cvetkovich embraces movement in the
everyday—even the slow movement of brushing her teeth—as a kind of
resistance both to the demands to be efficient and productive and to an
utter numbness within depression. The utopia of ordinary habit lets one
move with depression and so opens one to new forms of creativity not in
spite of depression but alongside and from within it.

Berardi and Cvetkovich are, of course, not in total opposition. For
instance, Berardi writes: "The passive estrangement named alienation, the
painful estrangement from the self, must then be overturned to become a
delirious, creative, refocusing estrangement."[98] Here we see traces of Cvetkovich's utopian thinking. Cvetkovich depathologizes and devindividualizes

depression. She rejects cure, or what we might call redemption, in favor of the utopia of ordinary habit. This utopia is inhabited by acts not of salvation but rather of *spending time* in manners that counter both panic *and* the frantic attempt to numb depression. Like in the previous chapter's example of the singing of cover songs which both expressed Cvetkovich's loneliness and made her feel a little less lonely, ordinary utopian habits are habits of spending time over saving it. Here, again, we might recall the difference between overcoming damage and persisting in spite of damage. To feel a little less lonely through this queer collectivity is not to resiliently resurrect in order to become a productive and efficient happy subject. Rather, it is to insist that the damage done by a society that demands such happy subjectivity need not be carried alone and therefore need not have the only or last word. Hence, this ordinary utopian thinking asks us to consider how we might begin to *feel* ourselves differently through quotidian moments of feeling otherwise in relation to that which has got us so lonely in the first place.

Cvetkovich's utopianism shares some sympathies with Kathi Weeks's "utopian demand." According to Weeks, "A utopian demand should be capable of producing an estrangement effect and substantial change, while also registering as a credible call with immediate appeal; it must be both strange and familiar, grounded in the present and gesturing toward the future, evoking simultaneously that 'nowness and newness' that has been ascribed to the manifesto (Caws 2001)."[99] Like Cvetkovich's utopian habits, the utopian demand is both ordinary and imaginative. It exists concretely in the present, attentive to the past, and yet without foreclosing on possibilities in the future. Whether as demand (Weeks) or habit (Cvetkovich), these utopias ask us to gravely attend to our estrangement by investing in that which makes us strangely alien from the system such that we might imagine our alienation as refocusing and delirious, and not only as a source of despair.

The alienation of our souls, taken to their poetic level, might be, for Berardi, a return to our soulfulness and the breaking-down of the systems that demanded we put such fullness to work. He suggests that:

> The collapse of the global economy can be read as the return of the soul. The perfect machine of Neoliberal ideology, based on the rational balance of economic factors, is falling to bits because it was based on the flawed assumption that the soul can be reduced to mere rationality. The dark side of the soul-fear, anxiety, panic, and depression—has finally surfaced after looming for a decade in the shadow of the much touted victory of the promised eternity of capitalism.[100]

The resurfacing of the dark sides of the soul, the breaking out of depression from within a Prozac economy that sought to quell the darker moods in order to keep the brain productive, can function for Berardi as a way into a refocusing estrangement. And this is indeed what happens for Cvetkovich when she writes of ordinary habits. For Cvetkovich, the question becomes not how to cure depression (rehabilitating Fisher, overcoming melancholy), but how to live in such a way that keeps moody possibilities open. In contrast, for Berardi, the crucial political question is how to heal depression.

In a chapter section titled "How to Heal Depression," Berardi offers up the Deleuzian/Guattarian schizoanalytic method as political therapy touched on earlier in this chapter. Such political therapy would, according to Berardi, start from desire, unlocking the pathological obsessive loci of desire tied to SemioCapitalism so that new investments in desire— for instance the desire for time as wealth, time to make love and to create— would become possible. These investments would be "autonomous from competition, acquisition, possession, and accumulation."[101] To get to a place where this reorientation of the field of desire becomes possible, however, the depressive must submit to such a political therapeutic process. For Berardi, the depressed person is one who lacks desire and, quoting Ehrenberg, "the depressed individuals are not up to the task, they are tired of having to become themselves."[102] While we might agree that the depressed are exhausted by having to become "happy," this might actually be because to be happy with what is on offer would be the opposite of becoming oneself. And yet, Berardi prescribes the following "simple steps" for the overcoming of depression and the reorientation of desire: "the deterritorialization of the obsessive refrain, the re-focalization and change of the landscape of desire, but also the creation of a new constellation of shared beliefs, the common perception of a new psychological environment and the construction of a new model of relationship."[103] These steps reflect steps taken by Cvetkovich in her construction of the utopia of ordinary habit. However, whereas for Berardi these are steps that would overcome depression, for Cvetkovich these are steps that can be taken not because one has overcome her depression, but rather because she has learned to live differently in relation to the demands of SemioCapitalism precisely because of her depression. Depression that seeks resistance instead of resilience involves fields of desire that refuse neoliberal demands that have nurtured in the social psyche such levels of panic, including those in which one's value is inseparable from one's productivity and efficiency. This is not a glorification of the suffering the depressed feel, but rather a reinvestment in ourselves over and against the systems that profit from our attempts to rehabilitate ourselves back into the social body.

Depression as a kind of resistant and persistent mood becomes a mode of communication unable to be recycled back into SemioCapitalism as surplus value. It resists the demand to be ever more expressive. Here the incommunicability found within depression is not something to be redeemed, overcome, and rehabilitated (made straight) such that better human friendship and allegiance might be found; rather, it is a mode of disorientation that can form assemblages (to borrow a term from Jane Bennett and William Connolly) of estrangement and so encourage collectives of singular rhythms to be ever more autonomous from labor relations. That the depressed woman is not up to the task is exactly the short-circuiting potency the crip, the disordered, and melancholic bring through a politics of the refusal of capitalist labor relations. In other words, bringing us back briefly to Rieger and Kwok, it could be in the invalid's inability to take his mat and walk that we might feel resistance to and a short-circuit of the systems of his invalidation. Such resistance takes the form of our sensitive attention to what had him sitting in the first place, and for what or whom he would be walking. To be sensitively attuned is to find within disability a crip poetics that opens new spaces for questioning and dreaming. This is space cleared through grave attending—attending to those bent on not laying straight in the grave.

To rethink one's value through invalidating systems of valuation is not as much the redemption of depression or its glorification as it is remaining with a difference from within moods, both depressing and hopeful. In attending to what depression and the depressed might become from within our estrangement, we might clear the imagination for formulations of value that ask not what we can *do* for one another or how in common we might be, but rather *how* we might become in coexistence alongside one another. To differently become is to unvoid the past by refusing to avoid it. It is to welcome hauntings of those subjectivities we've tried to flee. We welcome such a haunting, not so that we might vanquish our ghosts, but so that we might recover new ways of relating to past, present, and future selves and others.

At the end of *It Follows* Jay walks hand in hand with her childhood first kiss, Paul, whom she has now slept with and so we assume she has infected with *it*. At first blush Jay seems the image of innocence and beauty, her golden locks flowing down onto her white summer dress. But then we feel it, the affect in her eyes, she is exhausted from panicked fleeing and fearful hiding. As Paul and Jay walk, the audience sees a slow-moving "person" following them in the distance. *It Follows* and this poetics of disability does not offer a happy ending; both refuse to shake the specter of our own cripness. Jay has not overcome the damage that follows her.

At the end of *After the Future* Berardi acknowledges that proposals such as these often leave his audience with a sense of bitterness. He doesn't have a happy ending either:

> And I don't like to cheat at the game. I don't like empty words of self-reassurance, or rhetoric about the multitude. I prefer to tell the truth, at least, the limited truth as I see it: there is no way out, social civilization is over, the neoliberal precarization of labor and the media dictatorship have destroyed the cultural antibodies that, in the past, made resistance possible. As far as I know.[104]

And yet he persists. The crip persists. We persist not only through grief over a lost civilization, but perhaps more so because in our melancholy we realize what was on offer was never really that civil in the first place. To persist is to attend to what remains in the wake of crucifixions. For instance, in writing about Miller's poetry, Jill Alexander Essbaum acknowledges that "While [Miller's] poems are often grave and dismal in their imagery, by their tone they are backlit with hope."[105] While, as Essbaum notes, Miller's hope may come from her commitment to her Christianity, I want to offer an alternate theological reading.[106] Perhaps hope backlights the dismal and the grave, because it is through this gravity (a pulling down as opposed to a speeding up) that we might recognize, perhaps to our horror and delight, our own crooked natures. This recognition might better prepare us to willfully go our own autonomous (out-onomical, not individualistic) ways. In other words, perhaps this kind of hope, a hope that comes through and in our brokenness, illumines ways to remain *bent* on not lying straight in the end.

For Berardi this hope comes in the very fact that his brain is limited—that although "his knowledge and understanding don't see how any development of the social catastrophe could cultivate social well-being," he also knows that he doesn't need to know or understand how because "the catastrophe (in the etymology of *kata* and *stopherin*) is exactly the point where a new landscape is going to be revealed."[107] In attending to the catastrophe (of our own bodies, our psyches, our souls, our societies), we hold out faith that we might actually be able to reclaim the wealth of time and the beauty of our singularities. We might reclaim value outside our commodifiable surplus and worth outside our work. And we might push this faith even farther, asking how we can embrace the crip that follows, how we can attend to it. We might follow the following where it *wills*.

The willfully monstrous need not wander away from all senses of collectivity. Monstrosity might come apart from a risky commonality of productivity on offer by Rieger and Kwok, only to come noisily together in what Fred Moten and Stefano Harney name the Undercommons (a doing, a practice, of community from within the marooned community, particularly in the University, already considered to be fugitive invaders, never productive or professional enough—a doing of community that we return to in Chapter 6). For example, Halberstam notes in his introduction to the *The Undercommons: Fugitive Planning and Black Study* that "the disordered sounds that we refer to as cacophony will always be cast as 'extra-musical,' as Moten puts it, precisely because we hear something in them that reminds us that our desire for harmony is arbitrary and in another world, harmony would sound incomprehensible. Listening to cacophony and noise tells us that there is a wild beyond to the structures we inhabit and that inhabit us."[108] Halberstam continues, "And when we are called to this other place, the wild beyond, 'beyond the beyond' in Moten and Harney's apt terminology, we have to give ourselves over to a certain kind of craziness."[109] What if this craziness and this dream of another place came not only in a wild beyond, but also in a depressive attention to the everyday? Might a crazy beyond be a melancholic bad investing? Might it be a sociopathic refusal to be rehabilitated?

We can give ourselves over to this madness, to the ecstasy and depression of a chaotic cacophony murmured by those crip monsters on whose effacement harmony was built. This crazy (depressed, exhausted, inexpressible, and unreasonable) "we" is not a we that will come from a suppression of each singularity's maddening noise into a harmonious battle hymn of a productive multitude, even if we *will* wage our own, perhaps slow, war. For this cacophony is the sound of Sara Ahmed's willful politics, which "[refuses] to cover over what is missing, a refusal to aspire to be whole."[110] No common battle hymn, but rather "A queer army . . . that is not willing to reproduce the whole, an army of unserviceable parts. You can be assembled by what support you refuse to give. A queer army of parts without bodies, as well as bodies without parts, to evoke Audre Lorde's call for an army of one-breasted women."[111] This is a call to arms that, in its monstrous unproductive handness, is also a refusal. It is a refusal not of worth, but of the value on offer by neoliberalism. It is a refusal that demands and "exalt[s] tenderness, sleep, and ecstasy, the frugality of needs and the pleasure of the senses."[112]

   This refusal is the willfulness of affect alien prophets, figures of faith whose moody mattering have gone too long eclipsed in favor of making them productive parts of a mainstream theological narrative. Affect alien prophets are those who might pray for relaxation more than redemption; for sleep more than salvation; and for pleasure more than productivity. Such willful prophets, and the transformations we might find in even their most "negative" of senses, are whom we now turn to.

CHAPTER 4

Unwilling Feeling

To resist both the eschatological shadow of money and a redemptive work ethic is to flow against the temporal and emotional demands of capitalism. It is to live into the prophetic role and hence the space of what Sara Ahmed has termed "the affect alien." In *The Promise of Happiness*, Ahmed examines the affects and effects of happiness and how the objects it forms shape our ontological and political relationships with society. In her critical reading of happiness Ahmed identifies those who, through their distance from socially mediated "happy objects," are considered failures or threats. These threats, or affect aliens, include: the feminist killjoy, the queer, the revolutionary, and the melancholic migrant. Affect aliens are those who do not fit the affectual script handed down by mainstream society; they are those who flow emotionally against the normativizing tide. Conversely, the affect alien's opposite, the happiness-making subject, is shaped by and fortifies neoliberal capitalism and multiracial white supremacist patriarchy. For instance, the figures of the happy housewife or smiling domestic servant exist as products of the heteronormative white nuclear family. They fortify the idea that if one is not happy with one's gendered or raced position, then her unhappiness is her problem and not that of the societal forces that shaped the subjectivity of women in relation to the serving of men and children. A demand to be happy in one's present circumstance; it is a demand to let systems of subjectivization go unquestioned. Following on the previous chapter's suggestion that we listen for a cacophony of singularities, this chapter strains to hear where certain biblical affect aliens might be prophetically lending such alienation a prayer. In embodying counter-capitalist resistance, affect aliens act as prophets of another way. Ahmed's concept of affect alienation lets us touch on prophetic biblical laments from within unexpected textual terrains.

According to Ahmed, "to be a good subject is to be perceived as a happiness-cause as making others happy. To be bad is thus to be a killjoy. [*The Promise of Happiness*] is an attempt to give the killjoy back her voice and to speak from recognition of how it feels to inhabit that place."[1] From within this space of threat, the path tread by the killjoy, Ahmed finds possibility. This possibility rests in what can be learned from pausing awhile and inhabiting the Other's terrain or, if one can never fully inhabit the Other's terrain, then attending to the space of the affect alien. To emotionally attend to the alienated is to be willing to have our terrain up-tilled, reshaped, and differently plotted.

In this chapter I suggest that in attending to the prophetic call of the affect alien, we might learn to reorient our ordinary and extraordinary practices such that they better affirm a political theology suited to counter the affects and effects of neoliberal capitalism. Such a prophetic witness requires attention to both our own temporal, ontological, and emotional marginalization and to those who have come before, who have been willing to go and feel another way outside of normative biblical and neoliberal narratives. This grave attending, which in this chapter takes an allegorical form, listens for those affect aliens long ago buried and those who exist at the margins of our cultural or theological imaginations. To listen for the alienation, whether embodied by our fellows in the present or in the ghosts of the past, is to welcome the prayerful lament of those willing to invest in the damage, to take care of and for the exceptions to redemption, those who had or have become the bad investments.

Might welcoming such a haunting help us to feel our way through the world differently? This feeling may not be a happy one. And yet to give up a certain form of happiness (one dictated by neoliberal biopolitics) in order to get *a* life, as well as to live together differently, is the recognition that to remain alienated from the emotional flow on offer is to remain desirous of other options. Other options will contain a range of moods, including surprising joys and an alternative happiness. The feminist killjoy, hence, does not kill all joy out of hand, but rather short-circuits the joy of the system achieved through her marginalization. Indeed, Ahmed's recognition that "political freedom is the freedom to be unhappy" resonates with Berardi's insistence that our goal must be increased alienation from the modes of productive labor on offer. The freedom to be unhappy and the goal of alienation do not necessitate a nihilistic embrace of alienation for alienation's sake, but rather offer an amplification of alienation as resistance to those systems that alienated us in the first place. Hence, to emotionally flow in counter-capitalist streams is to attend to the prophetic weight of affect alienation.

The prophetic nature of unhappiness comes in its insistence that the happiness on offer can never fully capture alternate possibilities of joy. Unhappiness as prophecy is the prophetic negation of the neoliberal belief systems into which we have been inculcated. The demand to be happy by those who affirm the systems that have constructed our unhappiness serves a catechistic function. Feeling despair? Come to Jesus. Feeling unfulfilled? Come to Walmart. Feeling tired? Take a pill. Feeling envious? Get a job. Don't worry, be happy. But of course, each part of our neoliberal catechism multiplies worry as the solutions on offer rarely lead to sustained happiness or, more important, to one's present flourishing. As good pupils we come to trust our teachers, and so we blame ourselves when the solutions on offer leave us still in a state of alienation. We are promised wealth, worth, and happiness if we only follow the rules of both the neoliberal economy and the nuclear family, but when achieving such promises ends up being impossible, we are blamed; it is our fault for not being flexible, innovative, and productive enough to succeed.

It is perhaps in this dynamic between promise and threat that an investigation of affect is particularly appropriate. Gregory Seigworth and Melissa Gregg, in their introduction to *The Affect Theory Reader*, remind us that where affects are concerned, any dichotomy cannot hold. Looking to the work of Patricia Clough, they argue that even in the moments of utter despair and unimaginable threat there is always a chance for something different. The slipperiness of affect, its structural resistance to being merely good or bad, allows Seigworth and Gregg to affirm that "This inextricability of affect's *promise and peril* is . . . what is pried apart and/or relayed through the patho-logy of a body's doings in the pedagogic encounter with a world's shimmerings."[2] In other words, since affects arise between and besides bodies and make up the pathways of being affected and affecting, they can never be merely promise nor peril. They teach us what has been and what is, but they also open us to the possibilities of what might be.

Indeed, affects are instructive, and as such a faithful attending to the affect alien asks us what it means to learn from and therefore witness to the lessons brought by their/our alienation.

As detailed in previous chapters, the eschatological judgment of money formed under neoliberal economics holds us cruelly captive. Hence, can a salvation that comes through indebtedness to either the Market or a monarchic Christ ever fully liberate us from our chains? In this chapter I want to look to how moments of prophetic moody blockage within the Hebrew and Christian bibles insist that the breaking of the chains remains possible, if at times only through the limited freedom of willfully remaining enraged and depressed about our situation. To resist our marching orders by refusing to feel happy or even okay with the narrative of a salvific life dictated by Fundamentalisms, whether they be neoliberal or explicitly religious, is to prophetically say no to the redemptions on offer by secular and religious theologies that profit off cruelly optimistic attempts at becoming rehabilitated.[3]

Instead of looking to characters of hopeful resilience, this chapter reads for affect alien prophets of another way. I surmise that expressions of affect alienation can be read theologically as prayers of lament. To explore this supposition, I look to Jonah and Martha, biblical characters I name as affectually marginalized. Looking to biblical figures helps us to ask what moodiness has to teach us about political theology. In turning to the bible, I seek not an authoritative reading, as much as a thought experiment, one whose hypothesis suggests that, in finding representatives of moody and disordered prophecy in the bible, we can listen to theological affect anew and, in doing so, question contemporary emotional complacency with teleological salvation and divine obedience.[4] This critique of salvation and obedience follows the previous chapters' troubling of affectual demands—complacency with the status quo, docility in the face of suffering, and happiness in the face of oppression—made by the constructions of temporality and value on offer by neoliberalism.

Once again I place in conversation with affect theorists, philosophical theology—in this case that of John D. Caputo. Like Crockett and Robbins (and from a less theological standpoint, Hardt and Negri), Caputo writes in the wake of the death-of-God. A foundational thinker for the field of radical theology, Caputo finds theological potency from within the immanent world. His theology claims a radicalism and materiality with which I am in sympathy. And yet, like Crockett and Robbins, and Hardt and Negri, I find a lack in Caputo's thinking. There is a moodiness missing in Caputo's materiality. Hence, this chapter asks radical theology to be ever more radical in its attention to affect. It asks the field to gravely attend to the messy materiality of the moodiness of those of us its events have eclipsed. This chapter demands a radical theological hearing through its own attempts to listen anew to some affect alien prophets.

The Prophetic Potential of Affect Alienation

For Sara Ahmed, feelings are pedagogical. The promise of happiness teaches us what to associate with happiness. And as such it teaches us to desire to be associated with such associations. Through socially mediated emotions we are taught value, and through the learned experience of what society deems properly valuable we are engendered to be either satisfied or dissatisfied. Along with the epistemological and pedagogical force of feeling, Ahmed finds a sense of political possibility from within the ways in which we might reorient happiness: "we might need to rewrite happiness by considering how it feels to be stressed by the very forms of life that enable some bodies to flow into space."[5] The call to rewrite happiness is similar to my calls to rethink salvation and productivity. To rethink these terms is not to deny the interesting ways in which they function; rather it is to analyze to whom a normative construction of each has granted worth. To rewrite happiness is to follow happiness where it has wandered, to see around which bodies and objects of desire it has cohered, and to reopen paths for its incoherence. To rethink happiness is to look to the damming and damning of certain lives, in order to find cracks in the dam/n through which life might flow regardless of one's submission, or lack-there-of, to manufactured "happy objects."

For instance, in her discussion of Alfonso Cuarón's film "Children of Men," based on the book by P. D. James, Ahmed notes that the revolutionary character does not flow easily. The revolutionary is stressed, experiencing the world from the position of resistance. Ahmed asks what we might learn from this experience of counter-flow, and suggests that "we might revolt by revolting against the demand for happiness."[6] To revolt against the demand for happiness is not to reject the utility of happiness. Indeed, Ahmed finds happiness interesting. It is rather to reject the idea that to be happy is to be free. More authentic political freedom comes when we are free to be unhappy: "The freedom to be unhappy would be the freedom to live a life that deviates from the paths of happiness wherever that deviation takes us. It would thus mean the freedom to cause unhappiness by acts of deviation."[7] Deviants become freedom fighters. Those who find cracks in the dam/n expand the fissures through which the rest of us might follow. They fight for our freedom to be unhappy in the face of oppressive demands for docility and coherence.

In the creation of an archive of affect alienation (the collecting together of figures who flow emotionally counter to the historical narrative, deviants who deviate), Ahmed finds what Deleuze found in political cinema: the reappearance of the people that have gone missing from history. In this reformulation of political freedom, *The Promise of Happiness* aims to tap into bad feelings as creative responses to an unfinished history.[8] What types of creative responses might be found when one lives not only into a bipolar sense of time and into a crip sense of movement, but also the space of the affect aliens that embody moods of madness (mania, depression, stubbornness, shame, and anger)? And, in terms of theology, might deviation from the paths of happiness be deviation from happy-ending theologies, neoliberal, fundamentalist, and liberal sorts? This political freedom to be unhappy is the loosing of the chains that behold us to a theology that claims we must be saved from the dangers of an anarchic freedom, one which radical theologians find in the multitude, and which in the previous chapter I found in the singularity of each crip body illuminated in a poetics of unproductivity.

Reading Ahmed's description of the feminist killjoy in conjunction with Ann Cvetkovich's description of depression, the moods of depression and madness come to inhabit a renewed and reimagined feminist response to an unfinished history. Such a response takes shape below in two biblical figures. My first biblical feminist killjoy and bipolar prophet cries out through the manic—potent self-inflating, rapid, and melodramatic—feelings of rage found in the book of Jonah. We might say that the book of Jonah, at first blush, has an air of familiarity. Even secular children and adults have a sense of a man who, disobeying God, was swallowed up by a big fish. Jonah and the whale make direct and indirect appearances in great works of literature, in movies, and in popular contemporary children's cartoons. Yet this chapter argues that we become acquainted with a different Jonah, with Jonah as an affect alien prophet. I read Jonah's refusal to go with God's emotional flow as an act of pedagogical lament. I ask how Jonah's fear in the early chapters of the book, when he runs from God's command to save the Ninevites (enemies of the Hebrews), and his anger in the latter chapters over having been forced, in the end, to save them after all, can serve as affect alien laments against interpretations, ones that temper any sense of moral ambivalence within the text. Listening to both Jonah's prophetic mania and depressive silences reveals that although we might find in the God of Jonah a God of mercy—the popular Christian reading of the tale of Jonah—we might equally find a God who seems to choose cheap repentance over concerns for justice. In hope not to settle the issue of which God appears in Jonah, but rather to refuse such binary thinking, I seek to reclaim a righteous character to Jonah's anger. Jonah's rage, I surmise, may not represent a rejection of mercy, but rather a rejection of the need to feel happy in the face of the comfort shown to those who have caused his people such discomfort. Jonah's anger, his affect alienation, keeps questions about the present material well-being of those outside a normativizing script at the fore.

My second affect alien prophet similarly attends to present material well-being. This embodiment of the feminist killjoy takes shape in the character of Martha, primarily as she is depicted in Luke's Gospel,[9] as read through the lens of Caputo's *The Insistence of God: A Theology of Perhaps*. Affirming Caputo's assertion that Martha embodies a theology that keeps the question of the material world at the forefront of a life of faith, I argue that Martha's quotidian depression—represented in her insistence on going about the daily business of life when Jesus comes to visit and her complaint to Jesus over Mary's lack of help—has a prophetic character.

I read Martha's worrying and weariness in two key ways. First, I argue that her worry over the daily business of hospitality ties the question of faithfulness to the needs of the present world; in being what I'm calling "mad for the world," Martha resists the demands to be satisfied in a future resurrection and in a spirituality that ignores the material reality of the present. In this reading of Martha I do not refuse the possibility of Mary's own prophetic role. Rather, in looking to Martha's mood and to how her emotions are refuted, I hope to imagine Martha's own unfinished history. I want to imagine how we might hear her worry and dissatisfaction not as moral lessons for our own satisfaction, but rather as prophetic in their very worrisome and dissatisfactory nature. I want to rewrite Martha's unhappiness and Mary's "better part" in order to reimagine the pedagogical and hence prophetic promise Martha's mood might hold for both Jesus and reader. I turn explicitly to Martha not so much as to favor Martha over Mary, but rather to stem the tide of interpretations that either allow Mary to flow more easily into the role of faithful disciple or have "dammed/damned up" Martha's moody character, even as they have tried to redeem her fidelity.

Having established a biblical rationale[10] for a theology of affect alienation, and returning to Ahmed's work, this time on willfulness, I attempt a preliminary sketch of what this affect alien theology has to teach us about prophetically living in the face of coercive narratives of obedience, including those of neoliberal capitalism. I argue that while the Lukan Jesus and Jonah's God might seem like strange targets for such a counter-capitalist critique (Luke's Jesus encourages a detachment from material possessions and Jonah's God shows mercy to Jonah's enemies), an affect hermeneutic begs of more complexity. It looks to the moods of those characters that seem to have gone degraded even in the establishment of our more liberal theologies. It problematizes any clear moral lesson in these texts. Indeed, might learning to inhabit a rebellious mood even in the face of what seems like a friendly theological offering (service with a smile, resilience in the face of damage) be the type of prophesy we need from within the shadows of a system that hides its coercive nature under the guise of capitalistic freedom?

This chapter is shaped by the preceding question and a series of others: To whom or to what are these mad prophets lamenting? Might it be to a God *affected* by the madness as much as to those of us made alienated by such a world? Further, can God be made affectually alienated by theological demands for future-oriented salvation, emotional obedience, and the caged-freedom of capitalism? Can God be made alienated by theological propositions that resonate with neoliberal concepts of redemption and fidelity? If so, can God be made depressed? To approach these questions, a theology that critically interrogates the promises of both happiness and God will be key. Reading Ahmed's exploration of the "hap" of happiness and Caputo's theology of the "perhaps" helps us to open up such a theology.

What might a return to the "hap" of happiness do? This question drives the constructive and ethical turns made within Ahmed's investigation of the promise of happiness. According to Ahmed, happiness is etymologically tied to "the drama of contingency."[11] Stemming from the Middle English word "hap," which meant fortune, happiness in its original context would have meant having good fortune or luck.[12] For Ahmed, this understanding of the "hap" of happiness would suggest that although today we understand happiness to be the result of hard work or a cultivation of a certain outlook on the world, in its original intent happiness was a result of what *happened to* you. The experience of happiness was not your reward for fidelity to certain modes of living, nor was unhappiness your punishment for infidelity. To be sure, that happiness contains this sort of contingency might be profoundly troubling for some. If we have no control over our happiness, then what's the point in striving to be happy? Yet for Ahmed, it is the reaffirmation of the contingency embedded in the hap-ness of happiness that we can find different possibilities for thinking happiness—possibilities divorced from the assumption that those who are happy are good subjects and those who are alienated from happiness are bad ones. In resurfacing happiness's contingent nature, Ahmed hopes to "refocus our attention on the 'worldly' question of happenings."[13]

This form of hap-ness resonates with Caputo's understanding of the theological potential of the "perhaps." Compare Ahmed's assertions on the world reorienting and remaking of the "hap" with the theological reorientations of the "perhaps" in Caputo's material theology. Ahmed, on the potency of the "hap":

> The wretched ones might be full of hap, might be hapfull, because they deviate from the paths of happiness, because they live in the gaps between its lines. To be full of hap is to make happen . . . to make hap is to make a world.[14]

> When we are estranged from happiness, things happen. Hap happens . . . a stance toward possibility might be a happenstance.[15]

> We can value happiness for its precariousness, as something that comes and goes, as life . . . to turn happiness into an expectation is thus to annul its sense of possibility.[16]

> Hope is about desiring the "might," which is only "might" if it keeps open the possibility of "might not."[17]

And Caputo on the potency of the "perhaps":

> In a theology of "perhaps," we side with the infidels and we think the true faith requires more infidelity and less mystification.[18]

> If "perhaps" is a saving power, it is one that also means that nothing is safe.[19]

> If things had greater clarity and security and a more certain outcome, we would not need to make vows or to pray or, better, we would be unable to, as the vow and the prayer would suffocate with self-complacency.[20]

> The insistence of God means that God too is asking to be rid of the God of peace and quiet.[21]

The insistence of God read through Ahmed's hap-ness and Caputo's perhap-ness is the insistence that the character of happiness and that of fidelity not be tied to certain outcomes, actions, or people. Reading Ahmed and Caputo together, along with forms of prophetic madness (depression, mania, melancholy, ecstasy, crip monstrosity), we can answer the insistence of God with our own adherence to the mad imaginaries that might *happen* when we wander away from the happy theological scripts we have been offered. This adherence to what might happen is what I develop in the next chapter as unreasoned care, or a grave attending, by which I mean a mad desire to be brought down, to gravitate toward both the mattering of the material world and to those voices that we thought were buried and gone.

To attend to graves and gravity is to ask to be haunted; it is to be open to the gift of madness. Such a grave attending insists that instead of fidelity to the script we might be faithful to a hap-ness, which grants us the freedom to question given teleological narratives, including but not limited to a Christian telos and a captive adherence to the Market. It is the wretched ones (the infidels), full of hap, that might best answer God's request to be rid of the God of peace and quiet. As Ahmed and Caputo might jointly say, it is in giving up happiness for life that we might refuse self-complacency in order to pray. This prayer would not be, as Caputo makes clear, a prayer for salvation out of insecurity into security (a certainty that a rising tide will indeed lift all boats), but rather a prayer that nothing will remain safe. This would mean, most specifically for our purposes, that those granted the most security, those who make up what Ahmed has named "the institution of White Men"[22] and their hegemonic Christian accomplices, would never be safe. This would further mean that no construction of God, not even the one proposed in the following pages, would ever be safe. It is a prayer that we would give and be given space to see what can happen—for happenings to arise from places and sources not yet known. This arising will come with our maddening attention, our careful practices of attending to both the dam/ns and their cracks, our attending to the depressing state of the world *and* to the manic possibility (promise and threat) of what might be. For now, let us listen to two such prophets crying out to us from within the cracks of the biblical text.

"Angry enough to die": The Madness of Jonah

The book of Jonah, that story of a "foolish" prophet who ran from God and was swallowed up by a big fish, has been retold many times. One such telling is found in *The VeggieTales*, a popular Christian cartoon series in which adorable vegetables act out biblical stories. In *The VeggieTales*, Jonah's alienation is not prophetic; it honors what Jack Halberstam has diagnosed as the adult demands for "sentiment, progress, and closure,"[23] and what Ahmed might diagnose as the demand to be a happiness-making object for others. During the movie, when Jonah, a scared Hebrew asparagus, is in the belly of the fish, he is visited by a gospel choir. These veggies, acting out this *Hebrew* tale, are shaped like crosses. Chastising Jonah they, sing:

> You're feeling pretty blue, you didn't do what God requested o/Yea I'd
> be bobbin too if I was going to be digested./This ain't a pretty picture
> no, I said it ain't a pretty sight. /You ran from God this morning, and
> you're whale chum tonight. /But hold up, hang on, not so fast/You see
> God's a God of mercy, God's a God of love, he's going to help you
> *from above.* /Praise the lord he's a God of second chances, you'll be
> floored by how his love your life enhances. You can be restored from
> your darkest circumstances. Our God is a God of second chances.[24]

Similarly, another musical number goes: "Jonah was a prophet, ooo ooo, but he never really got it, sad but true, if you watch it you can spot it, doodilydoo, he did not get the point."[25] These two songs resonate with a body of Christian interpretation that reads Jonah as a foolish Hebrew stuck in a theology of vengeance. Jonah refuses to go to Nineveh because he thinks the Ninevites deserve God's wrath.

Yet, reading the book of Jonah through the position of the affect alien, this prophetic foolishness can perhaps be read as a lament against theological sentimentality, obedience, and closure. According to Justin Ryu Che-sung, we can read Jonah as a postcolonial subject. Israel was invaded and destroyed by the Ninevites in 722 BCE, and Nineveh (the Assyrian capital) was considered the "'City of bloodshed, utterly deceitful, full of booty—no end to the plunder!' (Nahum 3:1)."[26] And according to Yvonne Sherwood: ". . . reading Nineveh not as the exemplary 'gentiles' . . . but as 'the Assyrians' . . . The book can no longer be resolved into a simple morality play based around a triangulation of Jew, God, and gentile, but becomes a tortuous labyrinth of argument and counterargument."[27] If we follow this reading, the lessons of the text become more complicated. If Jonah was asked to save those who were slaughtering his people, then perhaps Jonah's anger is more justified than a mainstream Christian reading of Jonah as vengeful can contain.

We might find in his "negative" affect a demand for protection and justice, or at the very least a plea to not be the one to save the people about to slaughter or already slaughtering his people, particularly if God does not need Jonah in order to perform divine acts of mercy. This reading could be supported by Jonah's own words when he says in 4:2, "'O Lord! Is not this what I said while I was still in my own country? That is why I fled to Tarshish at the beginning; for *I knew* that you are a *gracious God* and *merciful*, slow to anger, and abounding in steadfast love, and ready to relent from punishing'" (emphasis added). If we are to take Jonah at his word, an issue to be further addressed in this chapter, then Jonah—despite interpretations like that in *The VeggieTales* and those of what Sherwood calls the mainstream—believes in God's mercy. What Jonah may reject is the necessity of it being Jonah's task, as a member of the colonized, to save his current or soon-to-be oppressors. It should be noted that others have read Jonah as representative of the powerful and the Ninevites as the postcolonial subjects.[28] Yet, following the possible timelines suggested by Sherwood and Chesung, this reading can perhaps be read as anachronistic, overlaying the current subjugation of non-Jews, and particularly Arabs in the "Holy Land," onto the Jonah text. Even if we find Jonah to be closer to the seat of power, Jonah's anger toward God and the ambivalent ending of the text beg for a different kind of hearing. To let Jonah's affect wander, following it where it *wills*, opens us to a multiplicity of peril and promise that cannot be contained by making Jonah, God, or the Ninevites easy victims or heroes.

To resist an oversimplification of Jonah's character, we need not negate the importance of God's mercy. Rather, in allowing Jonah his full due, we call for a dynamic narrative of faith, one that sees in each promise: peril, and in each peril: promise. Further, to attend to what Sherwood terms "the underside" interpretations that haunt the mainstream readings of Jonah is to impede the ability to co-opt the "moral of the story" into something easy to digest. To allow Jonah his due is to problematize theologies that turn even mercy into a biopolitical tool in an economy of exchange. In following Jonah's affect to unexpected places that question God's own affect (even that of mercy), we can resist our own inclusion as part of the faithful, when Jonah's effacement is the ransom paid for such inclusion.

One such alternate narrative, one I hope attempts to hear Jonah's complexity better, is the postcolonial reading of Jonah endeavored by Chesung and acknowledged by Sherwood. Through these readings we might entangle Jonah with other postcolonial subjects and affect aliens, or what Halberstam has named "shadow feminists" and "queer failures." For instance, Jonah's various acts of refusal resonate with those of the character Xuela in Jamaica Kincaid's *Autobiography of My Mother*, detailed by Halberstam. According to Halberstam, Xuela refuses her role as colonized by refusing to be anything at all.[29] This is an enactment of shadow feminism, which refuses the identity categories on offer by a society that has limited one's choices.[30] Perhaps in running away from God's command to warn Nineveh, Jonah similarly inhabits such shadowy terrain. In fleeing, he refuses to be Nineveh's savior or condemner.

Further, in his refusals, Jonah allows for the dynamic of argument/counter-argument suggested by Sherwood to *hap*pen; he inhabits a postcolonial position that refuses to acquiesce to a project that may have eclipsed the justice owed to those colonized. In this way, Jonah's infidelity better attends to a God of the "perhaps," one responsible to the "hap" allowed for by the wretched and the affect alien. The opening to a different hearing from a postcolonial underside continues to have consequences for a theology that remains faithful to the madness of what might happen, particularly when we differently hear the last lines of the book, the part of the story most prominently used to portray Jonah's "foolish" and "vengeful" nature.

At the end of the book, after God has spared Nineveh, Jonah is not pleased. He tells God he knew God would spare them and that this is why he fled. According to Jonah, his anger is not about the actual result of Nineveh's salvation, but rather the process of salvation. Perhaps it seems to Jonah that God would have spared his oppressors, whose repentance appears at best too easy and at worst inauthentic, all along. In 3:5–9, immediately after Jonah has proclaimed to Nineveh that they have forty days to repent or they will be overthrown, the narrator tells us:

> And the people of Nineveh believed God; they proclaimed a fast, and everyone, great and small, put on sackcloth. When the news reached the king of Nineveh, he rose from his throne, removed his robe, covered himself with sackcloth, and sat in ashes. Then he had a proclamation made in Nineveh: "By the decree of the king and his nobles: No human being or animal, no herd or flock, shall taste anything. They shall not feed, nor shall they drink water. Human beings and animals shall be covered with sackcloth, and they shall cry mightily to God. All shall turn from their evil ways and from the violence that is in their hands. *Who knows?* God may relent and change his mind; he may turn from his fierce anger, so that we do not perish." (NRSV; emphasis added)

God, through Jonah, has given Nineveh forty days, and yet almost immediately, without time for discussion and reflection, the Ninevites repent, going as far as to throw sackcloth over the animals. The extremity of this repentance can be read as a farcical swing of the pendulum—the city going from one of "bloodshed, utterly deceitful, full of booty—no end to the plunder!" to one of immediate and complete repentance. We might interrogate not only the sincerity of repentance, given the extremity of the response, but also whether it was widespread and lasting.

For instance, the king of Nineveh says, "Who knows? God *may* relent" (3:9), which could imply that his performance of repentance is an act of hedging bets. He does not claim certain belief in God's conviction and power, but rather affirms the threat of destruction and so takes action just in case. Indeed, as pointed to by Gerald O'Collins (albeit as a way to take the side of the Ninevites), "But in a *sudden* and total conversion, the *whole* people and the king of Nineveh 'believed God.'"[31] Is it unreasonable to assume that this suddenness was suspect to Jonah? Although a theology of the "per-haps," a mad attending to what might happen, may not reject such a hedging (a God that *may* be and so one who *may* save) or be in search of a complete repentance, we can find in this melodramatic tone and questionable sincerity a resistance to any clean-cut reading of the moral nature of the characters in the Jonah tale.

Additionally, we have no previous narrative of Jonah as hostile toward the gentiles. Those who are innocent do not get his wrath. In chapter 1 God sends a storm that threatens not only Jonah's life, but also the sailors with whom Jonah was fleeing. When it becomes clear that it is Jonah who is to blame, Jonah tells them to "'Pick me up and throw me into the sea, then the sea will quiet down for you; for I know it is because of me that this great storm has come upon you'" (1:12). Jonah here is willing to sacrifice himself in favor of saving the whole ship. Might we not then assume that something different is going on with his reaction to the salvation of the Ninevites? Additionally, although Daniel C. Timmer, citing Jonah's melodramatic tone, questions the sincerity of Jonah's statement, in 4:2, about how he knew all along that God was a gracious God, slow to anger, he does not allow for the same possibility in terms of the sincerity of Nineveh (an issue discussed further in this chapter).[32] Hence, might Jonah's anger be heard as a response to what I'm calling the cheap repentance of Nineveh and the risk of a too cheap acceptance of such repentance on the part of a safe God, as much as (if not more so than) a rejection of Nineveh's ultimate salvation?

Or perhaps Jonah's anger arises not only from skepticism over Nineveh's sincerity but additionally out of trauma from the divine ordeal endured in the process of being coerced into prophetic action. God threatened Jonah's life with a storm and the belly of a beast, and then made Jonah responsible for the lives of those who had been slaughtering or would slaughter his people. Might the affects of such a trauma be those that bubble up in the dialogue between Jonah and God at the end of chapter 4?

> "And now, O LORD, please take my life from me, for it is better for me
> to die than to live." And the LORD said, "Is it right for you to be

angry?" Then Jonah went out of the city and sat down east of the city, and made a booth for himself there. He sat under it in the shade, waiting to see what would become of the city.

The LORD God appointed a bush, and made it come up over Jonah, to give shade over his head, to save him from his discomfort; so Jonah was very happy about the bush. But when dawn came up the next day, God appointed a worm that attacked the bush, so that it withered. When the sun rose, God prepared a sultry east wind, and the sun beat down on the head of Jonah so that he was faint and asked that he might die. He said, "It is better for me to die than to live."

But God said to Jonah, "Is it right for you to be angry about the bush?" And he said, "Yes, angry enough to die." Then the LORD said, "You are concerned about the bush, for which you did not labor and which you did not grow; it came into being in a night and perished in a night. And should I not be concerned about Nineveh, that great city, in which there are more than a hundred and twenty thousand people who do not know their right hand from their left, and also many animals?"[33]

By refusing to be happy about being coerced back into the role of prophet (and to be comforted after God has granted him shade from the desert wind, only to cruelly take the shade away, exposing Jonah once more to the sweltering heat), Jonah is once again refusing to become what God has demanded. Jonah's repeated proclamation that it is right for him to be angry and angry enough to die can be read as an act of masochistic refusal. Jonah does not seek easy remedy (like the cheap repentance of Nineveh) for his anger or his discomfort at having been left unshaded in the desert sun. Rather, Jonah persists in his posture of refusal and so resists through his inaction and his affect.

This affect, as noted briefly earlier, can be read similarly to the excessive—and therefore comical—repentance of the king of Nineveh, and yet this does not dampen its prophetic character. We can affirm Jonah's melodrama, particularly since we have affirmed that of the Ninevites. Indeed, the parallel between the excessiveness of the two reactions, those of the king of Nineveh and of Jonah, perhaps strengthens the prophetic importance of Jonah's anger and depression. If the Ninevites repent so quickly, in a manner that may seem insincere, then even if Jonah's anger is itself an inflated performance, it is one that refuses to give this story's God too simple of an ending—a cheap acceptance of His command.

Jonah of course has already not made things easy for God, nor has God for Jonah—each killing the other's joy—but this moment, coming in the story's final lines, leaves a particularly lasting impression. To be sure, the impression left might be one in which we see non-Israelites understanding God better than this Hebrew Prophet ("Jonah was a prophet but he never really got it, doodilydoo"), a message that has been read as a pre-Christian acceptance of a merciful God. Yet there is another way to interpret this exchange. That the book concludes not on the turning of his heart, but rather in a question, may mean that Jonah's challenging of God (his infidelity) is his greatest act of faith. Like Martha, who we will see later in this chapter is dutiful, but with disdain, Jonah, once coerced back into his prophetic duties, complies, but with complaint. As Ahmed reminds us, sometimes being unhappily willing is its own kind of resistant willfulness.[34] Both of the biblical figures followed in this chapter found moody ways to keep their wills crooked in the face of the straightening rod of mainstream interpretation. Jonah will do God's bidding, but he need not be happy about it; his affect, perhaps all the resistance he has left, will not be swayed. And so even in the face of his God, and even in *silence*, Jonah may be refusing to go unheard.

The narrative complication brought when we follow Jonah's mood remains even if we read Jonah's affect as other than righteous anger. For instance, Michael Snediker, drawing on Eve Sedgwick's reading of shame in the writings of Henry James, offers us the possibility of a different account of Jonah's desire to die. Imagine a teenager embarrassed by a parent:

> *I could just die!* More often than not a performative of shame rather than a literal threat (shame, after all, is as Sedgwick suggests, the performative affect par excellence), this articulation of shame nonetheless speaks to the ways shame, as an affect, erupts not just in the space between one version of self and another (as in James), but also in the space where one *wants* another self, and more acutely, wants to give up the self one *has*.[35]

Perhaps Jonah is ashamed. Perhaps he wishes he were someone else, either someone more merciful, or someone who had not saved Nineveh. Perhaps the self that has come out of the fish and gone into Nineveh looks back on the self that fled with shame. In its performativity, shame "inhibits not only enjoyment, but continuity."[36] Shame disrupts the continuity of an unquestioned self and therefore the enjoyment of a safe self. Perhaps it is from this sense of a discontinuous self, one arising over the course of his journey, from where Jonah's joy is killed. Perhaps it is not God, but Jonah's own shame at his shifting position in relation to God that has got him so heated.

For Sedgwick, Snediker reminds us that "Shame . . . 'generates and legitimates the place of identity . . . but does so without giving that identity space the standing of an essence' (64). While identities are not to be essentialized, however, Sedgwick claims that 'at least for certain ("queer") people, shame is simply the first, and remains a permanent, structuring fact of identity' (64)."[37] While Snediker embraces Sedgwick's understanding of shame as a disruption to continuity and accedes to its place as a queer affect, he rejects shame as *the* queer affect par excellence and uncovers where affects like joy actually precede shame. And yet it is the disruption of joy that shame may bring and shame's queering of a sense of self that become important for our current reading of Jonah. Even if we decide Jonah's anger comes more from shame than from a righteous adherence to justice (or better, if we remain ambivalent about just what affects Jonah is performing), it is in the disruption of the continuity of Jonah's self in relation to God that we might still find in Jonah's affect a prophetic haunting of accepted histories.

In finding a queer sense of shame in Jonah's anger, we might see that not only does shame act pedagogically on Jonah, but also on God and reader. To feel Jonah's shame with Jonah is to ask what does he need to be ashamed of? What are the systems of subjectivization on offer that have constructed his actions and his characterization in the story as shameful? Is there shame in being afraid? In being disobedient? In anger? In vengeance? Is it shameful to desire shade for which he did not labor? Perhaps Jonah's shame is pedagogical toward God, asking God to be ashamed. What parent doesn't feel the force of the child's melodramatic wish for death at the moment of embarrassment? Even if one finds the other's shame ridiculous, the embarrassing action that has brought on such shame is still surfaced. Shame, like all affects, cannot be easily parsed—its pedagogical lessons are not clear-cut. It is both promise and peril. Indeed, the discontinuities of self, illuminated by Jonah's potential shame, may actually be like the postcolonial rejection of the choices of self on offer—condemner or savior—in which while the joy of the one shamed (Jonah) may be disrupted, so too might his affect disrupt any uncomplicated and continuous theological shaming committed against him. At the end of the story we do not get Jonah's final decision on whether it is right for him to be angry. We are left with God's questioning of Jonah's rage. To be left with a question and no clear answer is an affecting request that the reader sit with the force of Jonah's mood and the divine question it provokes. The question of mood, not its coherence, is most instructive.

The question of the question that ends the book of Jonah can fortify the importance of affect theory for biblical interpretation. To be sure, we might assume that Jonah's silence at God's final question is a sign that Jonah has lost the argument, leaving readers of the text with a clear moral lesson about Jonah's failing and God's just mercy. For instance, Albert Kamp argues that Jonah's silence at the end of the book, and the abruptness with which the book ends, allows for God's perspective to hang most heavy in the air; God literally has the last word.[38] And yet there is more to be found in Jonah's silence and silencing. Silence need not be acquiescence; it might be exasperation. Jonah's heart has not necessarily turned toward God. *Perhaps*, Jonah has become exhausted with a God who, he feels, does not get it. Jonah's silence may be another moment of the mad being unwilling to let (it) go. Additionally, Sherwood (whom I quote at length, since her reading exemplifies and inspired the counter-reading of Jonah I attempt here) argues that the interpretations of silence as acquiescence do not represent Jonah's intent as much as the wishes of Jonah's interpreters:

> A good pupil-prophet is evidently seen and not heard. When Jonah speaks uninvited the post of teacher-critics instantly tell him to sit down and shut up: his protest in 4–2 is dismissed as a "lame excuse" for disobedience or as an irreverent "attempt to limit the scope and intention of God's word." The hushed atmosphere of the classroom promotes quietism in the most literal sense. And as Jonah's speech is converted to silence, so his silence, ironically, is interpreted as speech . . . the space at the end of the text (where Jonah, for his own reasons, does not answer God's rhetorical question) is interpreted as either a moment where Jonah bows the knee and acknowledges his error, *or* a moment where the reader and Jonah's education come to a climax in an exam. "The reader has to carry away the question, think about it, and decide rightly," Wolff declares.[39]

Indeed, why assume that Jonah now affirms God's argument? His affect and actions have perhaps shown otherwise.

Rather than a prayer of repentance, what gets repeated is one of affect alien lament: "angry enough to die," "yes angry enough to die." Jonah's litany takes on a mix of rage and despair, a kind of bipolarity in which Jonah's depressive exhaustion becomes manic melodramatic rage. To refuse to be happy with God, to leave the space open for his unhappiness, but also for myriad emotional reactions in the reader, Jonah has gifted us the possibility to leave a happy-ending theology for a living one, for God's life with us to contain a promise that may or may not be fulfilled—a promise for justice, for mercy, for a different kind of faith.

The dialogical nature of this text allows, if not for total recovery, then at least for a kind of prophetic haunting. This is a haunting that would not assume we knew why Jonah was so heated, but rather would see what happens when we take up in hot pursuit of his anger or shame. After all, it is in attending to the wretch, he who will not be happy with a reading of God as one of peace and quiet, where things might happen.

The biblical Jonah does not have a happy ending. In contrast, *The VeggieTales* narrative is one in search of a clear moral lesson. Reflective of Sherwood's resistance to interpretations that view Jonah as a silent pupil-prophet we might, along with Halberstam, again find Kincaid instructive: "'I think in many ways the problem that my writing would have with an American reviewer is that Americans find difficulty very hard to take. They are inevitably looking for a happy ending. Perversely, I will not give the happy ending. I think life is difficult and that's that.'"[40] The happy ending provided by *The VeggieTales* is not a happy ending for Jonah, but rather one that hopes to make us feel uncomplicatedly good and certain about God. It is one that offers us a God of peace and quiet and not one of the hap, of potentiality. Ransoming Jonah, we are able to say, you with your foolishness and anger, it is your kind of attitude we have overcome. Hence, to refuse to empathize with Jonah's anger may be to theologically empathize with the mainstream and so with the victors.

In a theo-ethical reading of Jonah, Miguel de la Torre writes that Jonah has failed to understand God's message of mercy and chooses retributive justice instead of reconciliation.[41] Yet the request that the oppressed not make waves (not one specifically made by de la Torre), that they find "peaceable," "positive," or "productive" modes and moods of dealing with their oppression allows the very structures that demand such reconciliation to go unquestioned. An affect alien, Jonah refuses this type of liberal politics. He queerly fails, á la Halberstam, at a theological game, but in failing he reveals that this game was one he could never win.

In addition, Sherwood argues that while Jewish readings have historically embraced a questioning that leaves all involved (God, prophet, and reader) uneasy, "The [Christian] mainstream gratifies the reader, comforts and reassures her, places her above the vacillations of the text. The role of the book is not to teach, to surprise, or even less to dislocate us; the view of life is sanguine: God is on our side, the plot flows in our interests, it vindicates our position, and God throughout, is demonstrating his love for us, his Ninevites."[42] Here again we can call to mind *The VeggieTales'* need for moral closure versus Kincaid's refusal to give her reader a happy ending. In siding with Kincaid, via Halberstam, we can refuse the comfort on offer to us by *The VeggieTales* and other mainstream readings that sacrifice Jonah for our vindication. We can choose instead to make the bad investment of sticking with Jonah in all his moody tension.

Such tension is amplified by the volatility of Jonah's mood:

> Like all monstrous aberrations, Jonah is too hot and too cold: the excess is important, not the temperature. Thus he is situated at the heart of the anti-Jewish rhetoric in which "Jews are too smart and innately incapable of genius . . . over-intellectual but over-emotional, hyper-rational but superstitious". . . . The spectre of one who is at once too hot and too cold explodes the very binary system on which his existence depends.[43]

Jonah as a Jew, in this way, is already an affect alien. He is overly upset about his own life, but not upset enough about those of the Ninevites. He is foolish enough to think he can run and hide from God, but cunning enough to try and convince God he believed in God's mercy all along. He is melodramatically overheated (manic) when left in the sun and coolly detached (depressed) from the lives of the Ninevites who "do not know their right hands from their left" (Jonah 4:11). Jonah the Jew is already too bipolar, already too monstrously affected. Whether he would like to be or not, he has already been affectual alienated from the mainstream. What remains to be recognized within this bipolarity is a prophetic voice, a faithful refusal to get his disordered emotions in check and his moral lessons in order. Such refusals become prophetic when they refocus us on those whose complexity of life we have erased for our own "moral" formations of community and self. While not giving a clear alternate vision, I consider Jonah's anger prophetic because it troubles the stability of narratives and so asks for other options.

Read through Halberstam's "queer failure," Ahmed's "affect alienation," and Caputo's "theology of perhaps," in the book's final question we find a refusal to choose clear sides—fidelity or infidelity, obedience or disobedience, moral or immoral—and as such, a way of keeping the promise of God's mercy *and* justice alive. In other words, in his shamefully discontinuous self, Jonah opens alternate flows through the story that the mainstream had sought to dam/n up. In rejecting the mainstream premise of faith, Jonah opens us to the fracturing of the term, but also to the fecundity found in asking for other options. It is in finding power not in a successful political or theological program, but rather in failing to get (with) it, and refusing to be comforted, that Jonah becomes an affect alien prophet pushing our material theology to be ever moodier and ever more radical.

What May/be of Martha

We might rediscover another moody happening in the story of Mary and Martha in Luke 10:38–42. Jonah, himself, haunts Luke's gospel. Our affect alien prophet, redeemed as the symbol of the importance of repentance, is a warning about condemnation in Luke: "When the crowds were increasing, he began to say 'This generation is an evil generation; it asks for a sign, but no sign will be given to it except the sign of Jonah. For Jonah became a sign to the people of Nineveh, so the Son of Man will be to this generation. . . . The people of Nineveh will rise up at the judgment with this generation and condemn it, because they repented at the proclamation of Jonah, and see, something greater than Jonah is here!'" (Lk 11:29–33). Jonah has given way to something better; the Son of Man has arrived to turn even more hearts, to save even more sinners. Jonah's presence in Luke not only serves as a tie between our two affect alien prophets, but it also keeps the question of condemnation at the fore of this analysis. Just as we slowed down to attend to the complexity of Jonah's affect, what might happen if we were to attend not to the hero of the Lukan tale (the Son of Man), but to one who seems to go, if not condemned, then demeaned for not following the right signs? What might *hap*pen if we read Martha as one of the wretched, as an infidel (a reading Caputo has already begun for us), and as an affect alien prophet?

Following a rereading of Jonah's anger not as foolish, but rather as theologically fecund, we can read Martha's weariness with Mary and her frustration with Jesus not as problematic, but rather as prophetic. Perhaps Martha's moodiness is a prophetic lament against a structure of hospitality that risked slipping into coercive obligation instead of persuasive relation. In posing questions to the possible coerciveness of the demands of discipleship and hospitality in Luke we can rethink what has gotten Martha so down. In contrast to a madness that takes the form of crisis, Martha's steady commitment to the present moment is reflective of the type of affecting depression described by Cvetkovich when she notes that depression follows one home such that feelings of depression and anxiety become ordinary, infused in quotidian worries. Reading Martha's worries alongside Cvetkovich, we glimpse into Martha's busyness the formation of everyday habits that keep the body moving despite the weight of both ordinary worries and those of an extraordinary character. To read Martha's affect in this way is to uncover the possibilities for a more radical reading of the everyday within the biblical text. These possibilities would resist a sense of redemption out of depression and worry, the comforting salve that might come with interpretations of the Martha and Mary story that claim utter fidelity to Christ's promise of future salvation and to Mary having "the better part" of faith. To interpret Martha's affect as prophetic is, instead, to keep the question of what's going on right there and right then for Martha, Mary, and Jesus alive. But also, it is to keep our senses attuned to how narratives of faithfulness often transform prophetic complexities into historical complacency. Martha's affect alien lament can be read as that prayer invoked by the insistence that nothing, not even Jesus, be safe. In her quotidian refusal to ignore the material necessities of the world and in her refusal to be quieted in a structure of hospitality, she makes the "hap" happen. It is not obedience to a safe God, but rather madness for the world, for the present needs of daily life and for her own present condition, that Martha's response to Jesus invokes.

Of course, only a "safe" God and world can be placed into such a competitive relationship. Hence, it is not a God divorced from interpretation that this reading of Martha seeks to undo, but rather the God constructed from the follies of both traditional interpretations that position Martha and Mary into binary opposition (the material vs. the spiritual) and contemporary readings that, while embracing or "rescuing" Martha from her demeaned position, eclipse her mood. In other words, my reading of Martha's madness for *and* moodiness about the world might illuminate how she shows her fidelity to a God of the world and so a God willing to be made, unmade, and remade by the world. This God would bring less condemnation and more constructive contestation. Or as Caputo might put it, "to be faithful to the soul is to be faithful to the ground of God."[44] Taking Caputo a step further, we might say Martha's soulfulness is reflected in *her dissatisfaction* with both Mary and Jesus. In her *unhappiness*, Martha may be responding to the event of Jesus' arrival. Attending to Martha's alienating and alienated laments teaches us to resist the dichotomy between faith and unfaith, between comfort and confliction, between the spiritual and the material; it risks giving up happiness with God in order for God to live.

While traditional interpretations often placed the sisters Mary and Martha, who welcome Jesus into their home in the Gospel of Luke, as diametrically opposed—Mary the representative of the contemplative (and better)[45] life, and Martha the embodiment of preoccupation with the matters of the world—contemporary scholarship has taken a much broader and complex approach. To be sure, many interpreters, following a pattern already established in the ancient and medieval church, have read Mary and Martha in this dualistic way, placing Mary on the side of spiritualism and Martha (disparagingly so) on that of materialism. To do so, they have emphasized Jesus' assertion that Mary has chosen the "better part" (Lk 10:42). Additionally, some feminist interpreters read this verse as Jesus' encouragement for the breaking-open of gender roles, arguing that he urges Martha out of the kitchen and toward the role of spiritual disciple.[46] Yet, along with more recent readings of Martha, including that of Loveday Alexander and Caputo, we can request of this Gospel event even more complexity, allowing Martha her due.

I will read Martha's story through: Alexander, who attempts to "rescue" Martha through a reengagement with the text; an intertextual look at the discipleship in Luke; Caputo, who views Martha as the representative figure of a material theology, a figure, who, through a perceived infidelity, actually shows a greater commitment to the carnality of God;[47] and Ann Cvetkovich's discussion of the everydayness of depression. Reading with this constellation of texts, we might hear Martha's worry and anger as the prayers of an affect alien prophet, one who leaves open the potency of the hap of a material theology attentive to the mattering of our mood.

The Double Bind of Female Discipleship in Luke-Acts

An intertextual reading of the Mary and Martha story from within the larger theological discussion of discipleship within Luke-Acts helps to support an alternate reading of Martha's complaint to Jesus: "'Lord, do you not care that my sister has left me to do all the work by myself?'" (Lk 10:40). Read through the lens of feminist affect theory, this complaint becomes not only justifiable, but also prophetic and pedagogical. In order to flesh out some possible grounds for Martha's justified frustration, an exegesis of the consequences for women in terms of Luke's understanding of discipleship will be helpful. Particularly helpful is an investigation into verses 14:25–33, a direct statement in Luke-Acts on the cost of discipleship, and so one might say, criteria for "the better part" of faith granted to Mary by Jesus:

> Now large crowds were traveling with him; and he turned and said to them, "Whoever comes to me and does not hate father and mother, wife and children, brothers and sisters, yes, and even life itself, cannot be my disciple. Whoever does not carry the cross and follow me

cannot be my disciple. For which of you, intending to build a tower, does not first sit down and estimate the cost, to see whether he has enough to complete? Otherwise, when he has laid a foundation and is not able to finish, all who see it will begin to ridicule him, saying, 'This fellow began to build and was not able to finish.' Or what king, going out to wage war against another king, will not sit down first and consider whether he is able with ten thousand to oppose the one who comes against him with twenty thousand? If he cannot, then, while the other is still far away, he sends a delegation and asks for the terms of peace. So therefore, none of you can become my disciple if you do not give up all your possessions." (NRSV)

Reading the above verses in conjunction with further elaboration of discipleship in Luke-Acts surfaces issues of gendered alienation. One might find issues of alienation in terms of the role of women in the balance sheet of discipleship. In the Martha and Mary pericope the Greek reads, "But Martha was distracted with much serving [*diakonian*]" (10:40). Elisabeth Schüssler Fiorenza, in *In Memory of Her: A Feminist Theological Reconstruction of Christian Origins*, famously and influentially argued that *diakonia* here is a lightly coded reference to Christian service or ministry, and that Luke is engaged in a critique of women who took on active roles in the early Christian movement. Mary, who adopts a more passive, "properly subservient" role, is elevated over Martha.[48] This raises the question of who exactly was free or encouraged by the gospel writer to abandon kin in order to follow Jesus. What does it mean that Luke's gospel includes the hating of wives? What might this mean for those women who try to follow and those who are abandoned? Who served as ransom for the cost of discipleship?

Most important for our reading of Martha and Mary, although discipleship is available to some, it seems to be primarily for those unattached to households. According to Francois Bovon, since Luke describes Martha as the one who welcomes Jesus into her (singular) home, we can conclude that Martha was the household manager (Lk 10:38).[49] Further, he notes that the inclusion of what he names as the "event with unforeseeable consequences," initiated by the welcoming of a guest into one's home is representative of a critical concern in the early Christian community, that of providing hospitality to itinerant missionaries.[50] The requirements of faith necessary of those who join such itinerant missions—the injunction to "hate" family in Luke 14:26 and to give up all of one's possessions in Luke 14:33—carry implicit requirements for both those left behind (the hated) and those whom the disciples would have to rely on for sustenance, after having eschewed their own familial and material supports to follow Jesus. In Luke, in particular, that "wife" is one of the things that must be hated and left behind helps to place Christian women into two categories: first, those who had or felt they could take the freedom to follow Jesus, abandoning home and family; and second, those without or unwilling to practice this freedom, those who, while being a necessary part of the Jesus movement in their acts of hospitality, risked being considered to be taking part in the good, but not the better.

Although it seems that neither Martha nor Mary was tied to the household because of husbands or children, Martha, as the head of the household, may have felt unable to abandon the work of hospitality, on which Jesus, in visiting her home, would necessarily rely. We might go as far as to say that Mary had the freedom to take "the better part" because Martha took on the work of answering the event initiated by a guest coming to the door. Or, as Augustine argued, Martha and Mary were utterly connected and consequent to one another: "[Martha] is disturbed [with feeding], so that [Mary] may [simply] feast; this one orders many things, so the other may [simply] behold one."[51] The duties of Martha's hospitality allow for Mary's freedom to follow.

Loveday Alexander finds a similar double bind in the story of Martha and Mary. Her reading, which attempts to "rescue" Martha by honoring both the integrity of the text and that of her feminist concern, unearths issues within a dualistic reading of Martha and Mary that vindicates Mary by rebuking Martha. In such a dualistic reading, "Mary's elevation is only achieved at the expense of Martha's humiliation. Mary crosses the cultural boundary between female and male domains, and is praised for it, but what does this do for her sister?"[52] The making of Martha as an exception for the inclusion of Mary as the better disciple (perhaps Mary's "look I overcame gender" narrative) persists as long as Martha, while doing what was necessary, did not do what was better. And yet Martha's service is needed to support the itinerant Jesus movement. As such, "Told in this [dualistic] way, the story encapsulates an all-too-familiar double-think, whereby a dominant social group simultaneously assigns certain necessary but unpopular tasks to a helot class and denigrates their importance."[53] Alexander recognizes such a dynamic when male preachers, siding with Mary, chastise their congregants for making too much fuss over work in the world ("women's work" perhaps in particular); these same preachers then expect the table to be set and dinner to be ready when they get home. We might further see such demeaning today when during labor struggles, like the fight to raise the minimum wage to $15 an hour (the fight for 15), opponents ask whether fast-food workers (and other service laborers, who are often women of color and recent immigrants [authorized and not]) should really be making more than paramedics. We rely on those providing necessary service (servant leaders perhaps)—sanitation workers, janitors, those who prepare and deliver food—while demeaning them. We deem them to have the worse part (and so assume they deserve worse pay, which means they possess less value under Market Fundamentalism). Thanks to their service, we "professionals" (often also paid poorly) have more freedom to choose "the better." Allegorically speaking, we might say that the structure of discipleship in Luke, and under neoliberal economics today, remains unquestioned.

This is a structure of duty and freedom that is mirrored in Luke's larger concept of discipleship. Indeed, the Lukan Jesus assumes this sort of hospitality when in 10:8–12 he says:

> Whenever you enter a town and its people welcome you, eat what is set before you; cure the sick who are there, and say to them, "The kingdom of God has come near to you." But whenever you enter a town and they do not welcome you, go out into its streets and say, "Even the dust of your town that clings to our feet, we wipe off in protest against you. Yet know this: the kingdom of God has come near." I tell you, on that day it will be more tolerable for Sodom than for that town. (NRSV)

Here, the promise of God's blessing is followed by the threat of God's curse. In this passage one welcomes not merely through an economy of grace—that is, the kingdom of God given freely without obligation—but rather through an economy of obligation or threat: One will welcome or one will suffer worse than Sodom. Under such an economy of obligation, the women who are left behind implicitly must serve the disciples and followers who come to the town, presumably including men who have left other women similar to those who now provide the disciples with food and shelter. If they do not serve the itinerant movement, they do not fulfill their obligation.

Martha, as she who can offer hospitality, must do so or risk a fate worse than Sodom, but yet she still does not get the "better part." According to Bovon, we should not read this parable as one in conflict with the demands for hospitality, but rather against Martha's excessive worry, which helped to obscure for her the one essential thing: that which Mary recognized in her act of sitting down at Jesus' feet to listen to his teachings.[54] And yet, can we truly blame Martha for carrying the worries a head of household responding to the demands of hospitality might have felt? Does granting Mary here the better understanding of the essential not still leave Martha in a sort of double bind? Greet guests with hospitality or be considered worse than Sodom, but do not worry too much over the material acts that provide for such hospitality, for then you are mistaken in your faith. The double bind placed on Martha is key for coming to understand Martha as an affect alien prophet.[55]

For instance, in looking to Martha's alienating affect, might we read her inability to stop acting (even as her unwillingness to abandon the duties of the house prevents her from the actions of discipleship demanded by the Lukan Jesus) as a lament against the double bind inherent in a hierarchical economy of discipleship? Martha's worry over the cares of the household might indeed be a reminder that even my own injunctions to slow down imply a level of freedom of choice that, for many, is nearly impossible. Hence, we might hear Martha's worry as a lament that questions the structures of faithful subjectivity as opposed to the individual choices of each subject. Additionally, while Mary has perhaps come closer to reflecting the demands of discipleship laid out in chapter 14, and while we might acknowledge a reading of Mary as a theological rationale for freeing women from domestic life, the story begs for further complication. For instance, Elisabeth Schüssler Fiorenza has reminded us time and again that Mary sits silently, receptively hearing Jesus, but makes no proclamations of her own. Schüssler Fiorenza argues that a reading that privileges Mary and ransoms Martha privileges female passivity at the expense of female activity, and as such the Mary and Martha passage is best read with Acts 6, in which Mary is not presented as preaching along with the men, but instead remains silent.[56] In concert with such concerns Alexander notes that Mary, while getting out of the kitchen, is pliable to male authority. She abandons her sister for a man. She does so seemingly undisturbed. In terms of affect: "'In Peter Ketter's phrase, [Mary] is "a quiet, tranquil soul," who is dear to the heart of preaching theologians, in complete contrast to the self-confident and eloquent Martha'. . . . Martha, by contrast, is independent, feisty, argumentative, busy with her own world of work and refusing to subordinate it to male demands for attention."[57] Martha, when read through her affect, may appear more disruptive to cultural norms than Mary.

There are multiple ways to read Mary's silence and contentment with Jesus as feminist; we need not eschew such readings in order to read Martha as preaching or proclaiming through her complaints to Jesus both in the scene of hospitality depicted in Luke 10 and in the story of Lazarus's death and resurrection in John 11:21. In John, Martha meets Jesus on the road (while Mary stays at home) and laments, "Lord if you had been here, my brother would not have died."[58] To be sure, Mary also complains in John, but it is Martha who is more active, going out to meet Jesus and speaking up first for the sake of her brother. Caputo reads Martha's lament in John as a refusal to ignore the pain of death and loss in the present, even while she is assured of resurrection in the (very near) future.[59] The pain is not redeemed. Martha, once again, embodies a material theology that will not let the mattering of life and death *in the present* go.

This unwillingness to let go should remind us of the mad woman who cannot let go of the saliva on her tongue or the monstrosity of cripness that follows us wherever we flee. Martha's willfulness in this way can be read as a giving up of the happiness with a safe God in order to live, in order to make room for the hap of faith more than its certainty. Martha's worrying and weariness become prophetic laments on behalf of the world. Perhaps it is from within Martha's state of anger that the prayer that nothing remains safe gets launched; it is her affect that is full of hap.

Bipolar Busyness and Everyday Lament

To better understand Martha's affect alienation as prophetic, let us return to Francois Bovon's interpretation of her mistake being that of holding too many worries. According to Bovon, the Gospel writer wants us to conclude that through Mary's attentiveness and devotion to Jesus, she has understood the essential thing that matters most for faith.[60] Bovon's analysis of *pollēn* and the differing interpretation of "single thing" versus "few things" helps to bring this issue of what is essential to light. There have been four main ways these words have been interpreted, but according to Bovon only the first two can be legitimate:

> In the first case, the reading "a few things" encourages Christians to be content with having little here on earth. This being content with having little may be understood either from an ethical point of view (faith takes away excessive preoccupation that I have with myself) or from an ascetical point of view (I must practice self-denial).
>
> In the second case, the only thing that counts is the practice of one's faith. Caring about the Lord, expressed as fixing one's attention on what is important, puts the cares of this world into their proper perspective and transforms them into expressions of love. This is what it means to talk about the "one thing" that is necessary.[61]

This analysis, Bovon argues, does not mean that Jesus is telling Martha to care only about a few things, but rather points to how Mary understood that there is only one truly indispensable thing. Bovon further argues that Jesus' issue with Martha is not that she is too tied to the material, but rather that she is preoccupied, overly worried about everyday tasks of hospitality and so has not put the cares of this world in their proper perspective.[62]

Bovon carefully analyzes the Greek verb (*merimnaō*), which appears in 10:41 when Jesus says: "Martha, Martha, you are worried and distracted by many things; there is need of only one thing":

> *Merimnaō* ("to worry") is a verb with considerable implications. "*merimna*" pertains to someone or something, looks on the future with anguish, either blocking or precipitating action. A theological meaning was added to this secular one, discreetly in the Septuagint, then more openly in the Gospels: insofar as worries are oppressing, they are certainly not miraculously eliminated by faith, but can be entrusted to God . . . *Martha's many worries brought on an excess of activity (the Greek word thorubazō, which is less common than thorubeō, means, in the active voice, "cause trouble"; the first meaning of thorubos is "noise"; but then it also means "commotion," for instance of a crowd).*[63]

In understanding Martha's mistake to be an *excessiveness* of worry, Bovon urges readers to break free of a simple dualistic reading of Luke 10:38–42. He notes that we should come to understand that Martha is "a well-intentioned woman, threatened by her good intentions and her multiplicity of activities, who was in danger of becoming *ungrateful* toward the one whom she meant to revere, and unjust toward her sister."[64]

Alexander recognizes a similar dynamic, asking us not to read Martha's mistake to be that of her service—which being Christ-like Alexander argues cannot be at the heart of what Jesus rebukes in v. 40—but rather of her worry:

> It is only when Jesus begins to speak that we are given explicit clues about the nature of Martha's mistake. Martha is "called" by Jesus in this verse, and the attentive reader of Luke's gospel should already know that being "anxious" (*merimnas*) is not a good thing for the would-be disciple . . . (Lk. 12.25), a warning against worrying about food and drink which is embedded in a longer block of teaching on the dangers of riches as a distraction (12.13–34). Mary's "one thing needful" is echoed . . . in the ruler's "one thing" is lacking in Lk. 18.22, which also picks up again the theme of "treasure in heaven" (cf. Lk. 12.21, 33–34); but the theme of single-mindedness weaves in and out of Jesus' teaching in less explicit ways right through the central section of the gospel (cf. Lk. 9.57–62; 11.33–36; 12.30–31).[65]

In these readings the Lukan Jesus rejects not material service, but an anxious attachment to possessions.

But are these interpretations still too dualistic? Can worry over the material world and the material demands of hospitality be separated out from the essential thing, the worry over spiritual teachings? Can Spirit and World be so easily disentangled? Further, if, following Alexander, we are to read the freedom/obligation relation between Mary and Martha as reflective of how often the majority, while needing the minority, demeans them for fulfilling majority needs, then perhaps Martha's frustration cannot be so easily dismissed. Perhaps her worry cannot simply be tied to an issue of riches or single-mindedness. If one must serve or face a fate worse than Sodom, what else was Martha to do, but worry over material sustenance? If we were under such economy of threat, could we have found ourselves similarly single-minded? Hence, even though my reading of Martha is indebted to Alexander's, I *worry*, that while she upholds Martha's emotions (being feisty and argumentative as feminist and subversive), she still struggles to rescue Martha without ransoming her mood.

What if we read this excess of worry not as an individual failing, but rather as a moody lament against the dual bind that those tied to everyday material needs who wished to be faithful to the Jesus movement may have felt? What if we read an anguished look toward the future as a defense of material life in the present or put differently, an anger for the world—a fierce love of this world and a prophetic frustration flowing out of having to care for and therefore carry more than her share of the weight of the world? Further, what if in behaving "ungratefully" Martha, in dialogue with Jesus, through her words and affect, is reminding Jesus of economies of grace and not obligation? Would reading "to worry" as "causing trouble," "commotion," and "noise" help us to hear Martha as one who may be depressed, who may eschew happiness to live, and so who may challenge how we come to practice (in)fidelity to both God and world? What if Martha's excessive worry is the affect appropriate for a feminist political theology that takes the role of women in the biblical story seriously and sensitively?

Caputo reads Martha's complaint to Jesus as the embodiment of a material, if not yet feminist, theology. Martha's response to the event of God, he argues, reading Meister Eckhart's emphasis on Martha as the embodiment of both wife and virgin, makes room for the "perhaps":

> In a theology of "perhaps," . . . we take as a model the agency of Martha, the wife who was a virgin. Martha acts, but she acts from the

ground of the soul, which is one with the ground of God. That means she is an agent mobilized in response to a provocation, to an event, who gives existence to an insistence, and that existence takes the form of the most material and *quotidian* reality.[66]

For Caputo, Martha's infidelity is an act of faith against a spiritual demand that would take her away from the material reality of the everyday world. Martha's actions come in the form of a response to an event that "insists" on God "happening."[67] The event is a promise, but as a promise it contains the structure of the perhaps, the threat that perhaps the promise will not be fulfilled. Hence, Martha who responds to God with hospitality and with an insistence on the importance of the material sustenance needed for such a response, in her act of infidelity to Jesus' request not to be distracted, may actually be faithful to the material demands of the event of God.

According to Caputo, "The pulse of radical theology is taken by whether it has an impulse for the world, the stomach for flesh, the spine or heart—I multiply as many carno-corporeal images as possible—to displace the logos of two worlds, to transfer the funds of its heavenly treasures to earthly accounts."[68] It is in Martha's worry over the everyday material world where Caputo sees this kind of radicality and names it as a radicality that exposes a kind of bipolar disorder (and not in the constructive way we have explored previously) carried by any dualistic thinking between a world of faith and one of matter. Indeed, Martha's response to the event of Jesus' visit is the active response to the insistence of God through the material existence of God with world. In contrast, as noted by Bovon, "Luke did not distinguish between a Mary who preached and a Martha who served, but rather a Mary who listened and a Martha who wore herself out extending hospitality."[69] In other words, as touched on briefly earlier, the distinction can be read as the difference between one who shows faith through trusting reception and a praised inaction (an inaction that has both been blessed by traditional inter-preters as a support for placing the spiritual over the material and one that is opposed to the inaction of those made depressed through their mad adherence to the despairs of the present, those who have the wretched and not the better part), and one who shows faith through busying herself in actions (and affects) that address the demands of the immanent world.

While there are important arguments to be made about the potency of inaction, we can see two main problems with the distinction made between Martha's action and Mary's silence. The first, pointed to earlier, is that we should be wary of assigning to Mary a more liberating role for women. As Schüssler Fiorenza, Alexander, and Bovon have noted, Mary does not preach, she listens. She may be out of the kitchen, but she is not out in the public world. Martha, while remaining in the kitchen, *does* make her feelings known, if not yet fully heard. This is not to say that Martha is closer to public preaching, but rather that those who prioritize Mary's silent presence out of the kitchen over and against Martha's vociferous kitchen-bound lament miss alternate feminist readings of the scene, and so commit their own damning/damming up of Martha, allowing her complexity to be effaced in the construction of Mary as a feminist figure.

The second, reading with Caputo, is that to prioritize Mary over Martha is to support the dangerous kind of bipolar disorder that sees material action and faith as diametrically opposed. Because Martha expresses both faith and concern for material hospitality, Caputo argues, she exposes the falsity of such bipolar thinking.[70] And yet might we expose a different kind of bipolarity in Martha, one that not only turns our attention to the material world in such a way as embraced by Caputo, but also one that serves as a lesson *for* Jesus, a lament that might not only teach we readers of the text, but also God?

"Don't you care?" The Madness of Martha

For all of his reliance on Martha as the embodiment of a theology of "perhaps," I am left wondering whether Caputo's theology has, perhaps, given her the full prominence she deserves. Is there a sense in Caputo's radical theology that Martha's radicalism comes still as a more receptive agent, responding to the event *of* God, but not causing an event *in* God? What if instead of seeing the crux of the action being Martha's hospitality, we saw both her worrying and then her complaint as climactic? What if it is not only that Martha shows concern for the material well-being of her household (including the community and Jesus, whom she serves through such concern), but more so the very fact that she is so worried about the quotidian world and annoyed at Jesus and Mary, who show her to be a faithful embodiment of a theology of (per)hap-ness? Could Martha's "excess" actually be a kind of faithful attending to the madness of and in the world? Might her madness, at and about a world in which her attunement to the material everyday places her in the double bind of discipleship in Luke, in fact be prophetic? Further, might her anxiety and anger over this double bind be the lament of the feminist killjoy? Such a lament, I surmise, might kill even Caputo's theological joy when it arises at the very moments when he might seem to dehumanize Martha, even as he makes her his representation of a material theology. For Caputo, Martha is a figure standing in for the carnality of the present world, but the specificity of her mood—how she is affected by and affecting in the scene of material hospitality—is left under-theorized and so eclipsed.

Caputo's own "redemptive" reading of Martha draws heavily on that of Meister Eckhart. In Eckhart's reading, Caputo finds a material theology that is representative of the carno-corporeality, the stomach for flesh, and earthly accounting of radical theology. Yet when we return to Eckhart's own sermons and through them revisit Caputo's Martha, I am left to wonder just how much carnal flesh and earthly accounting we find. Despite Caputo's allegiance to the infidels, within both Caputo's and Eckhart's exegeses we can locate, perhaps, a problematic emphasis on obedience.

While Eckhart acknowledges Martha's commitment to hospitality and the specific historical position and wisdom she has as the elder sister, his reading refuses to let Martha's emotions be felt in a negative mood. Instead he redeems her anger and worry out of their negativity. Looking to the line in Luke in which Martha urges Jesus to get Mary to help her, Eckhart writes: "Martha did not say this out of spite. Rather, she said it because of endearment; that is what motivated her. We call it affection or playful chiding."[71] Martha has no contempt for Mary, only care. She has no frustration for Jesus, only favor. Similarly, Eckhart does not see Christ chiding Martha, but comforting her to ensure her that Mary, while not yet learning the lessons of life as Martha has, will still turn out okay.[72] Eckhart's reading stands in fresh contrast to the medieval reading of Mary and Martha. Yet we *sense* that something is missing. If we find in Martha the wisdom of age and knowledge of life, why not let the wisdom of her frustration be found in the moodiness of frustration rather than in its positive redemption? Why must anger be sublated into affection? Why not let anger stand as its own force of wisdom, an insight into the weight of the world placed heavily on Martha? Does Eckhart here really have the stomach for both the promise and peril of a fleshy Martha? Does Caputo?

Adherence to Eckhart's redeemed reading of Martha's materiality does not leave room for much to happen with Jesus. Jesus serves not as a dialogue partner, but more so as the voice of an omniscient narrator comforting those in the present about a future to come. Eckhart's redemption of the moodiness of the scene continues through his insistence that when Jesus names Martha twice in Luke 10:41, he does so "to indicate that Martha possessed completely everything of temporal and eternal value that a creature should have. When he said 'Martha' the first time, he indicated her perfection in temporal works. With his second calling out, 'Martha,' he affirmed that she lacked nothing of all that is necessary for eternal happiness."[73] Once again we are told from a seeming omniscient place what Martha and Jesus must have been feeling. But if we are to take seriously the promise and peril of affect, if we are to refuse to keep a God of peace and quiet safe, we must allow for the possibility that Martha was, in fact, not happy with the temporal or eternal objects of happiness on offer. In doing so we clear space for a Jesus, who says Martha's name twice in the way an intimate who thinks he knows better might. A caring, if condescending, friend might indeed say "Martha, Martha," shaking his head frustratingly and endearingly as he corrects what he perceives to be her folly. By making the saying of Martha's name a prescription about her temporal and eternal state, Eckhart actually sets up greater affectual distance between Jesus and Martha, eliding the intimacy of fellowship in which disagreement and dialogue might blossom even (especially) amongst heated affects of anger, frustration, condescension, and comfort. Further, whereas Caputo finds in Eckhart's reading of Martha an insistence on the material ground of God, in eclipsing her moodiness with God he may be missing the heart or spine of messy carno-corporeal relations.

In his reading of Jesus' response to Martha, Eckhart once again redeems any sense that Martha might be too materially tied to the world. His sermon continues: "Hence [Jesus] said [to Martha], 'You are careful,' by which he meant: You stand in the midst of things, but they do not reside in you; and those are careful who go about unimpeded in all their daily pursuits. Those people are unimpeded who perform all their works properly according to the image of eternal light, and such people stand in the midst of things, but not *in* things."[74] This reading of Martha as unimpeded can perhaps only stand if Martha's anger is redeemed as affection, and if we come to ignore the excessive character of the Greek for "worry" as explicated by Bovon. To actually pause in the emotional path tread by Martha is to feel a great sense of impediment. To worry to the point of "causing trouble" is not to flow easily with God, but rather to block such ease.

Further, while I would be wary of arguing for an over-attachment to one's possessions, to allow the things of the world to reside in you might actually be a more fitting description of the material theology Caputo seeks when he writes that "In Martha, God happens with all the robustness of mundane existence."[75] To emotionally engage with the mattering of the things with which Martha resides (duties of hospitality, the care of her sister, the grief over Lazarus's death) might be to reside with those "hated" and so abandoned by Jesus' disciples who had or took the freedom to follow him. This is not to say that there is nothing meaningful in following Jesus, but rather that in Martha's anger and worry we might find a prophetic refusal to let be and let go of the stories of those who stayed, the stories of the things of this world that went "hated" (including wife and child).

This is a haunting refused by Eckhart in his redemption of Martha's "negative" affects. Unlike the willfulness that I, as well as other feminist interpreters like Alexander, find in Martha's refusal to stay silent in the midst of her frustration, Eckhart found in her "playful chiding" an obedience to God's will: "Obedience is when the will satisfactorily carries out what insight commands."[76] Eckhart understood Martha's concern as arising from a fear that Mary was too quick to cling "to consolation and sweetness," and so would not learn to live the virtuous life of Martha and find what Martha had found in such a life: happiness.[77] The first way toward such a virtuous life, according to Eckhart, "is to give up one's will to God. This is necessary in order that one rightly know whether to perform or avoid an action."[78] Hence, for Eckhart, Martha is happy because she has aligned her actions with God's will, and this is the happiness she wants for Mary. It is "work and activity" that therefore lead Martha to eternal happiness.[79]

Again, this is a look at Luke's gospel from on high and not from the gravity and intimacy of a God who is at home with Martha; it is a view that obscures Martha's own words in favor of making Martha the "happy housewife." Such a reading cannot stand if we are to allow for Martha's affect to open us to the hap of both promise and peril. Yes, she is active in the house; yes she may, for Eckhart at least, have been a working "wife," but this need not mean she is happy. Indeed, it is the persistence of her negative affect throughout the fulfillment of the demand to be hospitable that opens a pathway to the questioning of both action and inaction within the scene. If Caputo wants a theology that sides with Martha as it "comes to grips with unrest and threat," he might be cautious of aligning too closely with Eckhart. Indeed, Caputo seems at times to advocate for a risky serpentine-like Martha, while simultaneously affirming her happy housewife status. He uncomplicatedly lauds Martha's work and activity: "Martha is busy about the many works, the many material things—meals, clean linens, a swept house—that are needed to welcome Jesus and make him comfortable (vita activa)."[80] For Caputo this activity is the response to the event of God, a response that honors quotidian material life.

In this responsive life he finds that "Martha knows that to ask for Jesus to come is to call for peace and accept trouble, both the promise and threat, and that peace cannot be purchased separately."[81] And yet, can we really say that it is just in her activity where Martha recognizes this promise and threat? An obedience to the structure of discipleship that has placed her in an economic relation to the material "costs of discipleship," what must be sacrificed (hated, abandoned, ransomed) in order for the tower of disciple-ship to be built, seems less like the welcoming of an earthly accounting and more like the settling of heavenly debts. Indeed, as Eckhart has it, Martha may be material, but she is also in her obedience to her role as both "wife and virgin" a figure of detachment: "A virgin who is a wife is free and unpledged, without attachment,"[82] by which Eckhart means that like a virgin Martha cannot be distracted by attachments to husband and child, but like a wife can produce fruit with God. It is Martha's ability to detach from the world as "a virgin" that gives rise to her function in a divine plan of making for God more product, producing material and spiritual fruit. Here, perhaps, Martha as divine instrument does not refuse a God of peace and quiet as much as she serves one.

This Martha too eerily falls prey to biopolitical and bio-Logos control, a control that asks Martha, "What have you produced for me lately?" In "On Detachment," Eckhart writes:

> I find no other virtue better than a pure detachment from all things; because all other virtues have some regard for created things, but detachment is free from all created things. That is why our Lord said to Martha: "One thing is necessary" (Lk. 10:42), which is as much to say: "Martha, whoever wants to be free of care and to be pure must have one thing, and that is detachment."[83]

Is the detachment from created things (particularly when it easily slips into the service of obedience to a husband God) truly the highest of virtues in a material theology that seeks an earthly accounting over and against heav-enly treasures? In eclipsing these moments in Eckhart's material theology, and in finding a radical theology solely in Martha's activity and not the emotion that accompanies such a material life, Caputo does a disservice to his prized figure.

Like Caputo, I find in Martha a stomach for flesh and the gripping allegiance to the very promise and peril that accompanies the event of God. But, unlike Caputo, I find it in the revelatory ambivalence of being dutifully hospitable, but being so with hostility. The tension created by hostile hospitality is the tension that might allow for the "hap" to happen, it is the prayer that not even God remain safe. Further, if even in theolo-gies that claim an allegiance to Martha, Martha's own moody reality must go silenced or under-theorized, then how much more closely and ardently must we readers of alienation attend to her affect? How much more might we read her anger as a prophetic voice from the past still haunting all her critics and saviors in the present?

Or perhaps I have just undone my argument. Must this critical look at Eckhart, Caputo, and Alexander convince me to cohere to interpretations of Luke that view Mary as the way out of happy housewifehood? I think not. For returning to the problematic elements of Eckhart's material theology reminds us that radical theology needs Martha's mood. We need to ponder what her anger can do. And, ask, where her worry might help us wander. To be both dutiful and dissenting at once, as Martha seems to be, is to open a dialogue on just what is demanded of Martha and of discipleship more generally. To let Martha's emotions remain negative without redeeming them into secretly happy moods, is in fact to feel our way toward different readings and hearings. It is to open ourselves and Jesus up to a hearing of Martha's lament such that we can affirm that from within her knowledge of life and her material attention to the things of this world we find righteous reasons to be angry. It is, therefore, not just that Martha is tied to the material, but more so that she is worried for and pissed at the matter at hand that makes her a theologically potent member of an archive of affect alienation. Martha's moodiness is perhaps a particularly poignant addition to our archive as we find her within a gospel that has in other passages excised "negative" feelings from Jesus. Jesus is permitted to cry out on the cross in Mark, "My God, my God, why have you forsaken me?" (Mk 15:34). In Luke he is tamed: "Father, into your hands I commend my spirit" (Lk 23:46). The pains of the flesh are erased. Martha's mood might re-enflesh a Lukan archive.

I want to suggest that the eclipsing of Martha's mood and the lack of theological attention to the question of what in life had got her so bothered, might reveal in part why some of us have flowed more easily into theological spaces, including those of political theology, than others. In an essay on mood, Ahmed writes, "How is it that we enter a room and pick up on some feelings and not others? I have implied that one enters not only *in* a mood, but *with* a history, which is how you come to lean this way or that. Attunement might itself be an affective history, of how subjects become attuned to others over and in time."[84] For Ahmed, attunement to the atmosphere of the room can mean learning to not bring up certain topics. What is it about historical and contemporary theological moods that impeded Eckhart and Caputo from picking up on some of Martha's moody possibilities? Which topics have we learned not to bring up from such redemptive readings of Martha's "hospitality," as though it shouldn't and therefore couldn't have been hostile? Which feelings are we afraid to follow? Whose affect alienation can we hear? Can we have a theology that welcomes not only Martha's hospitality, the material attention to the event of God, but also her hostility, the material attention to her own embodiment? Can we have a theology that recognizes that the two are consequent to one another?

To re-enflesh Martha in all her potent prophetic character is to look to her embodied response to the event, to her worry and her anger, to what I'm calling her madness. We can see two sides of madness in Martha. First is a manic sense (the excess illuminated by Bovon's reading) of busyness reflective of the many worries placed on Martha as the head of the household. Second is Martha's possible killing of Jesus' and Mary's joy through her unhappiness and complaint. These moments of madness can be read as Martha's prophetic affect alienation and so a different kind of bipolarity than that worried over by Caputo—one with the infidelity needed to leave room for the "hap" of the "perhaps."

Reading artist Allyson Mitchell's series, *The War on Worries*, Cvetkovich notes that "*War on Worries* is an apt description of [Cvetkovich's] *Depression Journals* narrative, whose stories are frequently about the logistics of housekeeping and self-care and the everyday habits of living inside bodies and houses that are the intimate and material locations of depression."[85] Cvetkovich describes part of the *War on Worries* piece:

> Two plastic toy soldiers fight it out inside the confines of a matchbox, which is mounted on a background of fluorescent print wallpaper from the 1970s that recalls the home front. Scrawled on the silver frames in the style of a things-to-do list are labels that structure the war on worries as a series of decisions to be made: organic meat vs. cheap groceries; clean bathroom vs. visit to art galleries; serenity vs. wild partying; work vs. vacation; casserole in front of the TV vs. outdoor picnic; suburban background vs. urban present; periodical upkeep vs. antipoverty actions.[86]

For our purposes here we might add to this list: household activity vs. spiritual reception; or life in the face of death in this world vs. new life in the next; or paying the cost of discipleship vs. practicing hostile hospitality. Hence, we might find in this piece a depiction of the tension between Mary and Martha, and so Martha and Jesus.

Indeed, *The War on Worries* depicts both the tension between everyday worries and the call to be involved in larger social justice struggles (periodical upkeep vs. antipoverty actions), sustainable consumer choices (organic meat vs. cheap groceries), healthier living (serenity vs. wild partying), and pleasure (work vs. vacation), as well as the way in which the domestic sphere is often anything but comforting. As witnessed in the previous chapter, everyday depression (and the many worldly worries which nurture it and which it nurtures) follows one home, breaking down the duality between domestic and public life. Hence, it is from within this quotidian reality that Cvetkovich looks to ways of acknowledging the pervasiveness of depression and finding persistence from within a worrisome world. Most significantly, she finds a persistent life in "utopia of ordinary habit," touched on in the previous chapter. For Cvetkovich habit and the everyday routine become a crucial way of keeping the body moving in the face of depression and worry. In various routinized activities, such as swimming, cleaning, going to the dentist, or just getting out of bed in the morning,[87] Cvetkovich finds "forms of transformation," which she then describes as part of the "sacred everyday."[88] She further asks "how it might be possible to tarry with the negative as part of daily practice, cultural production, and political activism."[89] And suggests that sometimes "magic and mystery sit alongside the banal and the routine."[90] Perhaps we can read Mary as that magic that sits beside the routine and banal that Martha inhabits. But for Cvetkovich it is precisely not that mystery and banality come to be opposed, but rather that sometimes in just keeping oneself moving and engaged in the world one allows for magic to *hap*pen; in this way, Martha's routine does not rule out her magic.

This reformulation of the sacred everyday performs a breaking open of a duality similar to that performed by Caputo. To carry magic alongside the banal is also to carry the material alongside the spiritual, but more so to come to see the two as not sitting alongside one another, but rather as intimately enfolded in and unfolding from one another. To respond to the promise of a God of "perhaps" is not to sit and wait for an event to happen from without, but rather to embrace the "hap-ness" embedded within everyday material life—life that comes with a vicissitude of perilous and promising moods. According to Cvetkovich, an aim of the Public Feelings Project is the articulation of new approaches to the relation between the macro and micro; in other words, a turn toward how everyday feelings of depression and worry might get reformulated not as distractions from more important macro issues (Mary's better part), but rather part of a new narrative that takes the micro material reality of those historical exceptions as important ways into macro transformations. For instance, Martha's everyday worries might be read as an acknowledgment of the importance of present activity and of the activities of all members of the community (those inside and outside the home—those itinerant disciples and those "hated" and abandoned) from within an incarnate faith. Martha, in this way, may carry within her worry over the everyday—what has too often been read as a distraction—a point of view on discipleship and faith within the Jesus movement that God and we needed and need to hear.

Additionally, it is not just in Martha's embrace of the everyday where we can see the breaking open of dualities; read through Cvetkovich's work on depression, we come to view Martha's "excessive" worrying and her refusal to give up the habits of the everyday as indicators of a refusal to give up on both the affects of depression and anxiety that mark a life responsible for the material sustenance of a movement and the rituals of remaining vigilant to a God of this world. Bovon recognizes the intensity of affect expressed by Martha in his description of Luke 10:40–42:

> *Fatigued* and *feeling abandoned*, Martha laid into Jesus, *taking him to task* for his indifference ("don't you care . . ."), and into Mary ("that my sister has left me . . . by myself"). Martha made a *pitiful sight* and called for help. Jesus' retort was more a diagnosis than a criticism. At first look, this retort appears severe, but it was aimed at redirecting Martha to what was essential, to that part that was singular and had priority, the part that Mary had chosen all on her own.[91]

There is some sympathy for Martha's feelings in this reading and in Bovon's affirmation of Jesus' care for Martha. Yet Bovon may be too quick to overlook the importance of Martha's taking of Jesus and Mary to task. Martha's words, but also her refusal to give up on worrying, can be read as pedagogical. She is teaching Jesus and Mary how it feels to carry the worries of the world, and what it has meant to be left to face such worries "all on her own." An interpretation of Jesus that sees him diagnosing Martha as having an excess of concern does not lessen the cares of the material world that remain in need of attention. This is not to say that the recognition of bad feeling has no use, but rather that in turning so quickly from the diagnosis of Martha's excesses to that of Mary's superiority in faith—which according to Bovon she chose all on her own, but which we might say she was able to choose thanks to the material labor of Martha—Bovon's Jesus, instead of alleviating Martha's worries, may have increased them.

Here the story ends; we do not know what each character has learned. As in the story of Jonah, we are left to sit with the mood and decide for ourselves how we have been affected. Has Martha given up on "excessively" worrying about everyday concerns? Perhaps, perhaps not. Has the Lukan Jesus come to a greater respect for the emotional effects the demands of hospitality and abandonment carry? Perhaps, perhaps not. Will Mary be more helpful to Martha next time? Perhaps, perhaps not. Will Martha get out of the kitchen? Perhaps, perhaps not. Have we adequately come to feel Martha's worry, listened differently for her lament? Perhaps, perhaps not. And yet in reclaiming Martha as a moody prophet we can indeed allow for this level of uncertainty, for a more dialogical faith in which the questioning of God is done by some of the most beloved (if also, and importantly so, wretched and pitiful) actors in the bible. Martha's manic worrying and depressing complaint leave open a greater possibility for alternatives to happen than more traditional narratives of fidelity can allow. That we cannot know whether her heart is turned from anger to affection leaves the space open for a reading of the Gospel in which part of the lesson is that there is an (in)fidelity in questioning God and in remaining affectually alienated from God as long as God may not yet have heard/felt our lament.

In other words, in the moodiness of this gospel tale we might hear an injunction to find from within Martha's embodied reality the spark causing an event *in* God. Martha affects God through her mood. Martha helps us to welcome a God of promise and threat (one who promises comfort and threatens the comfortable) by moving us to better attend to the moods of those we find threatening.

From Willing to Willful

Jonah and Martha's killing of joy—God's, Jesus', and the theological joy of mainstream interpreters'—are acts of will. They *will* not obey requests and demands made to them by Jesus and God. They *will* not give up on their material present realities and the maddening feelings that accompany such persistence. We *will* insist that how they feel matters for how they and we may continue to exist. Hence, we might place Jonah and Martha alongside Ahmed's archive of *Willful Subjects*. For Ahmed, collecting such an archive helps to mark how certain forms of what Caputo might call persisting and insisting are considered willful because they "pulse with desire," but it is a desire directed in ways other than what the mainstream has dictated as the right way. The gap between continued existence that subverts the norm and a continued existence that bends itself to the norm is the key difference I find between a sense of problematic overcoming and prophetic persistence in the face of damage. According to Ahmed, "If authority assumes the right to turn a wish into a command, then willfulness is a diagnosis of the failure to comply with those whose authority is given."[92] Willfulness, therefore, is not marked by strength of will, but rather by the aim of will. It is beyond the scope of this chapter to engage in a definition of the "will" or to give a proper genealogy of its terminological ties to freedom, direction, and desire. Hence, for the purposes of this reflection, I take Ahmed's attention to the difference between one's will aligning with (willing) or opposing (willful) the will of society. For instance, we might say that the structure of neoliberal capitalism critiqued in the previous chapters requires a large amount of desire-fueled will, but such desire is a form of willing that supports contemporary hegemonies, and so subjects are seen not as willful, but as willing to get with the program. Willful ones are those—like the feminist killjoy, the bipolar woman, and the monstrous crip—whose wills are disordered. From within this disorder, or what Ahmed describes as failing to take the right form, we might learn to tread different paths.[93]

In treading different paths with willful subjects, Ahmed argues that we are also able to find a form of subjectivity with an uncertain and more impulsive form of intent.[94] This does not mean that we find no motivation or intent behind Martha or Jonah's willfulness, but rather that following the will around, seeing where it might wander off the path, allows for a kind of resistant action that does not know where it will end up. It knows that it desires to not take part in what is on offer, but leaves open what might come from "coming apart"[95] in the face of such a desire. In this way, a willfulness archive might be an archive of the wretched that affirms the "hap-ness" described by Ahmed in *Promise of Happiness* and the "perhap-ness" that Caputo sees as necessary for the insistence of God as a promise that may or may not be kept.

Resonant with how the promise of God can serve as an uncertain gift is Ahmed's suggestion that the coming apart (as in the parting ways from the mainstream) of the willful part, as well as a mood of willfulness, "can be gift[s] given, [willfulness can be] a gift relayed between parts, a gift that allows noncompliant or resistant action to be carried out *without intent*."[96] This is not to say that wills of the willful lack desire or purpose, but rather that they resist the making out of the resistant will's direction a new program, one easily co-opted into another form of hegemony. Such wills might invest in damage instead of overcoming it.

A willfulness that opens up resistant action without intent might be a ground for a multiplicity of divergent becomings rather than a demand to be one way or the other. Willfulness without intent is not a program toward redemption out of our crookedness—a straightening salvation that comes from getting in line. Rather, such willfulness can allow each singularity to pulse at its own pace, to follow its own rhythm where it wills. We can see this sort of willfulness pulsing amongst Occupy Wall Street protesters who refused to have their program of resistance straightened out and made palatable. For instance, in response to a speech given by Slavoj Žižek during an Occupy rally in which Žižek warned that we should not forget to ask what happens the morning after the occupations when we return to normal life, Halberstam wrote: "Like many anti-colonial and anti-capitalist movements, these movements refuse to conjure an outcome, eschew Utopian or pragmatic conjurings of what happens on the 'morning after' because the outcome will be determined by the process. All we know for sure is that the protests announce a collective awareness of the end of a 'normal life.'"[97] In this collective awareness of the end of a "normal life," one which looks to the process and not to pragmatic conjuring, we can hear the affect alien laments of Martha and Jonah asking, through their hostility, that God and we take seriously the material present. They/we demand, through an attention to the affects and effects of our mainstream "normal" theological lives, an end to such lives.

The end of a normal theological life might be the killing of theological joy found in the moods of Jonah and Martha. Jonah's anger with God kills the joy of the Christian mainstream. This is a mainstream that rejoices in, and whose force relies on, Jonah being a foolish vengeful Hebrew unaware of God's merciful goodness. To follow Jonah's unwillingness to let such joy stand unquestioned might be to challenge mainstream joy. To hear Martha's excessive worry as her killing of the theological joy of those who wish to disentangle the banal from the magical might be to attend to and invest in the enfleshed burdens placed on those who have been left out of history—the women "hated" and abandoned, and yet relied upon, by the Jesus movement. Hence, to follow Martha's will around may be to question the erasures of the domestic worker, often a woman of color who toils away so that those in the household she serves may have the freedom of contemplation, or of the depressed woman who cannot let be long enough to become the model consumer.

This killing of theological joy is indeed a gift, one given from the willful part of society to those who have been all too willing to let be and let go. It is an offering from those who have been bowed down so that we might better walk the straight and narrow. It is a kind of blessed cursing given in the structure of lament, which says no to what is on offer as the only possible salvation. This "blessed no" allows for the impossible to *hap*pen, perhaps.

If willfulness is a gift given from willful parts past to willful subjects present, then might the willfulness of Jonah and Martha be holy offerings, ones full of peril and promise? This is a perilous promise that may or may not be fulfilled, but that still grants us permission to will another way. The prophetic willfulness of these biblical affect aliens can help to remind us that, as Ahmed writes, "Perhaps some have 'ways of life' because others have lives: some have to find voices because others are given voices; some have to assert their particulars because others have their particulars given as a general expression."[98] Our mainstream interpretations have given God a voice and left Jonah to fight for his. Our traditional interpretations have given a silent Mary or an obedient Martha the voice of the good and left the moody Martha to fight for hers.

An affect alien theology resists such univocity, even in those theologies that have been similarly alienated from the mainstream. To be sure, the affect alien theology proposed here risks its own slide into the univocity of the negative. This is a risk I acknowledge and hope to counter in not killing joy out of hand, but rather listening for the moods that surface at the site of the Other's erasure. Hence, it is a cacophony of feeling and not the harmonizing of thought that my theology seeks. I want a shameful and righteous Jonah. I want a dutiful and dissident Martha. This ambivalence in the archival ghosts that haunt and populate the pages of this book, an ambivalence surfaced through the very promise-peril structure of affect, is the one too quickly eclipsed by theologies that look to figures for material representation without questioning which moody histories they pick up on, and which they have let fade to the background.

In fact, could both the call to place utter faith in the Market—and that to place utter faith in any theology that too quickly eclipses contextual histories—fortify the very institutions and theologies leftist political theologies hope to challenge? This is what Ahmed gets but Caputo leaves unspoken. Ahmed's "hap" is fleshy with not only emotion, but also race, gender, sexuality, ability, and history, whereas Caputo's "perhaps" remains, perhaps, too spectral. For Caputo, Martha, as a figure of hospitality, insists on the event of God. For an affect alien theology, Martha's worry as a woman in a particular role within a particular movement and Jonah's despair as a Hebrew in the face of oppression matter for political theology.

A theology for the affect alien, for the unredeemed, might remind us that, even from a place of embodied will, intent and position remain in flux. To follow willfulness down the paths its "disordered" form takes us might be to allow a theology of perhap-ness to happen in such a way that challenges the normativizing theologies of neoliberal and orthodox salvation history. Yet in its affect this willful challenge will neither offer up a clear redemption narrative nor eclipse the contextual realities that make us not in the mood to be saved.

Refusing the salvation on offer, affect alien laments insist that whether or not we let a God of risk and uncertainty get *a* life matters for whether or not we call into question the certainty of our neoliberal Gods, that of Money and Market, but also of Whiteness, Ability, Productivity, Efficiency, Sanity, Straightness, Maleness, Youth, Reason, Health, Beauty, Wholeness, and Resilience. In order for those of us made unhappy by the demands placed on us by this pantheon to exist, we will insist on putting them at risk, through our persistence in the mad (depressed, manic, unhappy, unreasonable, envious, wrathful, impotent, desirous, and willful) state in which they have placed us. As Ahmed insists, willfulness is that which impedes the assumed happiness that is on the way. In other words, our madness (our killing of theological joy) poses a threat to these gods and their promises of happiness. In insisting that these gods not remain safe, we will come to exist as that which they have already labeled us to be and so will cease to acquiesce to the false promise that it is by following their demands that we will become happy. Instead we will persist in unhappiness, in bad investments, such that another way to wander (a possibly joyous way) comes into existence.

If happiness is pedagogical teaching us what we should desire to be associated with (wealth, beauty, whiteness, straightness, professionalism), then willfulness is pedagogical in that it teaches us to question the rods of association. Rods of association are often less obvious than those of coercion, like that of the Billy club. Rods of association are how systems like neoliberalism, which claim a democratic ethos, persist. Evidence of the rods of association might include: adjusting one's accent or grammar to sound "smart," refusing to cry in public, finishing work on deadline, wearing a prosthesis at the expense of comfort and mobility, marrying this person instead of "living in sin" with that one, or obeying laws of assembly. These rods of association are not those explicitly enforced on us by the outside, but rather come to be internalized techniques of repression such that, as Ahmed makes clear in her concluding chapter, our own arms become the straightening rod of the absent sovereign. The straightening rod of the absent sovereign is of course also the chokehold of the invisible hand of the Market.

This is not to say that all who seem to go willingly along, arm in hand with the Market, can be seen as lacking in resistant will. Sometimes, "subjects become willing if not being willing is made unbearable."[99] Indeed, we need not demonize those who find it impossible not to go with the flow. Still, we *can* learn from those who bear the unbearable placing their bodies dam-like across the rushing tide. And if it is impossible to stop the flow of the mainstream, it may still be possible to feel a different way through it: "It is thus possible that disobedience can take the form of an *unwilling obedience:* subjects might obey a command but do so grudgingly or reluctantly and enact with or through the compartment of their body a withdrawal from the right of the command even as they complete it."[100] When one must obey, one may do so unhappily, with expressions of unwilling acquiescence. This is the type of willing encased in the affect of our biblical characters who obey God, but do so with hostility. This is the sort of damming we see in Martha and Jonah. They dam the theological flow, not by denying God, but by damning God. Jonah tries to fully disobey and cannot bear/live in the face of God's coercive rod (the storm, the fish), but he still practices unwilling obedience through his affect. Similarly, Martha practices both disobedience—she does not cease in her worry—and an unwilling obedience to the demands for hospitality—she actively shows hostility toward the uneven burdens under which the obligations of hospitality have placed her. Damning her sister and Jesus for their lack of care, she also impedes the flow of the story. These affect alien prophets exist as blockage; their existence stops up or slows down the neoliberal flow. To *feel* rather than to *flow* is their prophetic character to persist, and so insist, and so exist, and so persist, per-haps.

In the persistence, rather than overcoming, of affect alien prophets, we should recall the crip sensibility that demands a return of singularity and the affirmation of the pleasures of a relaxed soul. We can find in the tapping into bad feelings a creative and, dare I say, crooked response to demands to straighten up and get in line with the panic and exhaustion inducing happiness on offer by neoliberal capitalism. Indeed, might we find in the bad feelings explored in these pages the specter of all those whose histories have gone missing from the historical archives? And if so, as I argue in the next chapter, might we find the potential for new ways of being from within these unfinished ghost stories? Might we be both haunted and halted by those who did not and do not go with the flow?

Prophetic madness (whether it comes in the form of the impeding neoliberal joy or of the ecstasy of breaking through biopolitical blockages to get a life) is the rejection of a theological certainty that says salvation will come through our fidelity, either to the supreme value of money or that dictated by exclusive and monarchic readings of the Christian Church and of Christ. The political freedom to be unhappy is not akin to the purported freedom of neoliberalism that rejects our relational responsibilities. Rather, as I argue in the next chapter, following Lynne Huffer's analysis of Eros in Michel Foucault's work on madness in conjunction with the polyphilia embedded in the Process God, the political freedom advocated for by the feminist killjoy and the bipolar prophet is one that requires a more faithful response to our entanglement with others. The freedom to be unhappy, while rejecting the demand to be happy for others, is actually the demand to attend to the suffering and flourishing of those others too often left out of both political and theological narratives of happiness and redemption. It is the call to attend to those bad investments. The freedom of the other to feel bad is our command to no longer ask to be comforted by another person's mood—demanding that those who are unhappy become happiness-making-objects. This command might be James's care work, Berardi's therapoetry, and my grave attending—all of which hope to find *a life* through our individual and collective discomfort (our madness). Whereas this chapter attended to the laments of affect aliens, the next chapter attempts to respond theologically to such cries.

CHAPTER 5

Unreasoned Care

What would it mean to hear the cries of all those whose lives have been ransomed for the construction of The Life? What theological grounding might instead ground *a* life? Just what kind of God might faithfully respond to such prophetic moods? Just what God might a political theology of and for the unredeemed imply?

Following Lynne Huffer into an erotic encounter with the Foucauldian archive, this chapter argues that it is from within the impossibility of ever making unreason (the limit of thought) fully speak that I offer an ethics of grave attending as fitting for a theology of unredemption constructed in these pages. It has not been my hope to surface affect alien prophets so as to make of them idealized subjects we might now worship, follow, or capture for our own knowledge. For instance, I sought to listen to Jonah's anger not to know him, know his mind, and so cure him, à la *The Veggie Tales*, nor to stabilize a reading of Jonah's anger in such a way that might efface the limits of his anger. Rather, we might listen for Jonah's anger (even / especially in his silence in the face of God) so as to keep the unlimited nature of thought alive even in a moment of God's limited mercy. In trying to feel Martha's mood, to be weary and worrisome with her, I sought not to redeem her as a model feminist citizen, nor to demean the affects of Mary, but rather to see where her moodiness might take us, and to ask what has been lost by covering over such a mood. In other words, in finding hope in what Huffer and Foucault might name as an eros in excess of bios, I find a resistance to a redemption of the suffering of the unreasonable, while at the same time an opening for the hope that their suffering might have been otherwise.

Hence, this chapter argues that we attempt, with Huffer and Foucault, a different listening to our own murmuring mad ones, to the unreasonable prophets that have populated these pages, and to those who have haunted it in the background. In an interview with Roger-Pol Droit, Foucault reminds us that "for twenty years now I've been worrying about my little mad ones, my little excluded ones, my little abnormals": "mes petits fous, mes petits exclus, mes petits anormaux."[1] It is my hope that in these pages I have joined Foucault in his worries for my own petits fous, those who I want to name as my little monsters—the monstrously unproductive, the crip waiting to be stroked gently open, Jonah the killer of theological joy, a worrying and worrisome Martha, the bipolar woman all too aware of the saliva on her lips, and Berardi's panicked and exhausted masses—monsters who, unlike Lady Gaga's, cannot or will to not grow up to be model citizens. Foucault's ethical attention to the archive, to history, to the little excluded ones, and to the powers of effacement enacted by sovereign secular reason will be a key frame for why and how we might begin to hear again so as to recover the possibility of what Foucault calls "becom[ing] again what we never were."[2]

Additionally, this chapter suggests that while Foucault, read through Huffer, seduces us into a practice of erotic listening for our irredeemably unproductive ghosts, Alfred North Whitehead's cosmology lures us to understand such ethical practices as also those on offer by a divinity whose actuality is dependent on our "making [God] feel."[3] A God that feels all of our becoming and perishing lures us to attend to how we affect and are affected by one another. An erotic Foucauldian ethic begs us to feel for all those ghosts that we have disappeared as inconsequential, but on whose effacement our becoming-subject has been built. Furthermore, I suggest that reading Whitehead along with Foucault and Huffer (perhaps my own kind of mad conjoining) illuminates the ethical import of a divinity that serves simultaneously as a limiting force for our actuality and an opening spark for our potentiality. According to Whitehead, in the Galilean origin of Christianity, in the figuration of God as Love, we might find a divinity which "dwells upon the tender elements in the world, which slowly and in

quietness operate by love; and [which] finds purpose in the present immediacy of a kingdom not of this world. Love neither rules, nor is it unmoved;
also it is [521] a little oblivious to morals. It does not look to the future; for
it finds its own reward in the immediate present."[4] God in the form of the
Eros of the Universe is freed from the orthodox Unmoved Prime Mover
and released into the present immediacy of what *might* be in this world.
The felt experience of the world brings God into actuality with the world;
but it is God as Eros, the appetition of Love in the world, where despotic
moralizing ruptures in favor of an ethics seeking erotic reward (what
Huffer names as a "yes to life") in the immediate present. God in process
with all other becoming subjects, both organic and inorganic (what Whitehead calls actual entities), takes care for all in the form of curiosity about
and desire for what has been, what is, and what might be. Indeed, we might
say that the Process God gravely attends not only to what has become, but
also to what was forced to perish in each act of becoming; this divinity
attends not only to the redeemed, but all those left unredeemed in redemption's wake.

The following pages, then, take care for what might be found when we
read Whitehead and Foucault together as erotically ethical aesthetes. In
the beginning Foucault comes closer to the surface, allowing Whitehead to
haunt in the background. As we move on the enfoldment shifts, with
Whitehead unfolding more clearly and Foucault haunting the edge of
Whitehead's thought. By the end, it is the two together that open my theo-
ethics—a theo-ethics in which a mad lament arises both through the careful contestation of what has been and as a grave attention to what might
have been. But, for now, let us attend to the Foucauldian archives that have
haunted Huffer.

The Mad Murmur of the Unredeemed

In *Mad for Foucault*, Huffer invites us to return to *History of Madness*, Foucault's early exploration into the shifting conception of insanity from the
Renaissance through the Age of Reason. Of particular significance to Foucault was the shift from the dark and untamable side of reason, that of
"unreason," to the category of madness, which in being diagnosed as such
was emblematic of both exposure and erasure. For Foucault, unreason was
the tragic underside of reason, that which hovered at the edge of thought
as the unthought. Madness was what unreason became through its pathologization and confinement. Madness was that which reason could distance
as other-than itself. Through the expulsion of madness from reason, the

moral subject was birthed. In making madness a recognizable thing, the forces of unreason, as well as the actual lives of those marked as mad, got silenced. As Foucault articulates this process, "If this evolution was to be summed up in one sentence, we might say that the kernel of the experience of Unreason was that madness was there its own subject, but that in the experience that came into being in the late eighteenth century, madness was alienated from itself through its promotion to a new status as object."[5] Huffer puts this turn thusly: "Both summoned and driven out, madness becomes a plenitude that can appear in the order of reason, as 'the opposite of itself,' to give science 'a rational grip' (M 243/F 261)."[6]

A long history of confinement, legalism, and medicalization took shape during this vital shift from the wild terrains of unreason depicted in the art and literature of the Renaissance to the making of madness into an object of study in the eighteenth and nineteenth centuries. In tracing the epochal shifts Foucault also begins to uncover ethical shifts and, in looking to the past, opens up possibilities for the future. Huffer finds in these shifts, and in Foucault's careful attention (or what she calls Foucault's curiosity-as-care) to the archives, a source of transformation through the possibility (and not promise) of resurfacing unreason as an inescapable part of reason, rather than as madness in need of expulsion and confinement.

Huffer further suggests that in focusing somewhat myopically on the histories of sexuality, queer theorists have overlooked the crucial tie between *History of Madness* and *History of Sexuality I* and, in so doing, have missed proposals that trouble a too-easy divide between a desubjectivating impulse and an ethical one. With philosophy's despotic moralizing as that which has caged and demands contestation, we are brought into contact with how the rise of rational man left victims in its wake.[7] A political theology of and for the unredeemed, for our purposes, differs from despotic moralizing because to take ethical care is to attend to particular interactions between self, other, and world; and not to presuppose a universal way of becoming the good subject.

In the move to madness as mental illness, unreason was tamed so that modern man as subject, what earlier in this book was named as "the good citizen," could come into being. In other words, it is through the making of subjects of the "mad" in their confinement and pathologization that rational man, the reasoned moral subject, is birthed. As Huffer suggests, "Madness is the 'ransom' paid by the 'other' for the historical rise of the rational moral subject."[8] In Foucault's formulation, "Unreason becomes the reason of reason—to the exact extent that reason only recognizes it as a possession."[9] To possess unreason for reason's own definition is to silence unreason and those parts of subjectivity that might trouble any sense of stable self, one closed off to our own transformation and to that part of life that awakens us to our responsibility to the other.

In returning to that part of subjectivity that undoes subjectivity, to eros more than bios, we return ourselves to the scene of the other's ransom, to the other's effacement, and ultimately to unreasons's potential to transform the violence of biopower.[10] In other words, we gravely attend to those who paid the price for our becoming and overcoming—or perhaps following Robin James, we take care for bad investments that become exceptions to neoliberal demands for resilience. It is in this sense of ransom, coerced from the violence of biopower, that Huffer locates one tie to the history of the queer. In this history "homosexuality" as a medical disorder is the ransom paid by the queer so that the reasonable heterosexual might be birthed. A return to the scene of effacement and to the powers of unreason, for Huffer, might be key for queer theory and a renewed sense that one can speak ethically without speaking morally, without capturing the subject in a system of moral principles which would demand another other's ransom, or which would fall into the same logic of violent biopower.

Following in Huffer's footprints, or archival hearings, we might better notice the ransom paid by the mad of this book, like the bipolar woman who cannot let go and let be. In particular, besides its queerness, a return to *History of Madness* returns us to the inescapable bond between madness and unproductivity. As we saw with our exploration of queer time and crip affect in Chapters 2 and 3, the queer and the crip have always already been a threat to the compulsory heterosexuality and compulsory ableism demanded by a neoliberal productivism. What *History of Madness* uncovers is how crucial productivity was to the establishment of reason over and against madness. Without such tie, the need for the confinement and pathologization of madness might have lost its moralizing vigor.

In *History of Madness*, confinement not only names and subjectivizes the figure of the mad, but also serves as an effacement of actual lived lives— those who went classed by madness in attempts to silence the power of unreason. A key figuration of unreason during the Renaissance was the "ship of fools," or in German the *Narrenschiff*. According to Foucault, out of all of the ships depicted in art and literature by such artists of madness as Bosch (whose painting *Das Narrenschiff* Foucault will continue to draw on throughout *History of Madness*), the *Narrenschiff* actually existed.[11] The mad were sentenced to an itinerant existence left to roam from one port to another, each port desperately protecting itself from the madness aboard the ship. Foucault admits that it is difficult to be certain of the meaning of such expulsions. He surmises that some may have taken sail in a kind of pilgrimage: the unreasoned in search of their reason.[12] In some instances it seems that the *Narrenschiff* may have been a way of expelling unwanted foreigners.[13] But beyond these practical reasons Foucault offers the insight that the ship of fools also took on a ritualistic form of passage and exile. While some might see this as a similar form of confinement as that which Foucault argues arose in the shift to the Classical Age, Foucault marks crucial differences between the ship and the asylum. The ship was confinement as passage; the mad were sent out to the other world and arrived from the other world. They were not contained or cured, but roamed the sea, representing the ever present unreason at the border of reason, the borders of ports, cities, and towns.

Furthermore, according to Deleuze, for Foucault, perhaps the ship is also the sea such that the two are symbolically enfolded: "folds and foldings that together make up an inside: they are not something other than the outside, but precisely the inside *of* the outside."[14] In other words, unreason was not that which could easily be objectified, contained, or cured because it was the underside of reason, a part of subjectivity that threatened but could not be sublated into reason. It could not be possessed.

Unreason's inability to be contained was to be suppressed in the epochs that followed such that thought's ability to think, or better feel-think, the unthought (to touch its limit) is lost when the ship of fools disappears into an unmediated dialectic. According to Huffer, "The ship of fools is thus 'the unreason of the world' (M 12/F 23; translation modified); its navigation is the creative but shattering movement of thinking itself toward its own limit as unreason."[15] Hence, at the very moment that madness is freed from its itinerant journey through the watery shadows, it is captured and drained of its transformative power. Exposure and enslavement fortify one another: "Repression and productivity work in tandem: the repressive gesture of confinement produces madness."[16] Naming as production is also the creation of a kind of captivity, even as it frees the mad from the chains of unreason. Being brought back into the fold of reason—being contained back on the shores—robbed unreason of its power to enfold back out of madness to move at the limit of thought and not as the rationale for its stability. Exposure and erasure work in tandem as an inseparable couple.

This coupling is what sets the stage for Huffer's ethical reading of Foucault:

Faced with an objectifying language of reason for the telling of history, *History of Madness* refigures those sexual subjects transformed by

science into objects of intelligibility—as homosexuals, onanists, perverts, and so on—by allowing them to hover as "fantastical" ghosts.
They haunt our present, but we can't quite grasp them.[17]

In their haunting, those subjects transformed into objects demand an ethical hearing. It is one answered by Huffer in her reading of an erotic ethic
from within the Foucauldian "archaeology of alienation," or his archival
attention, his curiosity as care.

It is my hope that in these pages we have begun to glimpse some other
ghosts, not just sexual perverts, but theological and economic ones—those
whom in their refusal to be productive and whole cannot be objectified
into the machines of production. Indeed, it is in this play of captivity and
freedom, in repression and production, that we get glimpses of those
unreasonable prophets that have haunted these pages refusing to come
fully enough into view to be studied as objects of knowledge, and yet of
whom neoliberal capitalism has so desperately tried to capture, fix, and
redeem. Here we might recall disability theorist, Henri-Jacques Stiker's
assertion that "Paradoxically, [the disabled] are designated in order to be
made to disappear, they are spoken in order to be silenced."[18] We might
recall Noëlle Vahanian's observations that "what is called reason is a form
of blindness, a suspension of thought which produces sanity—the ability
to desist from willing, a 'being caught up and carried along.'"[19]

Might this willing—one that, à la Ahmed, willfully wanders away from
the norm and persists in its affect alienation—be an erotic life force that
gravely attends to that which has been, is, and might be? We can see the tie
between the freedom of naming and the capture of being in Negri's
acknowledgment that if we are not careful, the monstrosity of the multitude will be reappropriated into a eugenic logic of Power that fortifies the
Empire. Negri warns of the monster becoming a tool in the eugenic narratives of the Empire; we can think here of Lady Gaga's use of Goth monstrosity to exhibit her ability to overcome damage. We might even glimpse
our too frequent theological capture of the biblical figures of Jonah and
Martha into logics we believed would be liberative, but which bypassed the
under sides of our reason. Perhaps it was the prophecy of unreason that
bubbled in Jonah's anger and Martha's worry.

In each of these formulations of alterity traced throughout these pages,
it is the violence of biopower, at the heart of the projects of Western civilization and neoliberal capitalism, over and against the transformative
force of eros, that creates the affectual alienation these monsters of mine
have endured. It is the ransom they paid for the rise of the eugenically

approved model citizen, able worker, and good Christian. In other words, with the help of Foucault and Huffer, we might begin to see the historical and philosophical matrices faced by those still holding tight to the capture of unreason. This hold is a desperate attempt to resist being freed into the grips of madness. This chapter looks to Huffer's reading of *History of Madness* as the opening of an ethical response to the unreasonable laments of those I have (drawing on Ahmed) named affect alien prophets.

Huffer proposes that we might find a discursive justification for a different practice of ethics in Foucault's attention to the historical shifts from unreason to madness, and the archival accounts of the simultaneous subjectivization and erasure of the living mad. Huffer names this practice as Foucault's ethics of eros. An ethics of eros will not be bowed to the moralizing powers of modern philosophy or sovereign secular reason.[20] According to Foucault, in the loss of unreason madness also lost its voice; it cannot speak; it remains an object of study, and not a subject in dialogue.[21] How can we be reoriented toward the lives of those who cannot speak? To those who are never supposed to be in dialogue? For Huffer, this is where Foucault's attention to the archive becomes key. Huffer proposes such archival work as the opening to "a pathway for a different hearing."[22] This hearing thirsts erotically not for the familiar figures of madness to rise from the dead and into productive life, but rather for the unraveling subjectivity of the listener, the one who has been birthed through the erasure of those our ears now seek to hear. This is because the voices of the mad, of the unreasonable, can never fully speak. But in their "murmurings"[23] they *do* haunt, and in their haunting they invite an erotic attention.

The theo-ethic embedded in erotic attention is amplified, I argue, when we begin to listen to the cacophonous sounds produced in the intensity of thought and unthought achieved in bringing together Foucault with Whitehead. The tie between Foucault and Whitehead is by no means obvious. And yet, both understand an unreasonable desire to be at play in how we might be and might have come to be differently. For instance, thought as propositional, for Whitehead, is thought as a lure toward feeling and is therefore perhaps erotic. Is there not, after all, an interesting resonance between the injunction to "become again what we never were" and God's conceptual feeling as "the sense of what might be and of what might have been . . . the entertainment of an alternative"?[24] According to Isabelle Stengers, God's conceptual feeling has the character of the "what if?," such that "In the constitution of an actual entity:—[sic]whatever component is red, might have been green; and whatever component is loved, might have been coldly esteemed."[25] To become again what we never were or what we might have been, in this sense, is a desire at the heart of both God and an erotic listening.

God's conceptual feeling as characterized by the what-if cannot be divorced from what has been. Indeed, for Whitehead, novelty and actuality are inseparable because actuality is necessary data for novelty and novelty is necessary lure for actuality: "Freedom, givenness, potentiality, are notions which presuppose each other and limit each other."[26] In other words the what-if arises from both what has been (determinate ingressions of what has been positively prehended or felt by the actual entity) and what might have been (the indeterminate that did not make the cut into determination, but rather remains as a negative prehension in the state of potentiality and not actuality). A freedom that arises from within the drama of actuality and potentiality is a grave freedom, one that is grounded in that which, if buried over, was never fully gone. This kind of grave freedom is reflective of Foucault's eros, which according to Huffer "articulates an ideal of freedom that hovers in the moment before its separation into pain and pleasure, dissolution and connection, the forces of undoing and merging."[27]

This freedom might hover in the middle spaces of God's dipolar nature, reminding us that while things today are thus, they might have been otherwise.[28] For Whitehead, perhaps like Foucault, this "otherwise" is opened by moments of madness, or what he calls folly: "It is true that advance is partly the gathering of details into assigned patterns. This is the safe advance of dogmatic spirits, fearful of folly."[29] Whitehead rejects this fear, insisting instead on the, perhaps foolish or *mad*, possibility of novelty as "a new vision of the great Beyond."[30]

The crest and trough of reason and unreason, and those of actuality and potentiality, enfolding within one another like waves, cut to the primacy of becoming in Whitehead's cosmology. Like the erotic ethics that relies on a desire to hear the murmurs of the archive in Huffer's reading of Foucault, Whitehead's processual cosmology relies on the Eros of the Universe, or God's desire for novelty within actuality. God as Eros of the Universe is key for our understanding of how the primordial and consequent natures of God depend on one another, in that the Eros of the primordial pole keeps the thirst for novelty alive within God's and our own actualized becoming. God ensures that actuality and potentiality continue to fortify one another in their coexistence. According to Faber, Whitehead calls this processual, nonformal unity creativity.[31] God's role in such a creative process is that "particular power that preserves precisely *this* unity by *keeping it open* (Faber 2000e)."[32] Keeping the whole open both preserves what has been and ensures that what might have been will not be lost. God's appetition in God's primordial nature refuses the closure of what has been, whereas God's consequent nature takes the "tender care" that nothing of what has been or what might have been be lost.[33]

Reading Whitehead's erotic divinity, one that simultaneously limits and is unlimited, along with Foucault's erotic ethic, reveals a crucial resonance between the Process God's "tender care that nothing be lost" and Foucault's "care as curiosity." From within a folding together of these two thinkers a political theology response-able to the laments of the unredeemed might (re)surface, even if it does so like a wave, only to wash over us momentarily, before being dragged back out to the watery, unspeakable abyss of thought-at-its-limit, of unreason. Let us welcome the monstrous waters.

My Little Monsters

According to Foucault:

> The fact that internees of the eighteenth century bear a resemblance to our modern vision of the asocial is undeniable, but it is above all a gesture of segregation itself. . . . It is the gesture of confinement, in short, which created alienation. . . . It follows from this that to rewrite the history of that banishment is to draw an archaeology of that alienation.[34]

What would it mean to rewrite the narratives of the affect alien and mad prophets that have peopled these pages as an archaeology of their alienation and, in doing so, look not to the nature of their madness, but rather to the situations of segregation—the moments they were ransomed for others' becoming and overcoming—that led to their being named as such? If the inextricable tie between the mad and the queer was essential to Huffer's return to *History of Madness*, then a tie between the mad and the unproductive fuels mine. I suggest this tie poses a theo-ethical question. If the unproductive and unprofitable have paid the ransom for the rise of the biopolitically affirmed model citizen and model theology, then might an exploration of why that ransom was paid help us to hear differently those whom have been wounded by such violence? Might such archaeology help us to rethink the given-ness of our theo-logical orders?

According to Foucault, in the late eighteenth century madness no longer took the form of the bestial nature of man. Rather, it was the result of—or perhaps better, it was that which needed to be resisted in the construction of a milieu.[35] Adherence to the milieu marked one's ability to resist madness. This adherence was not only to the social norms of the family (a point made by Huffer), but also to productive work. From within the archives Foucault notes that at the end of the eighteenth century "madness was lost nature, misplaced sensibility, the wanderings of desire, *time disposed of measure*."[36] Madness could be abolished through a return to one's proper nature, "a happy return of existence to its closest truth."[37] The truth of existence could be found in proper (natural) relations and the proper use of time, which included work appropriate to one's status and gender. For instance:

> "Come, you lovable, sensual women," wrote Beauchesne,
> "And flee the dangers of false pleasures, fleeting passions, luxury and *inaction*; follow your young husbands to the countryside, and on journeys; race them across grassy, flower-strewn prairies, then come back to Paris as an example to your companions, showing them the *beneficial exercise and work that befits your sex*. Love, and bring up your children above all, and you will learn to what degree this pleasure is greater than any other, and how *it has been reserved for you by nature*; you will grow old slowly, if your life is pure."[38]

Here, we might see a glimmer of the ship of fools, in that madness there, too, threatened societal order. And yet by the late eighteenth century the unreason inhabited by the ship of fools was no longer part of one's nature; rather it was one's fall away from the *natural social order* that marked one as mad. This shift meant that one could be trained, cured, and redeemed; one could be brought back into order. No longer an essential part of our natural subjectivity (the limit of the subject and of thought that persisted in the shadows), madness was a danger you could flee. The marks of madness here, those false pleasures, readily support Huffer's thesis of the importance of madness to sexuality, but it is also striking that along with sensuality—which might draw sensuous women away from the pure life of the domesticity nature reserves for their sex—rests the pleasures of luxury and *inaction*. Once inaction is no longer an essential part of action, it becomes the marker of a fallen nature, an issue of morality. The refusal of work marks one as corrupted and unfaithful. Hence, listening to this piece of the archive differently hears not only Beauchesne's moralizing voice, but also the ghosts of sensual women. If these ghosts had not been refusing their domestic labor, had not been falling into pleasurable inaction, there would be no need for Beauchesne's instruction.

Additionally, my sense of bipolar temporality can be considered a call to rethink time out of its measure. Might mania and depression be contemporary embodiments of the "misplaced sensibility, the wanderings of desire, *time disposed of its measure*" which in the eighteenth century marked the milieu constituted by madness?

The history of confinement might be a history of the refusal of bipolar time; time in which one does *not* get up out of one's (lonely or full) bed in time to get the domestic labor done. For instance, as part of his discussion of the tie between madness, religion, and time, Foucault notes that:

> In 1781, a German author evoked the distant happy times when priests were granted absolute power, and idleness was unknown; each instant was marked by "ceremonies, religious practices, pilgrimages, visits to the poor and the sick, and feast days on the calendar." *Time was thus fully dedicated to organised happiness, leaving no leisure for empty passions, boredom or disgust with life.*[39]

Time out of joint was to be organized, no day left idle, all passions directed toward order. Imagine what affect aliens lurk in the tale of these distant "happy" times. We hear what might have been the feminist killjoy giving up domestic "bliss" in order to live. We feel the gravity backlit with hope when the disgustingly crooked—who being herself disgusted by the straightening rod—remained bent, even in the end. Our little monsters are haunting Foucault's archive.

If the importance of use-value of the mad took on a striking significance as a rationale for confinement, it is one that has by no means abated today. Consider the threat to our economy made by the bipolar woman who falls back into the bed; and the crip who says, "Fuck employability, I'm too sick to work." What would it mean to be unable to work? Of what use could we possibly be if we remained idle? The salvation of the neoliberal city, like that of the eighteenth century Protestant one, depends on functioning labor; it depends, as Robin James makes clear, on being resiliently flexible and therefore malleable as the tools the neoliberal economy needs us to be. Even so, why confine the idle, unless the very presence of and the voices of the bodies of those who cannot or will not labor threatens the laboring of those whom have not *yet* been alienated from the narrative of work as redemptive?

Eventually, confinement was not enough to prevent the creep of alienation. Even those in such houses needed to be redeemed back into the moralizing system of work. If to work was to be redeemed, then within the houses of confinement, "cure" came through productive contribution to

society. Here a split in the forms of madness once again took shape. Those
from within a state of confinement who could learn to labor productively
(if uncompensated) and attend worship services (often on the importance
of work) without disturbance could be redeemed into good moral standing. Those whose madness was beyond reach were condemned to alienation: "In the workshops where [the mad] were expected to blend in with
others, they often signaled themselves through their inability to work and
to follow the rhythms of collective life."[40] Unproductivity was, in this
sense, a sign of an irredeemable madness.

Hence, the mad who could not work were now left with the imperative
to be cured. No longer necessarily controlled by a house of confinement,
they were left not to the powers of the state, but to those of shame: "But
when morality formed the substance of the State, and public opinion was
the most solid link in the chain that held society together, then scandal
became the most redoubtable form of alienation."[41] Work was worth, and
labor salvation. And thus the importance of a theology that resists this
moralizing tie bubbles to the service once again. If labor is redemptive (a
source of salvation), then for those who suffer from their own inaction, pay
may matter less than one's salvific election. Flourishing on one's own terms
is unimportant. Either one wants to be saved or not, and if not, they must
be mad and, therefore, scandalous.

This problem does not disappear with the rise of mental illness as a
diagnosable "natural" state, which now might be cured and, therefore,
arguably redeemed. According to Foucault, once mental illness was an
object of knowledge the actual lives of the mad, rather than resurrected or
redeemed, were in their salvation out of illness silenced further: "The
nineteenth century constituted mental alienation as one of the immemo-
rial truths of its positivism."[42] In other words, the progress of rational man
could be built on the recognition and so rehabilitation of mental alienation.
Unreason, which was always close at hand during the renaissance and
undoing the order of the world from within the tragic cosmic rhythm of
unreason's enfoldment in reason, was now able to be objectified, parsed,
and hence distanced from the world. One could escape one's madness,
because madness could be fixed (contained, stabilized, and cured). Unreason was a cosmic part of reason, while madness became a defect from
which we might get distance. If one could not get distance, one could not
be rehabilitated and so redeemed.

That madness could be medicalized and therefore neutralized implied
that those who did not or could not overcome their unreason were condemned. When madness takes its distance from reason and hence

overcomes unreason, those who stick to their madness become the exceptions to resilience, as outlined in Chapter 2. Might we therefore cling anew to the mad? How can we hear those who did not take leave of their unreason, those who could not get proper distance?

Indeed, what is to be done? If we cannot/should not redeem the mad back into a society, are we left to nihilistically watch as our little monsters fade even farther from view? If to name them and bring them to light risks a redemption that is actually their objectification and condemnation, is there any point in looking, listening, and feeling for their ghosts? Perhaps it is the refusal to stop looking, or in Huffer's formulation, to stop hearing, or reading for affect—refusing to stop touching and feeling for our monsters—that such impossibility of ever fully presenting them calls us to enact. Just because we cannot make them speak does not mean we cannot reorient ourselves ever more toward the fading background. According to Foucault, "What classicism had locked up was not simply unreason in the abstract where the mad, the libertine, the criminal and the sick all intermingled, but also a prodigious reserve of fantasy, a sleepy world of monsters, which were believed to have sunk back into the Bosch night from which they had first emerged."[43]

It may be time to wake the monsters, or if not fully wake them, to listen for sleepy murmurings, for the sounds of their dreams.

Erotic Listening

To hear the sleeping monsters would be to listen again for that which has been reduced to silence. Huffer notes that early in the text and "throughout the pages of *History of Madness* [lepers] will silently and invisibly haunt the arid landscape of a world that repeatedly rejects them . . . the leper is the 'ghost' (*M* 3) who hovers at the margins of the inhabitable social world that rejects him, a figure of the 'inhuman' (*M* 3) who will continue to haunt the sun-filled spaces of a Western humanism Foucault spent his life critiquing."[44] Like the "*it*" of disability that follows us home, the leper, as the figure of the inhuman, haunts even as Western humanism silences him by marking him as "inhuman." Indeed, like in the horror movie of our own making in which we flee from the creep of unproductivity and so unmeaning, "The fear of the other—of unreason itself—becomes the fear within, marked by 'the imaginary mark of an illness' (*M* 358/*F* 377; translation modified) to which everyone is susceptible . . . the dangers of unreason's contagious effects on positive reason."[45] It is this fear of becoming leper, of becoming mad, that shores up our drive to be ever more reasonable—that which I have named here and elsewhere as the drive to be redeemed as a productive and efficient member of society—the drive to *mean* something, to *matter* to a society that measures such worth as what we can *do* for the machine rather than *who* we are singularly and in our singularity also for one another.

Hence, the unspeakability of unreason does and should not mean that the leper and the mad who haunt have no impact on the future; it is quite the opposite. That they *still* haunt creates the possibility of transformation. Here, I quote Huffer at length, because this passage is crucial for the understanding of the Foucauldian ethics she hopes to unearth:

> The conception of an open future traces the outline of an erotic alterity whose presence is crucial in Foucault. The glimmers of eros that episodically burst through the pages of *History of Madness*, and Foucault's writings as a whole, point to what I will call an erotic other as the figure for an ethical love conceived as freedom. She corresponds to what Caputo calls, in the later Foucault, "the murmurings of a capacity to be otherwise." I argue here that this murmuring of otherness is there, from the start, as a consistent presence in all of Foucault's writing, as "scintillations of the visible" and a "style of life." For, if that otherness is silenced in the great confinement, that closeting is never total.[46]

If the closeting is never total, then it begs for our peeking in, for our straining to hear the monsters that go bump in the night; it requires us to be spooked by its openings. Glimpses of this spooking can be found in Foucault's straining to hear those who, at the limit of their thought, murmured to Foucault (and to us) in the language of unreason: Sade, Nietzsche, Artaud. For instance, it is in the moment of Nietzsche's breakdown, that of his bodymind and that of his thought, that Foucault sees him finally able to speak of the madness of which he has been philosophizing. Indeed, Foucault asks, "[might] this madness so foreign to the experience contemporaneous with it . . . utter to those who can hear . . . a point from which all contestation becomes possible, as well as the contestation for all things?"[47] In tying the scarcely audible words of classical unreason to the contestation of all things—a whisper to a roar—the Foucauldian ethic curves and knots with my own, dividing and undoing neoliberal time through embodiments of contestation. Might we see Nietzsche and Artaud, at their very moments of maddening breaks with modern secular reason, as affect alien prophets? And if their lament (their contestation of all things) is heard in barely audible words, then perhaps they beg from us a straining of the ear. Perhaps they lure us to gravely attend to today's breaking down and whispering mad—those whose laments come in barely audible words, but also as I have been arguing here, in affect—in the emotional expressions of the breaks.

This willingness to be spooked might be another name for the "style of life" suggested by Foucault in his exploration of Stoic and Cynic self-cultivation in *Hermeneutics of the Subject*. This cultivation, Huffer argues, is undertaken through practices of the care of the self, as explored by Foucault in the 1981–1982 lectures at the Collège de France collected in *Hermeneutics of the Subject*. It is cultivation reflected in Foucault's attention to the archive and his twenty years of worrying about his little mad ones. The tie between the care of the self and the archive denotes an erotic attention to the other. The care of the self, from which one might "become again what we never were," is an "an invitation to curiosity-as-care."[48] Curiosity-as-care might be Foucault's insistence on "the care one takes for what exist and what *might* exist."[49] Curiosity-as-care enacts a becoming that is at once a desubjectivization of the curious listener and a becoming-plural of both the ghost whom we try to hear and the "we" who are haunted by such ghosts. We might—even if it represents a rupture with Foucault's resistance to subjectivity—rewrite such desubjectivization as a re-singularization in the Deleuzian and Berardian sense. To desubjectify the knower might be to ask into what type of subject the knower has been coercively constructed *and on whose effacement* has she been birthed. To re-singularize the knower is then to re-singularize the ghosts she (im)possibly strives to know, touch, feel, and hear.

The importance of the "we" arises in Foucault's exploration of the care of the self in *Hermeneutics of the Subject*. Reading Seneca's letters, Foucault notes that for Seneca, "Even if we are hardened, there are means by which we can recover, correct ourselves, and *become again what we should have been but never were*. To become again what we never were is, I think, one of the most fundamental elements, one of the most fundamental themes of this practice of the self."[50] According to Foucault, for Seneca, and aligning with the Cynics, "the practice of the self will become increasingly a critical activity with regard to oneself, one's cultural world, and the lives led by others."[51] The care of the self, in this way, is a readying of the self for a transformation that would open us to a different kind of hearing. To become again what *we* never were is that care for what might have been, but also an erotic opening to the archive in that the becoming will happen in the plural form: we.

We could assume that the care of the self does not in fact necessitate a "we"; or that such a "we" in terms of Seneca's letter and Foucault's formulation is a "we" in reference to how *each* of us within the "we" might become what *each* of us never was. However, reading with Huffer and with Mark Jordan's explication of *Hermeneutics of the Subject* and *The Courage of Truth: The Government of Self and Others II*, the *we-ness* of such a style of self-care becomes more evident. In *Courage of Truth* Foucault suggests that there are two ways of reading the Greek conception of philosophical training in the care of the self: that which follows Alcibiades and that which begins with Laches. If we take Laches as our starting point: "The care of the self does not lead to the question of what this being I must care for is in its reality and truth . . . but the questioning of what, *in relation to all other forms of life*, precisely that form of life which takes care of the self must and can be in truth."[52] From Laches, Foucault follows to the care of the self in Cynic formation in which such care shapes a style of existence. Such a style of existence, while beginning through one singular life of the Cynic, is directed toward the embodiment of truth, the style of living that tells the truth, in *relation to all other forms of life*.

Cynics, Foucault argues in *Courage of Truth*, served as "scouts" going ahead to encounter the truth and report it back. They went beyond themselves into the world, but in doing so retained a style of life that would confront the world and its given orders with a truth beyond such orders. This confrontation is a bodily comportment, one that in its care of the self opens itself to desubjectivization such that the "body [becomes] a reservoir of alternate lives."[53] Such alternate lives are not only the ones that for each individual never were but might become again; the alternate lives in relation to the truths of the world that resist given orders are also lives on offer through an erotic encounter with our own others and with other selves' others, with the subjectivities ransomed for our redemptions. As Foucault argued, "By basing the analysis of Cynicism on [the] theme of individualism . . . we are in danger of missing . . . the problem, which is at the core of Cynicism, of establishing a relationship between forms of existence and manifestations of the truth."[54] Such framing is ethical. The problem of establishing a relationship between the style of *a* life and the myriad manifestations of the truth is a problem that might clear a pathway to a different hearing for such manifestations. It is a problem that demands grave attending to the archive.

Therefore, the care of self that allows the self to be transformed by a meeting with alterity is both a practice of eros and an ethic. Care of the self is a critical practice because it begins with a stripping away of the stability of one's current subjectivity as an act of desire to be transformed through an encounter with alterity. The practice of the self must be "a stripping away of previous education, established habits, and the environment."[55] If we apply this sense of stripping away to the curiosity-as-care that Huffer finds in Foucault, we see how the concept of the care of the self in Foucault cannot be divorced from a care for the other and hence forms a style of life that might be embodied by a "we." Such self-care is not a coming of the subject, but a stripping away of the habits of subjectivization that prevent us from "becoming what *we* might have been."

Like Foucault's earlier return to unreason, this call to return to a becoming that never was is seemingly impossible; it is an unattainable imperative to re-inhabit the ghosts of selves and possibilities gone unrealized or unredeemed, those who were never allowed to exist, what "we *never* were." And yet it is here where Huffer finds the ethical key to madness, the alterity of which, "articulated as a 'we,' . . . is transformed, in a time we cannot know, to become something other than the object pinned down, the straitjacketed psychotic or the convulsing hysteric on the scientific stage."[56] Becoming mad, we might become knowers of our unknowing, we might be open to rupture and not certainty, we might remain willfully unredeemed together.

We might find such mad rupture in Foucault's reading of Cynicism as "the idea of a mode of life as the irruptive, violent, scandalous manifestations of the truth."[57] This is a living truth, which, as Jordan understands it, is "not a plot of progress or of managed expenditure for the sake of a greater profit,"[58] but rather as Foucault makes clear, a revolutionary militancy that is a "bearing witness by one's life in the form of a style of existence . . . ensuring that one's life bears witness, breaks, and has to break with the conventions, habits, and values of a society . . . [One's life] must manifest directly, by its visible form, its constant practice, and its immediate existence, the concrete possibility and the evident value of an other life, which is the true life."[59] This style of life takes form in a care of the self that, in relation to all other lives, might insist on the concrete possibility of another life through bodily practice. This is a truth in rupture, not a plotted certainty. It is an ars erotica (in Huffer's terms) because it is practiced through the style of bodily existence inhabited by the Cynics. The desire for truth in this way is performed as much as spoken. It is not a desire for contained knowledge as much as for existence.

Perhaps surprisingly given their varying intellectual trajectories, we see a similar diagnosis of problematic historical knowing in Whitehead: "the moderns had lost the sense of vast alternatives, magnificent or hateful, lurking in the background, and awaiting to overwhelm our safe little traditions. If civilization is to survive, the expansion of understanding is a prime necessity."[60] Whitehead's processual scheme, including his critique of "the fallacy of misplaced concreteness" (the willful elision of aspects of actual entities that do not fit into stagnant conceptual frameworks), is a critique of the modern substantialist subject and its objects of certainty.[61] Indeed, we can read, turning away from our safe little traditions in order for understanding to be expanded, as an erotic practice in that in turning we are moved toward the lurking background.

Whitehead's thirst for an expansive understanding can be read as a thirst for that alterity which may be barely visible and yet in which there is both promise and threat (magnificence and hate). Aesthetic intensity, and so satisfaction of God's primordial aim, necessitates that we clear pathways for the hearing of alterity, that which, being thus, might have been otherwise. Such alterity, the otherwise, might lead to disaster, but the promise of intensity trumps the triviality of remaining within our safe little traditions.

In short, in the middle ground between promise and threat, what I have named in Chapter 2 as a bipolar sensibility, there lies a chance for the transformation of the self and the expansion of understanding. Knowledge arising through a care of the self that is also critical would demand the altering of the knower's being. *We* can only become *again* that which *we never* were, if care for the self is desubjectivating. This care for the self might begin with an erotic listening for those lurking in the background and result in a challenge to the subjectivities we have built for ourselves through the effacement of such alterity on the paths to our own redemptions. This is where Huffer finds Foucault's archival work so key to his ethics. Read in the wake of our analysis of Whitehead earlier, this erotic lure to become again what we never were, a call to attend to the past and the present so as to rethink the future, takes on not only an ethical weight but a theological one.

Huffer names the archive another heterotopia because it is both "utterly real" in that it is the space in which we might note the wounds inflicted by rationalism in its effacement of the unreasonable and "utterly unreal" in that it is the site of the potential of a different type of hearing—one which, unlike from within our "safe little traditions," this archival listener would "'agree to receive, as true, the wounding truth he hears.'"[62] Agreeing to be wounded by the truth murmured in the archive is the agreement to be altered by the other in an erotic encounter. For Huffer, it is in this erotic encounter that the possibility of "beginning again" or "transformation" might take place.[63] This transformation cannot be read here as a kind of redemptive resurrection, or as a programmatic ethical call. Rather, it is an invitation to embody the self differently, in a way that Huffer names as "a 'poetic attitude' and practice, recalling the etymology of *poiesis* as making: a making or fashioning attitude."[64] In this fashioning attitude or "style of life" (à la Cynicism) we are engaged in the type of spirituality Foucault saw eclipsed in the Age of Reason.[65] The style of existence that arose through the care of the self practiced by the Cynics was one that did not redeem philosophical knowledge as reasoned truth-claim, but rather served as "the grimace of philosophy staring back at itself in a curved mirror. Cynicism presents a series of breaking points at which philosophy must confront its own inconsistencies. It is a carnival but also a race to the limit."[66] The Cynic style of life was not one in search of rehabilitation into civil order, but rather one embracing of "nakedness . . . public ingestion, copulation, secretion, excretion . . . refusing tasteful privacy."[67] To bare the body of truth was to declare "fierce allegiance to truth" and to perform a transvaluation of philosophical values.[68] The transvaluation of value and the grimaced smile staring back at philosophy are not new regimes of philosophy being resurrected out of the grave, but the haunting of order by those who would live more nakedly. To be naked in public in this way might be to declare allegiance to the truth, even when that truth means remaining open to being undone in further transvaluation. The care of the self is the preparation for such undoing. We engage in an openness to be transformed, and yet this open possibility is not as much a promise of certain truth as it is a risk; to risk that things might become again what they never were is to risk that this becoming will end in tragedy.

This is true for both Foucault and Whitehead: What lurks in the background might be magnificent or hateful. And yet this threat is precisely where the theo-ethical attitude comes in, for the threatening of order— even the novel orders established in each moment of transformation— might just be how we ensure that our resistance to effacement does not become its own effacement of new others. To acknowledge that new moments of becoming result in new violence is to gravely attend to those ransomed (acknowledged or not) as the price of our becoming. In this way an ethics of eros is reflective of Robin James's call for a more evenly distributed care work, in which the care for the exclusions to rehabilitation is done without profit sought in return. To gravely attend in this way is affective and erotic because we are brought down by our desire to hear again that which never was. To hear again might be to imagine big rooms of becoming. Hence, crucially, "Foucault's eros is not a redemptive cure for that which ails us; it does not provide us with an essential plenitude to which we can cling for solace in these modern, science-dominated, seemingly loveless times. . . . If erotic generosity makes us want to cling to its promise of transformative connection, the violent force of erotic irony reminds us that the thing we're clinging to is a stick of dynamite."[69] The grimaces of our own philosophies smile back at us, through cracked mirrors, ready to explode.

An erotic ethics, my grave attending, is an unceasing demand for perpetual hearing. That the unreasonable can never be fully spoken means that our erotic curiosity must never end. If we were to fully resurrect or redeem the wounds inflicted by rationalism, we would no longer be listening for the wounds of new orders that arise in the vacuum created when we rupture old ones. The limit to our knowing allows for the unlimited.

A yearning eros is also apparent in Whitehead, as Stengers notes: "The justification of life does not require a 'higher freedom' that would see farther and wider than we. It requires 'yearning' as such, a yearning directed both to what is done and to what is undone, in the 'here and now' of decision: thus and not otherwise."[70] Whitehead's yearning and Foucault's listening begin to surface, if momentarily, the murmurs of the lurking background; or in Stengers's words, they reveal the undone from within the done. But in these moments of surfacing, both Foucault and Whitehead remind us that what might have been otherwise, might have been hell. This dual movement of promise and threat within Whitehead's cosmology opens theological possibilities. One such promised possibility is the political theology of and for the unredeemed and the practice of grave attention here offered. In the refusal of the clear division between promise and threat, we are brought down to the ways in which the grave is backlit with hope, and hope infused with gravity.

The (Un)Limiting Divine

Unlike Foucault, Whitehead does think in propositions, but ones that are felt as malleable moments of truth. For Whitehead, propositions are lures for feeling and, as such, they resonate with queer affect theorist Eve Sedgwick's desire to think both propositionally and affectually. Indeed, for Whitehead it is more important that a proposition be more interesting than that it be true. In her consideration of the issue of truthfulness and "truthiness," both in terms of Whiteheadian thought and that of poststructuralism, Catherine Keller notes, "We feel our propositions are truthful to the extent they dis/close the fullness itself: as articulated in the subject's interdependence with its others, its neighbors, strangers, enemies, its world."[71] The quest for what she names "trusty propositions," or dis/closive truths, is not necessarily, Keller and I argue, antithetical to poststructural-ist ponderings. Indeed, propositional thinking à la Whitehead might remain for us in an erotic and ethical register, resisting any moralizing dogmatism. Such eroticism, according to Keller's reading of Whiteheadian propositions, might be trusty in how it "faithfully [narrates] what has been in order to keep open the democratic space in which the shared future is negotiated."[72] This is an allegiance to the flesh, to the muck, to the archive, and to all that is given, but it might be—and might have been or yet become—otherwise.

The Cynic might have embodied these trusty propositions when, as "the man of parrhēsia, [he cannot] promise to remain silent . . . [he] cannot promise not to say anything . . . the Cynic does appear in fact as the proph-etēs parrhēsias (the prophet of free-spokenness)."[73] To be a prophet of free-spokenness is not to be held captive to a straw reading of Foucault or poststructuralism, in which to speak any form of truth might be to assert despotic moralism. Rather, the style of existence lauded by Foucault is an art of truth telling (and truth embodying) that prepares us to become again that which we never were. As Keller notes, we might need "to get our hearts and heads together, in truth, for the sake of that 'more' that we so becomingly, and never quite, are."[74] This is truth as a pathway toward a different type of hearing, a grave attention to what was, what is, and what might be, and not the establishment of a rational moral order.[75]

For instance, Faber reminds us that while the image of love or eros in Whitehead's cosmology is essential for God's "tender care that nothing be lost," the terms of love and tenderness are often too narrow, aligning with a kind of favoritism (the love of a particular actual entity over and against others). Hence he suggests that we "[negotiate] 'love' *only as polyphilia*, that is, as love *only* of *multiplicity*, and for understanding . . . polyphilia."[76] The eros of the universe and the tender care that nothing be lost are love and tenderness for multiplicity, by which Faber means for an open whole that resists favoring one entity over another. Such polyphilia desires the multi-plicity, the open wholeness, of becoming on offer in the play between actuality and novelty. Such love might be that found in the erotic ethics in which Foucault thirsts for the singularities of the archive that have been closed off; or by the Cynic attitude in which the Cynic "cannot have a family because, ultimately, humankind is his family."[77] To be a truth teller is polyphilic, it is to be in relation with the world's other lives. The care for the self in this way may be the aesthetic and ethical practice, an *ars erotica* or spirituality, of polyphilic attention to the truths that rupture order. It is to feel and listen for what was thus and what might have been otherwise.

That Whitehead's aesthetic cosmology recalls the opening made by the care of the self reminds us that we might become again that which we never were. The "again" here is of particular import for the mixing of tenses in both Whitehead's and Foucault's formulations of the play between finitude and infinity. Such a temporal mixing is key for the resonance I find between them and the affect-laden political theology I embrace in bringing the two together. The possibilities unrealized in the past imply the chance for novelty in the future; *again* and *never* stand in rational opposition, demanding instead an aesthetic style of being rather than a logical one. The tension between *again* and *never* reflects Isabelle Stengers's reading of the Process God's appetition as having the character of the "what if?"[78] This allows Whitehead to posit that "There must be value beyond ourselves. Otherwise every thing experienced would be merely a barren detail in our own solipsist mode of existence."[79] The value beyond ourselves is what lures us toward ever more penetration and hence the expansion of understanding. It is our thirst for higher values of intensity. The development of contrasts resists the fallacy of misplaced concreteness that coerces us to eclipse that which is in discordance with a given order. In contrast, Whitehead argues that "if there is to be progress beyond limited ideals, the course of history by way of escape must venture along the borders of chaos in its substitution of higher for lower types of order."[80] Thus, the thirst for higher orders of contrast represents God's threefold character as Eros, Adventure of the Universe as One, and the Harmony of Harmonies, which together represent a tender care for what has been, what might have been, what might be, and the intensity birthed from the integrated differences between the actuality and potentiality these three states represent.

The thirst for higher order intensity (one perhaps not unrelated to the manic side of bipolarity) is fundamental in Whitehead's aesthetics, and the goal of Beauty is found in each decision within the process of becoming. This Beauty is no guarantee that in each becoming anything of the past will be utterly redeemed. Rather, it is in the entertainment of multiple factors in each experience—while always limited, where we might take a theo-ethical stance that while in actuality things had to be for this moment thus, in potentiality they might have been otherwise. For instance, looking to Nietzsche, that prophet of madness, affect theorist Eugenie Brinkema discusses the ethical attitude of Nietzsche in terms of joy. According to Brinkema:

> Nietzschean joy is also an ethic, for he is explicit on this point: the eternal recurrence is not a strict return of what has taken place only,

but also a beam cast out on the future . . . in the joyful ethic of the "what-might-take-place" of any situation. . . . Joy, then, after Nietzsche, does not recuse itself from the messy facticity of being a Being-in-time, nor [does it] bracket the actual or active, either suffering or becoming. Rather, it places the infinity of chance and possibility into an existence marked by finitude.[81]

Finitude here is the affirmation of infinity. Nietzschean joy spurring from the entertainment of all possibilities for the what-might-take-place of any situation is willed through the finitude of situations actually taking place. Indeed, this Nietzschean joy may be the joy available to the feminist killjoy when she gives up the happiness on offer (a happiness unreflective of pains inflicted on her life) in order to *live*. The Nietzschean joy may be the impulse behind the Postwork Manifesto command to get *a* life.

The ethical entertainment of possibilities Brinkema finds in Nietzsche can similarly be found both in the Process God's character of the what-if, and in what Whitehead marks as "His [sic] tender care that nothing be lost." Both the what-if and God's tender care arise from God's dipolar nature. God's dipolarity, when read beside Foucault and Huffer, can imply an ethical style, a different kind of hearing. This tender care that nothing be lost might just be a glimpse into a political theology attendant to the murmurs of our little monsters, to the laments of affect aliens. After all, to gravely attend to what we thought was buried and gone might be to clear the pathway for a different hearing, one that in what might have been we find what might be. The coexistence and inseparability of caring for what we have lost, a looking back that opens the possibility of the what-if, cosmically inhabits the Process God's dipolar nature. God's dipolar nature consists of the mental and physical poles, or what Whitehead names as God's primordial and consequent nature. As God is also an actual entity, it is in our ability to make God feel that God's consequent nature becomes actual in the world. If God were not actual, God would not be able to feel our joys and sorrows, every moment of the world's becoming. In other words, all actual entities, including God, require others to make them feel and to feel them in order to have actuality in the world.

Without such a feeling (what we might also call a hearing, a touching, or tasting), existence is impossible. And yet, because of God's primordial nature, that which prehends all possibilities for each occasion, the limiting decision necessary for actualization does not have the last word. From this point of view, Stengers troubles an emphasis on this primordial nature or any attempt to separate out the two poles (a risk she finds in Whiteheadian philosophers, who, she worries, do not avoid the powerful attraction of the notion of "Unmoved Prime Mover") and, instead, thinks with Whitehead in a manner that she considers the "reverse" of such a stance: "[T]he point is to accentuate the inseparable character of the two 'poles' of divine experience, the pole called mental and the pole called physical, and therefore to go right to the end of what Whitehead proposed when he made God an actual entity (almost) like the others."[82] It is the inseparability of the two poles that keeps the inseparable aesthetic and ethical open.

Such an ethical force can be seen in Faber's development of God's "in/difference" in *Divine Manifold*: "In its movement of undoing any unifications or identifications, this 'indifference' is not carelessness, but translates the Buddhist 'detachment' (*viraga*), which *is* universal compassion (*karuna*)."[83] Here we are reminded of the Cynic who is in love with all of humanity. Universal compassion is the polyphilia, or love for multiplicity, that Faber hopes to illuminate. This is an ethics of care for all, including those made exceptions by lower order orders that seek to elide intensity in favor of concreteness. Put perhaps more politically, this is an ethics of care for all those neoliberalism has deemed too messy for redemption, those that are not profitable. This polyphilia may be the redistribution of care work sought by Robin James's melancholy, Huffer's erotic ethics, and my grave attending. This care is unreasoned care for *what is* in such a way that opens us to what *might have been* and *what might be*.

Even if in God's mental pole there exists a sense of the infinity of possibilities, since the mental pole is inseparable from the physical pole, these possibilities are dependent on yet-to-be-felt actualities. As such, while God is a source for novelty, God cannot be considered a pure or efficient cause of what is to come. If God were to have chosen the one possible universe that was best, à la Leibniz's divinity, God would not be *moved* by our feelings. In contrast to the orthodox reading of God as the Unmoved Prime Mover, who could from the start choose and ensure the best possible universe, Whitehead's God is dependent on being affected and affecting, being moved and moving in co-creation with all other actual entities in the world. If God is to be actual, God must be *moved*.

That this God preserves what might have been does not mean that we might resurrect those ghosts, as though the cut—the decision to feel one at a particular time—were reversible. The past is not repaired: "But if God enforces the irreparability of the past, he also guarantees the openness of the future, and invites the transmutation in the present of the effect of the past. And in this role, he stands for an inclusive and nonrestrictive use of the disjunctive synthesis. God 'embod[ies] a basic completeness of appetition'

(Whitehead 1929/1978, 316)."[84] The irreparable past might be like the impossibility of hearing the mad that were not given voice. The irreparability and impossibility perpetuate the need for grave attention. That what has been thus might be otherwise is what fuels a desire to lend an ear, to be willing to be subjectively undone by a different hearing of that which cannot be fully resurrected, but which can haunt.

Novel but Not Saved

According to Whitehead, God's initial aim can be thought of as that which is "best for the impasse."[85] Is this aim too teleological? Is the harmonizing of contrasts even as it is an intensification of those same contrasts, a kind of saving, a redemption of that which never was, but might have been? Is this not what, throughout these pages, we have been trying to contest? Stengers refutes or complicates our worry: "[W]hat emerges from this weaving, the feeling of what would be best 'for the impasse,' does not correspond either to a transcendent knowledge or to a determinate anticipation. Instead, this feeling has the features of a question of the 'what if?' type."[86] To ask what might have been is not to guarantee that we will indeed become again what we never were. Nor does it guarantee that our "never was" would not be tragic. The what-if does not save the past as much as it insists that transformation is possible—possible, but not promised. This is a saving that is a salvaging of possibilities for becoming from what might have been and not the redemption (the making okay) of what was. This salvaging more than saving is perhaps what Whitehead means when he writes of the everlasting life of what perishes. According to Whitehead:

> Throughout the perishing occasions in the life of each temporal Creature, the inward source of distaste or of refreshment, the judge arising out of the very nature of things, redeemer or goddess of mischief, is the transformation of Itself, everlasting in the Being of God. In this way, the insistent craving is justified—the insistent craving that zest for existence be refreshed by the ever-present, unfading importance of our immediate actions, which perish and yet live for evermore.[87]

Sensitive attention to the temporality in such formulations and to Whitehead's attention to the differential intensity that arises from such opposites as distaste and refreshment complicates any sense of a transcendent salvation or complete redemption.

Perhaps actions that perish live for evermore because of God's tender care that nothing be lost, including the pain of what has been. This pain

may be irredeemable in the sense of its unfading importance in our immediate actions, but yet live for evermore in its ability to haunt us as what was
and as insight into what might have been. That which is immediate in its
importance and which simultaneously perishes and lives seems to me to be
more reflective of Holy Saturday, a day in which we have become from our
past crucifixions, feel their immediacy of import, and yet are open to what
might be in the face of the promise and threat of what will be. The zest *for*
existence, or an erotic yes *to* life, comes from within the pain of perishing,
of death, and *before* the certainty of life.

In a discussion on love and power, Faber draws on the following sense
of aesthetic harmony in Whitehead's *Science and the Modern World*: "'The
aesthetic harmony stands before' multiplicity with the polyphilic divine 'as
a living ideal molding the general flux in its broken progress toward finer,
subtler issues' (*Science*, 18)."[88] Whitehead ties such progress to attention to
the things of the world, what we might call a grave attending to the muck
of the world. Faber ties such progress to a polyphilic resistance to violent
power in that, as Whitehead notes in *Adventures of Ideas*, "'enjoyment of
power is fatal to the subtleties of life' (84)."[89] In other words, if there is
something salvific in God's tender care that nothing be lost or in the lure
toward differential intensity, it might be an attentive salvaging of the sub-
tlety of issues of the world. This attending is not a redemption out of the
muck and into glory, but a being drawn back to the graves of that which
God prevents from ever being fully lost. This gravity is backlit, perhaps, in
God's character as the what-if and each actual entity's insistence on the
"Yes, but."

The sense of the what-if is further explicated by Whitehead in *Modes of
Thought*:

> The decisive consciousness that *this* is red, and *that* is loud, and *this
> other* is square, results from an effort of concentration and elimination.
> Also it is never sustained. There is always a flickering variation varied
> by large scale transference of attention. Consciousness is an ever-
> shifting process of abstracting shifting quality from a massive process
> of essential existence. It emphasizes. And yet, if we forget the back-
> ground, the result is triviality.[90]

Might we think of this flickering variation that lies in the background as a
haunting? It is the background we are warned not to forget; it is that which
keeps us out of solipsistic dogmatism. And so it is that which is not so much
a resurrection or redemption, but rather a refusal of the closing of the

closet. To welcome the flicker is to welcome the truth of the wounds inflicted on those effaced through biopolitical violence.

Let me surmise that this attention to the wound can be found in God's "tender care that nothing be lost." My pain is not redeemed, the leper is not resurrected; they have already undergone their fates, and yet, still, God's tender care just might mean that these wounds inflicted on our/we little monsters will never be insignificant. The background cannot be forgotten, or else we slip into triviality. Once again we see that actuality is necessary for transformation, for "whatever 'making feel' may mean, it is a vector. And in fact, the argument according to which the vectorial dimension of feelings disappears with satisfaction may be repeated with this new question: what if its disappearance were not its death?"[91] Negative prehensions (meaning those not ingressed and made actual as opposed to those that we would deem as negative experiences) retain their positive potential. This is the potential that might set the stage for a care for the self that would seek ever more contrasts and therefore ever more possibilities for its own undoing, a breaking free of our safe little traditions, such that we might become again what we never were. God's tender care that nothing be lost and our care of the self might work in conjunction for a practice of grave attention, a frank style of existence, that is willing to become—mad.

Can this becoming-mad, a becoming which is not the cause of a resurrection but of the insistence of unreason's significance to God, be a call to God that God take tender care that its historic wounds and the potential for future otherwise not be lost? But also, can becoming-mad be a model we follow such that we more consciously feel the significance of madness? In the moments when feeling moves to thought (not mere reason, but also thought in unreason's power to think the unthought) might we better raise the question of the what-if even/especially with God? Reading with Foucault, I believe perhaps we could.

Curiosity as Our Tender Care that Nothing Be Lost

Let us recall Foucault's curiosity as care: "a habit of thinking [he] describes as 'the care one takes of what exists and what might exist.'"[92] If there is no one ideal perfect world demanded either by God or by History, then we have two choices. One is a nihilistic rejection of any play with ideals; a fear not just of Truth proposals, but also trusty propositions. The other is a perpetual listening, a different kind of hearing for those (for we) that *for now* have not become again what they/we might have been. The space cleared by a belief that we actually could become again grants permission to *feel* for the cracks in the archive, to touch what might happen when the story of order is blasted open such that unspeakable languages of alterity and unreason bubble, if only momentarily, to the surface. In this sort of care for the self and its ghosts we can find from within our limits: murmurs, glimpses, tingles, and tastes of the what-if.

Touchy encounters with the what-if may come less from reasoning our way toward these cracks and more from an aesthetics of feeling our way there: "If Foucault is a thinker of the limit, that limit is not defined by thought alone, but includes an affective dimension . . . As Nietzsche puts it 'we have to learn . . . to feel differently.'"[93] Might learning to feel differently in terms of philosophy be to remember with Foucault, via Jordan, "how close the Cynic's truth telling stands to the edge of the tolerable, of the audibly human?"[94] Returning us to Foucault's deployment of the raped Creusa's hymn of lament in *Ion*, Jordan suggests:

> If Creusa's agonized transit from cry to confession was required for
> the founding of philosophy, the continuance of philosophy requires a
> series of performances at the edge of sight or of hearing. Truth telling
> will always demand that someone cry out—and that someone register
> the cry. What if philosophic writing—or philosophic writing so far as
> it is resistance—is more like a convulsed cry than voluntary speech?[95]

What does it mean to register these cries? The cries of today's lamenters and of those like Creusa, long gone, yet, perhaps, from tender care never lost? Is the registering of the cry God's feeling of our joys and sorrows, and so that which makes God actual?

Yet, even as God becomes actual through these feelings, and even if these feelings illicit God's tender care, it is still a care that, as the marker of God's Consequent Nature, is indifferent; it is in/different to *nothing*; it feels *all*. Hence, this ethic of care, this grave attending, permits infinite possibilities, which take shape through a polyphilic desire for the world. We can embody this erotic ethic. If God helps to set the limiting and unlimited terms of our decisions, it is still we who decide. And this is where curiosity as care and self-care must come rushing to the fore. We can do the work—work that Foucault aligns with the work of spirituality and what Huffer aligns with the art of *feeling* differently. We can register the cry. We can feel our way toward an undoing that is theo-ethical.

In addition, if we are to follow a Foucauldian ethic as part of our response to God's in/difference and to our own aim at novelty, we will have to acknowledge the systems of power that have made of some of us mad, crip, impoverished, hysteric, enraged, dead, and ghostly. Ironically, we will need to respond to divine *in/difference* with a persisting penetration of the workings of biopower that have made all the *difference* for those whom have been silenced. For Whitehead's cosmological order recognizes that the situations of those that murmur from within the archives (archives of history that never wanted to preserve us in the first place) might have been otherwise. Jonah might have been considered right; the depressive might have been appreciated for the strength of her will; and the crip might have been slowly stroked open.

Hence, if philosophy as resistance needs to both cry out and register the cry, perhaps we philosophical theologians might respond to divine in/difference with just this erotic attention to alterity. As the purpose of *Modes of Thought* reminds us, "The use of philosophy is to maintain an active novelty of fundamental ideas illuminating the social system. It reverses the slow descent of accepted thought toward the inactive commonplace. If you like to phrase it so, philosophy is mystical. For mysticism is direct insight into depths as yet unspoken."[96] While Foucault may have taken issue with the possibility of "direct" insight (except perhaps for the likes of Nietzsche and Artaud, mystics of a sort) into the unspoken, we cannot deny the reversal of moralizing secular reason Whitehead's concept of philosophy here, in direct disregard of the canons of reason, instantiates. What might it mean for philosophical theologians and philosophers of religion, we serious academics, to listen to the unspoken mysticism within the overly articulated thought? What might it mean to register—or in other words *feel*—the cry?

Contestation as Care

"[Each occasion] has to decide how it will have been obliged by what it, *de facto*, inherits. "*Yes, but.*"[97] How might we embody this "Yes, but"? How might we persist even as we have had to say yes to certain actualizations that have been harmful, that have wounded? Is there a "yes" to life in the cry of Creusa?

In a 2012 roundtable discussion published in the *Drama Review*, initiated and edited by Jasbir Puar in response to the austerity measures being implemented in Europe, Judith Butler ponders the political significance of "assembling as bodies, stopping traffic, or claiming attention."[98] She asks whether instead of saying "we are here," might these actions actually be saying "we are *still* here"—meaning "we have not yet been disposed of"?[99] She writes, "Bodies on the street are precarious—-they are exposed to police force, and sometimes endure physical suffering as a result. But those bodies are also obdurate and persisting, insisting on their continuing and collective 'thereness.'"[100] It is this tie between precarity and persistence from where I propose we can find the promise/threat nature of both divine polyphilia and the function of unreason for a Foucauldian erotic ethic.

The "we are still here" of the bodies assembled might also be an injunction to "become again what we never were," or an insistence that things having been thus, might be otherwise. To theo-ethically reread, with Whitehead and Foucault, "we are still here" is not only to understand the persistence of prophetic affect aliens, but also to both read God as having a correlating affective orientation and insist on a more erotic and ethical way of encountering such prophets. For instance, as Stengers notes, the limit created from an entity ingressing certain characteristics and not others, ensures that God's feeling of "what the entity has done with itself, 'its sufferings, its sorrows, its failures, its triumphs, its immediacies of joy,'" matters to how novel possibilities come to be. Stengers continues, "From this viewpoint of his consequent nature, God may thus be said to be conscious because of his experience of contrast between the 'impasse' that is and a possibility that turns this impasse into a 'means' for new realizations."[101] The impasse, a contestation to the flow, is the datum needed for the transformation of the flow. The impasse as a means for new realizations is a cosmological fact for Whitehead, but it might be, for us, a lure toward those strategic contestatory practices that Huffer finds in Foucault, which open pathways to the transformation of the self with interventions into larger structures of power.[102] In other words, perhaps the divine recognition that the impasse is also the datum for the what-if is a holy affirmation of the practices of lament that *in* despairing of the world create a manic hope *for* the world.

The laments whispered and wailed by affect aliens *persist* in claiming that, "we are still here." They resonate with a God who, through tender care, *insists* that in the face of our depression, rage, and anxiety the possibility of joy, ecstasy, and peace not be lost. Indeed, along with selves willing to be undone in an erotic exchange with the other, it is God as Eros for the world that similarly ensures that the closet created by the capture of madness in the eighteenth century remain open enough for murmurs of unreason to slip out. I argue that this is a slipping out that comes not as much through chance as through contestation. Reading with the precarity roundtable, we might take this even further and surmise that the exposure to precarity (to be vulnerable to the truth of the wounds created by the rise of rational man) is that which creates the obdurate persistence of the what-if. All philosophy as resistance starts out with a cry. And why shouldn't that cry be contained both in a convulsing body and in the stubborn query "Yes, but"?

Hence, acts of impeding—ones embodied through the affects traced in this book—come to add another layer to the ars erotica proposed by Huffer and the style of life proposed by Foucault. Might even the impeding of joy performed through its killing be the kind of thirst for life that an erotic ethic and a divine Eros propose? Perhaps the giving up of happiness, as the refusal to limit the manifold hopes of a big big room joy, is the excitement of life named by Whitehead when he writes that "Order is never complete; frustration is never complete. There is transition within the dominant order; and there is transition to new forms of dominant order. Such transition is a frustration of the prevalent dominance. And yet it is the realization of that vibrant novelty which elicits excitement for life."[103] If one gives up the orders of happiness in order to live, it is in the frustrating of order that excitement might be found.

Further, what if we were to look beyond happiness to a kind of Nietzschean joy? As Brinkema suggests reading Nietzsche in her examination of the forms of joy: "[while] happiness tethers itself to the ill or good fortune of what happens to some someone (*hap*—being their common root, so that happiness, happenstance, and what happens to a self ultimately are all the same), joy's merriment hovers in the pleasure of gladness in the glittering surface of *things*."[104] This immanent joy is a grave one, one which is "brought down to the surface of the world—the *there is*, the *once more* to life, the thinginess of the gaud?—Nietzsche's contribution to the history of joy adds one more crucial dimension: an affirmation that takes the form of a repetition of that immanence."[105] The registering of the repetition of immanence that is attentive to the thinginess of the gaud might require a spiritual practice that, through care of the self *and* God's tender care, the past retains its present immediacy, while casting a beam out on the future. In this grave joy, we might be haunted by a future historic.

If novelty can be elicited from the play between order and the frustration of order, and if joy might come in immanent thingy repetitions from within which we might become again that which we never were, then we who are despairing of today's orders are tasked with its frustration, but also with attending to that which might be repeated. For as Whitehead rightly notes, the frustration of order is never complete; it also will turn itself into new orders. This is where we might return to Foucault's care of the self that undoes the self. We are at risk of turning our refusal of morality into a new morality. A novel order is also an order, one that in its time will become old. But if we can remind ourselves that frustration is never complete, then perhaps we can hold on to a perpetual contestation that would mean our undoing, but also our care: "It is a long road from that contestation of limits to the freedom Foucault associates with self-undoing in *History of Sexuality II* and *III*. But, however long the road may be, contestation is a place to start. Contestation can produce what Foucault described toward the end of his life as 'kinds of virtual fracture which open up the space of freedom understood as a space of concrete freedom, that is, of possible transformation.'"[106] The long road of philosophy as resistance begins with a cry.

Thus, acts of impeding are not calls to rebuild the system as much as they are to rupture it. To contest and frustrate is not so much to speak but to reach for the limits of speech. Through our unreasonable affects we might find "the promise of a contestation that would summon unknown existences, drag them from their sleep, or even—all the better—invent them."[107] What if the care for the limit of thought that summons and invents unknown existences grounds the ethic of, as Faber puts it, letting the other be/come?[108] God's tender care that nothing be lost and Foucault's desubjectivating rupture can cultivate in us what Halberstam calls, in his introduction to Moten and Harney's *The Undercommons*, "a new sense of wanting and being and becoming."[109] This new sense is, for Halberstam, its own kind of madness; it takes a certain kind of craziness.[110] A cultivation and not a confinement of this crazy is what is sought here. Such cultivation takes a grave attending.

And yet, even if this cultivation summons unknown (or unactualized) existences, it should not be read as a resurrection of the system that denied our brokenness, nor as a redemption of our madness as though the mad are in need of redemption. That is because "We must confront [the undoing of the subject that is reason's other] for what it can tell us about a form of contestation that negotiates an opposition between tragedy and irony—grief and laughter, the sadness of acceptance and the exuberance of rebellion—to become a kind of resistance that is neither acceptance nor rebellion."[111] In this middle space between the sadness of acceptance and the exuberance of rebellion flickers the Holy Saturday of a bipolar time. Between grief and laughter, refreshment and disgust, there exists simultaneously an embodiment of prophetic despair of the world as thus and the manic hope that it might be otherwise.

CHAPTER 6

Unattended Affect

Scene Seven: The Confession

"I wish I could, but I just can't trust white women. And I feel I'm drowning in a sea of white womanhood."

The words of my student, Zamoria Simpson, one of two Black women in our political theology class, hung thick in the air. Seated that particular day in a conference room dedicated to the class of 1968, the year the first five African American women to graduate from Wesleyan College had entered the school, we were indeed drowning in a sea of white womanhood. The first five, as they are known on campus, being first-years, did not appear in commemorative photos of the graduating class. Instead, the blown-up images depicted the height of southern white womanhood. They included both a close-up of a well-manicured white hand donning a large diamond ring surrounded by beaming white "sisters," and a photo of the class known as the Green Knights standing over the juniors, the *Tri-K* class—Tri-Ks emblazoned across the sweaters of young white women, smiling inattentive to, uncaring for, or proud of what message they bore on their chests. In a year in which Wesleyan was addressing some of its white supremacist past, the class of '68 had asserted their presence; hanging over the students of today were the ghosts of what Wesleyan was built to be, but which many of us were now trying to transform.

The week prior to this confession of mistrust, Zamoria had offered the breaking of windows (a destruction of private property that would let in new breath) as the doing of Black political theology. Now, she was giving breath to a needed admission: She found most of her colleagues (at least in this particular class) and her mentors (at least in this particular college) untrustworthy. Her refusal to let "good white women" go uncontested is an insistence that although Wesleyan and this country have been thus, we still might become otherwise. Once again, the emotional labor of a Black woman was leading us out of the enclosures of the institution and into the places where we have been afraid to be halted and haunted, but where precisely some air might be let in—a place from where new breaths of being differently together might fill our lungs.

Zamoria's breath, what Christina Sharpe might name aspiration, "the word [Sharpe] arrived at . . . for keeping and putting breath back in the Black body in hostile weather" (a concept to which we return below), troubles this book.[1] My requests made for our grave attention cannot be divorced from my own positionality, from the place of white womanhood in which I have stood. The redemptions on offer by neoliberalism exist in the quotidian atmosphere, in the oxygen we breathe. The redemptions critiqued in this project are part of what Sharpe calls the weather, in which "antiblackness is pervasive *as* climate."[2] While often not named directly, climates of antiblackness and coloniality pulsate at the heart of neoliberal redemption narratives. Hence, my lament over the gap between the redeemed model citizen and my own feelings of irredeemability—too moody, too manic, too depressed, too unproductive, too mad—is grounded in a presumption that I was supposed to be one of the redeemed in the first place. What might it mean, instead, to have always lived under the presumption that you belong in the abyss, not risen from the cave, but always already destined to lie in the tomb? In other words, what might grave attention and practices of willful unredemption mean from the space and place of Blackness?

Perhaps Zamoria's aspiration unsettles the previous pages, where, for all of my talk of the ransom of subjectivities on which the construction, resilience, and redemption of good citizens has been bought, for all the murmuring monsters I have begged us to hear, there remained a resistance to the haunting of Blackness that whispers, whistles, and wails behind every construction of unredemption on offer. I have cared for the insights brought to me by my own disordering moods—my manic uplifts and depressive falls, the ransoms paid by a mad woman out of joint with the temporality of, and crip sensitivity to, the world. I have listened to the mad ones confined on ships of fools, but not those enslaved in the abyssal holds—"the *hold* is the slave ship hold; is the hold of so-called migrant ship, of the prison; is the womb that produces blackness"[3]—nor those sacrificed into the watery depths of the middle passage. I have prescribed, but have not fully filled my prescription; I have (if subconsciously so) resisted the bitterness of the pill. I have asked us to come closer to the graves, but have avoided what Sharpe calls the wake. The wake is the wake of slavery, where "The ongoing state-sanctioned legal and extralegal murders of Black people are normative and, for this so-called democracy, necessary; it is the ground we walk on. And that it *is* the ground lays out that, and perhaps how, we might begin to live in relation to this requirement for our death."[4] The wake is also the space and place where Black life continues to insist, where aspiration might breathe new life: "And while the wake produces Black death and trauma—'violence . . . precedes and exceeds Blacks' (Wilderson 2010, 76)—we, Black people everywhere and anywhere we are, still produce in, into, and through the wake an insistence on existing: we insist Black being into the wake."[5] Sharpe's project tarries with similar questions of this one—questions of care in the midst, not in spite of, trauma; refusals of the redemptions on offer; and practices of attention (keeping wake)—but it does so much more firmly from within the position of the unredeemed. Therefore, while our projects result in similar calls to a Saturday life in which salvage and survivance are much more viable than the resurrection or redemption of an imaginary wholeness, the distinction of positions from which we write matters. Sharpe has had no choice but to commune with the dead. Hence, it is her work, and that of others from whom the very weather tries to suffocate breath, to whom political theologians, those who are writing farther from the traumas of the wake, must attend.

Improper Innocence

Too often, those of us who work in progressive, political, and postsecular theologies hesitate to identify ourselves with the unsavory roots of political philosophy, U.S. Protestantism, and Western secularism. We have engaged the philosophies but have forgotten to re-hear the cries of the convulsing bodies on which they were birthed. By under-identifying with the ways in which the disciplines and faiths we inhabit are infused with legacies of white supremacy, we eclipse our responsibility to dismantle the systems that grew from the toxic soil. In the proclamation of our relative innocence, we risk cheap redemption, when deep reckoning is what is due.

The interconnection between white supremacy and the U.S. Protestantism that haunt political theology can, of course, be traced to the very establishment of the United States as both a sovereign nation and an economic power. In *Stand Your Ground: Black Bodies and the Justice of God*, womanist theologian Kelly Brown Douglas explores the genesis of what she calls our "stand your ground" culture. "Stand your ground" culture marks whiteness, and white Protestant Christianity, as sovereign property. As Brown Douglas notes, "for [the Puritans], building an Anglo-Saxon nation . . . meant building a Protestant Christian nation."[6] Such religious legitimation marks white supremacy as divinely ordained. It ties Christianity to the construction of "whiteness as cherished property."[7] When such property is trespassed on, white Christianity has God's permission to "stand its ground." As Brown Douglas starkly puts it, "a myth that declares the 'supra-status' of a group of people compels a sense of destiny that is bound to turn deadly."[8] In a stand-your-ground culture, George Zimmerman can kill Trayvon Martin with impunity, while we all know if it had been Martin who shot Zimmerman, the same would not be true. Having no rights to even self-possession, self-sovereignty, means that under stand-your-ground culture, there is no property Black people are supposed to count as theirs; there is no ground on which to stand.

Brown Douglas traces the development of this culture to American "founding fathers" who were enamored with the myth of Anglo-Saxon purity held over from Tacitus's *Germania*, the 98 CE treatise that marked ancient Germans as an exceptional race.[9] The same founders' fears of the mixing of the blood of European colonists and African slaves amplified the ability of non-Anglo-Saxon European immigrants to become white, while non-Europeans could not.[10] The transcendence of European immigrant identity into that of whiteness, and so Americanness, was fortified through the religiosity with which the Puritans and Pilgrims imbued the myth of the nation. This mythico-history becomes a liturgy, ritually repeated as justification for who could count as properly American, and so who could be redeemed out of their immigrant status and into salvific whiteness.

We see a similar mythico-history in religion's supposed counter. As Jonathan Kahn puts it, "the long arc of the twentieth century's secularization thesis, with its claim that religion is irrational, on the wane, and inappropriate for political work in the public square, should be called for what it is: a version of whiteness, if not white supremacy, that served to question the right of political place of African American citizens."[11] Under such a thesis, whiteness continues to stand its ground.

So what, then, of the postsecular thesis? What then of those theologies breaking open the binaries between theistic metanarratives and those of secularism? Can a discipline forged at the crossroads, if also the deconstruction, of two fields invested in whiteness, adequately address a stand-your-ground culture?

In other words, if a return of sovereignty to the people is at the heart of recent leftist forms of political theology, and if sovereignty itself is built on the effacement of blackness, we must ask, "Who counts as the people?" Can we political theologians, grounded in such mythico-histories, adequately attend to those eclipsed by conceptions of "personhood" built on marking some for political work, while rendering others disposable? And how might we better attend to the ways in which our own attempts at distance from such markings have left us culpable?

If our civil religion and Protestant Christianity are handmaids to, or perhaps the architects of, a white supremacist and nationalist culture, then there is no easy way out of the structures the two have built. White Americans, and particularly white Christian Americans (Christian by practice or by heritage), cannot distance ourselves from this history (no matter how leftist or radical we feel our theologies to be); it is our collective inheritance. It is the liturgical stuff in which we have been forged.

In his essay "From Political Theology to Vernacular Prophecy: Rethinking Redemption," in the volume *Race and Political Theology*, George Shulman outlines two overarching approaches to the concept of redemption. The first is the struggle to get free from the past, to redeem past discretions. We can see this in secularized theological registers when disgraced celebrities and politicians speak of being redeemed — of becoming changed men and women. We love a comeback story. But such a comeback is often highly commodified and done on the timeline and terms of the ones in need of redemption and not of those ransomed in the name of such resilience. This perhaps neoliberal form of redemption does little for the second form Shulman describes. Drawing on James Baldwin and Friedrich Nietzsche, he argues "that Baldwin . . . like Nietzsche . . . depicts a coming-to-terms with a past that is haunting and imprisoning because it is horrific and because it has been denied. The problem is an unredeemed past, and the question is not how to get free from it but how to redeem it in the sense of changing our relationship to it, both how we imagine it and how we bear and use it."[12] In other words, there is a crucial difference between being redeemed from our guilt and being redeemed only through a grappling with, and addressing of, the harm we've caused. Shulman rightly recognizes here how redemption can go awry—how one might desire to be free of the past, without attending to how we come to relate to the past differently. Such a desire for the freedom from damage without attention to what it has meant to be damaged, risks a cheap and also violent redemption. From the standpoint of the willful unredemption offered in these pages, there remains for me an unease with any conception of a redeemed past in that redemption might contain too much of a pull toward a sense of overcoming that wishes we'd forget the past. Still, Shulman's insistence on the need to grapple with the damage resonates with my own calls for acts of grave attention that would unvoid the past only by refusing to avoid it.

One way we might attend to the risks of redemption is to ask: In what ways have white political theologians sought to be redeemed? Has our field relied on practices of conditional inclusion for its redemption? I surmise that many of us have at least understood, consciously or not, our redemption as a liberation from the past more than as a reorientation to our past. I suggest that we have viewed our work as a breaking free of the ontotheological God and traditional sovereignty, but have not yet, or not consistently, attended to how such redemption has done little to challenge the mythico-history of whiteness and masculinity in which these disciplines have been forged. The proper standing of Anglo-American thinkers, methodologies, and bodies remains too innocent, too redeemed, or not undone enough. Such standing has certainly not been undone in the previous chapter's claims to radical witness through the work of Foucault and Whitehead. And so perhaps, and problematically so, I have not challenged my own sense of innocence, and my own needed undoing. I have not practiced the self-care that might allow us to become again what we never were through an erotic listening to those confined and ransomed for my becoming.

An affective drive toward innocence is the terrain my students, colleagues, and I have been treading at Wesleyan College in Macon, Georgia. Recently, our community has begun to acknowledge our twentieth-century ties to the Ku Klux Klan and the symbols, rituals, and institutional sensibilities that have persisted. For instance, so-called sisterhood traditions included the class name, the "Tri-K Pirates," and rituals of initiation that involved upperclassmen donning hooded robes and leading freshmen around by nooses. These traditions continued well after the first African American women entered the college in the 1960s. Even with a student body that is today at least one-third Black, it was not until the 1990s that some of the Klan iconography and the nooses and hoods were forbidden, and it was not until the 2018–19 school year that the class names were retired (class colors remain).[13] The history of these traditions and the abhorrent iconography and images that accompanied them have mainly lived "peacefully" in our archives for 180 years. Each time this history was surfaced, those raising the issue were met with moods of denial, including accusations that they were "spreading false information." Claims to religious and gender innocence were proffered: Methodist *women* could not have done this. While many on campus are finally open to reckoning with this history, others—including some alumnae, current students, faculty, and staff—still do not acknowledge the scope of the problem, nor how denialism and minimization allow white supremacist legacies to continue. The cries of "It wasn't me!" have been legion.

In an interview given to Bill Moyers on the then upcoming book *The Cross and the Lynching Tree*, James Cone warned us that if America could not get over its "innocence," then we would never be able to build the beloved community.[14] Obstacles to claiming our guilt are fortified by our stand-your-ground culture. Brown Douglas suggests that "[white space] travels with white people. It is the space that white people occupy. This space is not to be intruded upon, hence the right of whiteness to exclude."[15] If it is my God-given right to exclude, then there need not be a feeling of guilt or shame. I am innocent. At Wesleyan, White Christianity inhabits innocence. A mood of innocence pulses in the covert and overt Christian supremacy that imbues the atmosphere of the campus. Christian sensibilities show up in rhetoric around faith and servant leadership, in the invocations that open faculty meetings, and in the deployment of "good Methodism" to claim racism could not have been at the heart of our sisterhood traditions. To claim otherwise is to shake what is owned by Wesleyan sisters (at least its white sisters), the cherished property of womanly civility and Christ's blessing. The need for both collective and individual pardon, the fear of shame and guilt, risks killing Wesleyan's soul; it has been killing our country and literally many of our country-people.

To confront our discomfort with the mood of guilt, we must also acknowledge additional moods—those of possessiveness and persecution. For many white people, and white Christians in particular, it seems as though proclamations of innocence are not sufficient; one must also proclaim the guilt of those pointing out the fallacy of such innocence. Whiteness and Christianity are innocent, those who trespass on their grounds are guilty. This dynamic is at play whenever someone calls Black Lives Matter a hate group, or when right-wing pundits pontificate about "the war on Christmas." It is at play in the rallying call: "Jews will not replace us." It pulses behind: "Make America Great Again," because it affirms that "America" is under attack by the very idea that non-white people and non-Protestants might have their own ground in this country on which to stand. This persecution complex is the inevitable affective combination of the divinely ordained right to kill those who would challenge our standing and the much subtler affective attachment to innocence over guilt. The former is easier to identify because it manifests itself quite literally in a body count. The latter takes more careful attention, because it involves a more expansive reckoning; it involves realizing where we, too, have wanted to have our debts forgiven, and so where we, too, have had blood on our hands.

So what is to be done? Are there alternative affective registers with which we might become more finely attuned? Can I gravely attend to the debts I owe? Can my innocence be undone in favor of my accountability? Can I take account and truly refuse my own redemption?

According to Fred Moten and Stefano Harney, so-called bad debt is used to mark the unpropertied, to mark blackness as precisely that which does not have proper standing. Moten and Harney encourage those already marked as unprofitable to remain fugitive from sovereignty, so as to resist the very modes of relation that marked them as a bad investment in the first place.[16] But this need not mean that those of us marked as good investments should ignore to whom our profitability is indebted. We must reconcile with just how bad our credit is. To do so would be to sit with our sin. It might be to refigure figurations of atonement that ask not for a clean bill of account, one that could be paid and forgotten, but rather look for what might happen when we recognize that to atone is also to attune; it is to pay greater attention, to materially attend to all those for whom we were never supposed to stand.

Perhaps this is what is requested in the 2018 *New York Times Op-Ed*, by feminist essayist Roxane Gay. In her response to President Trump's infamous "shithole countries" comment, Gay writes:

> I am tired of comfortable lies. I have lost patience with the shock supposedly well-meaning people express every time Mr. Trump says or does something terrible but well in character. I don't have any hope to offer. I am not going to turn this into a teaching moment to justify the existence of millions of Haitian or African or El Salvadoran people because of the gleeful, unchecked racism of a world leader. I am not going to make people feel better about the gilded idea of America that becomes more and more compromised and impoverished with each passing day of the Trump presidency.

> This is a painful, uncomfortable moment. Instead of trying to get past this moment, we should sit with it, wrap ourselves in the sorrow, distress and humiliation of it. We need to sit with the discomfort of the president of the United States referring to several countries as "shitholes" during a meeting, a meeting that continued after his comments. No one is coming to save us. Before we can figure out how to save ourselves from this travesty, we need to sit with that, too.[17]

The call to sit with our humiliation, to feel the pain of what it is to inherit whiteness as cherished property, an inheritance that justifies Trump's comments, and which cannot be divorced from the inheritance of political theology, is the call this book asks us to follow.

If grave attending is a caring for the gravity, the pulling down to the material world, listening and feeling for what all its myriad emotions have to tell us, and where they have to lead us, then where we must be led is into the moods of blackness—moods founded and funded by the property-relations of slavery, and so marked as inescapably improper. If to gravely attend is to train the body and soul to welcome the penetration of lamentant cries, the cries of those who have been crucified by the construction of whiteness as cherished property, then I have to practice an erotic listening to an archive of murmurs which I have so far eclipsed.

Attending to the Grave Attention of Black Studies

According to Fred Moten, "Black studies is a dehiscence at the heart of the institution and on its edge . . . this emergent poetics of the emergency in which the poor trouble the proper, is our open secret."[18] He continues, "With its vast repertoire of high-frequency complaints, imperceptible frowns, withering turns, silent sidesteps, and ever-vigilant attempts not to see and hear, black studies, that vast, pleasurable series of immanent upheavals and bad, more than subjunctive moods, *is* the critique of Western civilization."[19] Black studies is the moody poetics arising from the open wound created by the cuts on which Western Civilization is built. It is the sound of this sutural rupture and the feel of this overflowing flesh, which (even) we so-called critical academics have refused to fully hear and to intimately touch. As an open secret that pulses at imperceptible frequencies, Black studies and blackness are at once omnipresent and invisible; they are at once the very possibility of sound and a penetrative silence. Blackness, for Moten, acts paraontologically both as that which must come first before Western Civilization and as the very chance a new world might be possible.

That Western Civilization was built on and finds redemption in the ransoming of blackness as criminality (as the improper challenge to cherished property) implies that the fugivity of blackness is the very place in which we might find a bipolar hope: a depressive attention to what is and a manic chance at what might be.

Such a moody hope might be found in the Black optimism of Moten's "Black Op." The title of this essay implies the fugitive movements of a stealth operation. From such fugivity comes a mood of optimism that is counter to future-centered cruel optimism—an optimism structured on lack, and one which fortifies neoliberalism as theorized by Lauren Berlant. Instead:

> Black optimism persists in thinking that we have what we need, that
> we can get there from here, that there's nothing wrong with us or
> even, in this regard, with here, even as it also bears an obsession with
> why it is that difference calls the same, that resistance calls regulative
> power, into existence, thereby securing the simultaneously vicious and
> vacant enmity that characterizes there and now, forming and deform-
> ing us.[20]

Black optimism does not wait for a savior. Black optimism refuses the naiveté of any uncomplicated sense of resistance, as though resistance escapes the logics of the power at hand, and as though "freedom" is not its own form of fortification of the rights of those who hold captives to capture. Rather, Black optimism rests in performances of Black sociality, of Black fugivity, of blackness's refusal to lie straight in the end. It is a collective embrace of the improper and so the nonparticipation in the rights of the propertied. Black optimism is not about the promissory nature of future desires, but rather about presentist need: "There is cause for optimism as long as there is need for optimism. Cause and need converge in the bent school or marginal church in which we flock together to be in the name of being otherwise."[21] Hence, any chance for some bipolar hope might come from listening for where fugitive blackness flocks together.

Perhaps Black optimism is there in Gary Fisher's big big room full of everybody's hope. This room is made big, not in spite of Fisher's self-claimed sociopathic, black, and queer identities, or his HIV; rather it is stitched together precisely from the flesh of these wounds. Such a backlit hope (perhaps a crip hope) is lighted from the high-frequency tones of what Moten names "Black mo'nin'." In the very last lines of his essay "Black Mo'nin'," in writing of his favorite aunt's funeral, Moten concludes:

> Ms. Rosie Lee Seals rose up in church, out from the program, and said, "Sister Mary Payne told me that if she died she wanted me to give a *deep* moan at her funeral." And, at that moment, in her Las Vegas-from-Louisiana accent, condition of impossibility of a universal language, condition of possibility of a universal language, burying my auntie with music at morning time, where moaning renders mourning wordless (the augmentation and reduction of or to our releasing more than what is bound up in the presence of the word) and voice is disso-nanced multiplied by metavoice, Sister Rosie Lee Seals mo'ned. New word, new world.[22]

Such a new world, from a new word that is, at once, both less and more than language, is possible not because the past has been redeemed, but through the refusals of redemptions on offer. Black mo'nin' is the murmur that conditions language and undoes proper speech.

Perhaps Black mo'nin' was present in the breath on offer by my student. Such breath was released both in her call for the breaking of windows as political theology and in her confession and contestation of untrustworthy white womanhood. According to Ashon Crawley, breath represents a double-gesture, in which we "gulp in, pause, until lungs—no longer able to contain that which is held—release, bursting forth and free from the flesh."[23] Breath that fills the lungs until it must break out of the flesh is the pause in the wake of that which tries to rob us of breath, and it is the chance of an uncontained new life.

In his essay "Breathing Flesh and the Sound of BlackPentecostalism," Crawley marks how the *black pneuma* of BlackPentecostalism is "the capac-ity for [this] double-gesture of inhalation and exhalation as the hint of life, life that is exorbitant, capacious and, fundamentally, social, though it is also life that is contained and engulfed by gratuitous violence."[24] Crawley looks closely to the whooping that happens within BlackPentecostal wor-ship. Such whooping is an act of breathing that both breaks open theologi-cal boundaries and ruptures the bounded liberal subject. Such opening, represented in breath's ability to pass flesh to flesh, marks a desubjectiviz-ing encounter grounded in Black sociality that challenges the very defini-tions of subjectivity on offer by Western Civilization. Breath further marks for Crawley a temporality divorced from Western teleology, one that might find a middle way between "forced recall and compelled forget-ting."[25] He calls such a middle "rememory." As an act of rememory, "the intentioned performance of breathing—whooping, for example— produces another narrative, one not dependent upon Newtonian physics of smooth, linear, contained time and space."[26] Breath in these ways contains a Holy Saturday character. Holy Saturday is indeed the day of the Spirit. Biblically speaking, it is the Spirit who remains and sustains in the wake of Jesus' crucifixion. And *black pneuma*, fugitive from linear narratives and alive where blackness flocks together in an always-already improper sociality, is what remains and sustains life in the midst of trauma. This breath, this whoop, this moan, this murmur is what we need to offer an erotic hearing to. It is to such aurality that we must attend if we are to risk going willfully unredeemed, so as to gain a chance at becoming again what we never were.

As touched on briefly earlier in this chapter, Christina Sharpe finds breath to be a similarly important site from which to challenge the pervading climate of Western narratives that produce and perpetuate antiblackness. She calls such narratives the orthography and dysgraphia of the wake. Sharpe's *In the Wake* is structured in four parts. The first part traces her own family's experience living and making life in the wake. The next three parts center on images all tied to watery wakes of the slave ship and the middle passage, as well as the ways in which these ships and holds repeat. In the chapters "the Ship," "the Hold," and "the Weather," she traces the orthographies of the wake and their impact on Black life, and she helps the reader to see the aspirating strategies of persistent and insistent Black life. One way she draws attention to such orthographies is in drawing our attention to the repetitive horror of the archive constructed in the wake of Black death. Such death accumulates to the point where murder becomes mundane and execution expected. For instance, in examining slave ship and auction manifests, she points out how in many cases the names of the enslaved, and even their descriptions (age, temperament, etc.), are left off in favor of the marking "ditto." She ties the ditto of the slave manifests to the repetitive death dealing forced on Black life in the wake: "The details and the deaths accumulate; the ditto ditto fills the archives of the past that is not yet past. The holds multiply. And so does resistance to them, the survivance of them."[27] The ditto ditto of the multiplying holds are made possible through orthographical and dysgraphic constructions. Such constructions can be seen, for instance, in the thinking that allows for the Pre-K to Prison pipeline, demonstrated in the example Sharpe gives of the teacher in Paterson, New Jersey, who posted on Facebook that she views her first-grade students as "future criminals."[28] "Future criminal" is the error in spelling for the writing of child in the dysgraphia of the wake. The un-childing of the first graders in Paterson constructs the narrative of innocence we presume in white children. We might find such dysgraphia in the January 18, 2019, incident in which white teenagers from a Catholic high school, donning MAGA hats, taunted a Native American elder in the midst of competing marches in front of the Lincoln Memorial. After moments of condemnation of the white boys, the discourse around the incident quickly became overwhelmed with proclamations that more information was needed and the situation was more complicated. The boy at the center of the controversy, Nick Sandmann, was even given an interview with Savannah Guthrie on NBC's *Today Show* to explain his side of the story. Narratives that proclaimed nuance judged the white teens to be young people who made a reasonable mistake in judgment given their age and the volatile situation they were in.[29] But as Elie Mystal points out in "Black Children Don't Have Nick Sandmann's Rights: And they definitely don't get the chance to redeem themselves on national TV with the help of Savannah Guthrie," "Black children have their side of the story too, but they don't get to go on *Today* and explain their actions, because they are dead. Their side of the story is left to bleed out in the street long before a compassionate white interviewer calls them for comment."[30] In other words, the white teen's right to be a boy, his redemption from bigot to child, is bought through the dysgraphia that permits the crucifixion of the Black child, through the misnomer of "future criminal."

To counter such narratives, Sharpe, like Crawley, draws on breath. She offers "aspiration" as a driving ethical call of the book. To aspirate is to care, it is to slow down enough to attend to each person in the wake, to every member of the archive who was supposed to remain breathless:

> To the necessity of breath, to breathing space, to the breathtaking
> spaces in the wake in which we live; and to the ways we respond,
> "with wonder and admiration, you are still alive, like hydrogen, like
> oxygen" (Brand 2015). As Philip says, the pause in the poem, the
> breath, "is totally subversive in the face of the kind of broad-brush
> brutalizing where people just get reduced to Negro man, Negro
> woman, and ditto, ditto, ditto. You pay attention to one, and it is such
> an amazing act—and one that spills over to all the other dittos—pay
> attention and taking care with just the one. Because that's all we can
> do is care one by one by one. . . . Breathlessness and the archive; the
> archives of breathlessness." The details accumulate in *Zong!* and for
> us, what might it mean to attend to these archives? What might we
> discover in them?[31]

Such aspiration, the care for, the breathing of names and narratives and life back into each ditto ditto in the archive takes a particular kind of seeing and

hearing, one beyond mere looking. Such a seeing is tied to Sharpe's practices of Black annotation and Black redaction, to which we return below,
but also to the kind of erotic listening called on both in the previous chapter
and by Moten's attention to the aurality of Black life. Such practices are
erotic and ethical because they force us to behold and take hold of, in
Crawley's words, "the hint of life" that remains.

The works of Moten, Crawley, and Sharpe flock together with the work
of others like Saidiya Hartman, Hortense Spillers, Sylvia Wynter, and Alexander Weheliye, to whom we might also look for models of grave attention.
These thinkers pose questions of what scenes have set the stage of, and who
has been ransomed for, the subjectivization and construction of proper
"humans." Such questions might count for Moten as,

> the open set of the Negro Question, where color and democracy are
> situated relative to a gender line, where the historical and ontological
> relation between blackness and radicalism is set to work. Perhaps
> their effectivity can be maximized if in posing them one understands
> radicalism to be a kind of outrootedness, an irreducibly interior and
> transversal transformationality, and blackness to be an archive of per-
> formances, at once disrupted and expansive, moving by way and in
> excess of its points (Africa, the Antilles, Arkansas, Amsterdam [Ave-
> nue], the city, the City) and events (confinement, transport, exchange,
> confinement, employment, emancipation, confinement, the city, the
> City) of origin.[32]

In other words, Black studies is an intra-, inter-, and extratextual archive of
performance and fugitivity whose radicality comes in neither a return to a
supposed purity of roots (à la radical orthodoxy) nor a clear exodus from an
ontotheological origin that risks, in its very claims to freedom, affirming the
spectral hold of origin and telos (perhaps à la radical theology). Indeed, as
Sharpe asks, "But who has access to freedom? Who can breathe free? [Nar-
ratives of freedom] do not ameliorate this lack; this lack in the atmosphere
of antiblackness. Recall, too, that captive Africans were brought out of the
hold, weather permitting, to put fresh air in their lungs and to be exercised."[33] If radical theology is to take up the rhetoric of exodus, of freedom,
it must better attend to all those left breathless in its wake.

In contrast to more Western and teleological injunctions to abstract freedom, Black study pulses through the fleshy interiority within and beyond
particular historical points. Further, its fleshiness—a porosity impossible to
code as the proper body—marks a refusal of the propertied body, and as

such is also the condition of transformation. Hence, to become again what we never were, relies on a better attending to (a hearing of) such an archive. For the purposes of this chapter, such a hearing focuses particularly on Sharpe and Moten. It is precisely in Moten's attention to the aurality of such an archive that he is, for me, the exemplar (a prophet) of grave attention, whereas it is in Sharpe's attention to the wake—the witness to how "the past is not yet past"—that she serves for me as a prophet of unredemption.[34]

Black Murmurs, Moans, and Maternality

Moten's propositions closely align with the call of our previous chapters. Chapter 5 called us to witness to the cries of convulsing bodies, and to the murmurs of the ghosts that demand we be halted and haunted not only by what follows us, but more so by what we, those of us more closely aligned with the Model Citizen, have followed. Moten's insistence on the aurality of blackness and Black social life is exhibited across the essays found in the middle volume, titled *Stolen Life*, of his trinity of works collected under the title *Consent Not to Be a Single Being*. *Stolen Life*'s position as the middle volume is consequent to this book's insistence on a Holy Saturday theology that thinks by the middle. Moreover, it is perhaps this middle book whose mood I most need to hear. For one, it is in this volume where Moten forcefully warns of projects where critical engagement with redemption winds up being crypto-redemptive. These essays mark how the instrumentalizing of pain often ends up valorizing that which it disavows (something to which this project certainly may have fallen prey). For another, as Moten puts it, "The essays are, more pointedly, concerned with how it is that a kind of impossible publicness emerges in and from the radical exclusion from the political, as the refusal of that which has been refused. . . . If a certain devotional and club-like buzz is alive and well here—because rubbing, worrying, brushing, and handing bear certain irreducible phonic effects—it is in echo of everything I've been taught on various dusty roads."[35] At the heart of these essays is both an exposure of the processes of subjectivization built on exclusion, what I would name as redemption bought through ransom, and the noisiness (the phonic effects) of a willfully unredeemed life. Indeed, it is the aurality attended to in two essays in particular—"Uplift and Criminality," and "Erotics of Fugivity"—where Moten most particularly embodies the grave attention called for in this book.

In "Black Op," although Moten explicitly names the importance of the sound of blackness, "night vision given in and through voices that shadow legitimate discourse from below, breaking its ground up into broken air; scenes rendered otherwise by undertones that are overheard but barely,"[36] it is in his exploration of the haunting murmur that is embraced by and simultaneously undoing W. E. B. Du Bois where the experience of such broken ground is most forcefully felt. In "Uplift and Criminality," Moten explores the politics of uplift within Du Bois's earlier work and its rejection of socialism. Further, in exploring Du Bois's transition away from an anti-socialist stance, Moten engages the ways in which a murmuring and haunting maternality can be heard as the possibility and rupture of Du Bois's positions. For Moten, "The murmur is a sound, a rumble, given on the outskirts of normal, as opposed to the center of (speech) pathological, articulation."[37] Looking to the murmuring of Bottom in *A Midsummer Night's Dream*, he insists on, "(. . . a constellation in which animality, sociality, criminality, blackness, and femininity circulate around a sound against or above speech, one that has, as Akira Lippit points out, the effect of making possible the construction, deconstruction, and reconstruction of the human, a project in which black radicalism is intimately engaged)."[38] The murmur that both makes possible and undoes sound is the break in the human that makes possible both the human's undoing and the chance that the "human" might become again what it never was. Moten draws on the rupture between Du Bois's embrace of the importance of the murmur for the construction of Black identity and his own refusal of the murmurs of Black women who remained fugitive from Black uplift. Indeed, Du Bois offers us "a murmur of ages" that "is laden with history, is the dubbed and overdubbed recording of a history of complaint, where the phonic *materi*-ality of song operates, again, over the edge of speech, over the edge of meaning."[39] And yet, he does not adequately attend to the murmurs out of joint with his own sense of redemption.

Du Bois's fear of the disordering moods of Black fugivity are traced by Moten from within Du Bois's formulations of the "Negro Criminal" in *The Philadelphia Negro*. Here, Du Bois is critical of Black social gatherings for their refusal to participate in social norms. Such normative participation, Du Bois assumes, might decriminalize blackness and supplement his desire for a respectable Black domesticity. For Moten, this represents Du Bois's own refusal to embrace the impossibility of a proper Black public. Recalling Brown Douglas and Sharpe, we might say, with no ground on which to stand in the wake of slavery, Black publics cannot be decriminal-ized. Or, as Moten puts it, "To be black, to engage in the ensemblic—nec-essarily social—performances of blackness, is to be criminal."[40] For Moten, it is in Du Bois's distaste for supposed disorderliness, where he reveals the heart of his issue, that of Black sexuality:

> The black woman's transgression of domestic respectability—in work-ing outside of the home, in seeking public and communal forms of sociality, amusement, and pleasure—is problematic for Du Bois in a way that recalls the ambivalences of normative uplift in Douglass when music and the discourse on music and rebellion in the second chapter of the *Narrative* emerge from a black woman's assertion of sexual autonomy and the resistance to sexual violation recorded in the first chapter. In that first chapter, the one who is constructed as property causes the very idea of the proper to tremble between the poles of appropriation and expropriation.[41]

It is the tremble and aurality of disordering moods, as enfleshed in this case by Black women, where we might say Black study offers us a willful unre-demption. But this criminality is one the early Du Bois rejects and hence ransoms on the way to his own "Look I Overcame" narrative. As such, for Moten, Du Bois misses his own criminality and therefore the full force of Black sociality. This criminality haunts Du Bois, who "intimately knows and obsessively indexes and represses this maternity. It is an inheritance that touches and unmans him, something handed to him that cannot be han-dled."[42] It is precisely the inheritance that undoes us that I hope this book asks us to attend to.

In trying to lend such an ear, Moten describes a moment when Du Bois is unmanned by the sound of the inheritance he cannot handle. During a 1961 recording of Du Bois, in which he speaks of the rupture in his own faith in reform, a rupture prompted, according to Moten, by the lynching of Sam Hose, Du Bois's voice cracks, or rather whistles. On the recording, one hears what Moten refers to as "a sound-image of Du Bois's scholarly and political intentions and commitments not only pierced but constituted by the low's high pitch."[43] In other words, without intention, Du Bois's speech is haunted, pierced, and constituted from within by a whistle—a high-frequency complaint. It matters not to Moten whether the whistle is actually a technical malfunction, or a sign of Du Bois's age (he was in his nineties at the time of the interview); rather, he cares for the uncontain-ability of speech revealed through the breaking in of a disordering sound: "In the end, it's as if he can't help but make this dirty sound, the black noise of overdubbing and overcoming, the disruptive addition to the instrument or the instrumental, the irruptive, resistant aurality of a runaway tongue in all its phonoerotic, pathographic materiality."[44] Perhaps, such high-frequency complaint, marks not just the material, but also the maternal, which Du Bois cannot handle and yet on which his becoming man is built and from which it might be undone. Moten's act of witness not merely to Du Bois's speech, his proper language and coded body, but also to his flesh, to the noises that undo the proper, is an act of grave attention. It is the possibility that with Du Bois, both as man and as unmanned, we might become again what we never were.

Later in the essay, Moten refers to another figure of the haunting murmur of Black women's criminality—that of the impossible domestic, who is the female slave. For Moten, "Impossible domesticity begins with irruptive reconstruction. It's marked and instantiated by a fugitive sound that is not just on the run from ownership but blowing a run that enacts a fundamental dispossession of ownership as such so that owning is, itself, disowned."[45] In other words, the impossible domestic, the enslaved female, is always already unpropertied and so improper. She embodies the impossibility of a respectable domesticity and a proper Black public. Hence, "It is in the imagination of the impossible domestic, the lawless freedom and/of the law of motion, her (every)day work, the work of the ordinary, the ordinary outwork, the madness, the flight, the criminality, in the presence of (the) work."[46] The mad, criminal, everydayness of the impossible domestic should call to mind the hostile hospitality of Martha, the double-bind of a woman always-already refused the better part of faith. No event from the outside adequately represents the power of the impossible domestic to undo the relations of property on offer. Rather, it is in the very criminality of her quotidian existence that the improper property disowns the rights of ownership. In Moten's words, "This means to think criminality not as a violation of the criminal law (however il/legitimate one thinks such law to be) but as a capacity or propensity to transgress the law as such, to challenge its mystical authority with a kind of improvisational rupture."[47] It is my contention that it is precisely in this improvisational rupture that the divine character of the "what-if," and the "yes, but," might be found. The nonlinear character of this rupture calls to mind the melancholic care work of Robin James, the postcolonial refusals of subjective prescriptions made by the characters in Jamaica Kincaid novels, the shadow feminists and queer failures of Halberstam, the political freedom of the feminist killjoy, Jonah's inflated rage, the crip who is too sick to work, the bipolar woman's fall into the bed, and the time of Holy Saturday more concerned with proper witness to the crucifixion than the certainty of resurrection. All of these modes of being and feeling refuse happy endings, in favor of asking for other options.

Making Ways in the Wake

At the heart of Womanist theology, as Monica Coleman makes clear from the very title of her book, is the African American saying, "Making a Way out of No Way."[48] This is the heart of Sharpe's work as well. Sharpe's attention to the terror of life lived in the hold, as the ship, and within the climate of antiblackness, remains coupled to the ways in which black people have made ways out of no ways, have mapped routes of insistent and resistant existence. Sharpe points to works of poetry and other forms of cultural production as maps handed down within the wake for such way-making. For instance, in the long poem by Dionne Brand, "Ruttier for the Marooned in the Diaspora," the "'Ruttier' is a guide to indiscipline and lawlessness; a map of disinheritance and inhabitation; a guide to how, traveling light, one might just live free of, 'refuse, shut the door on,' the weight of responsibility for one's planned demise."[49] For Sharpe, the ruttier is not a guide to redemption or resurrection. It does not represent an exodus from the wake. Indeed, she distinguishes her work "from those scholars and those works that look for political, juridical, or even philosophical answers to this problem. [Her] project looks instead to current quotidian disasters in order to ask what, if anything, survives this insistent Black exclusion, this ontological negation, and how do literature, performance, and visual culture observe and mediate this un/survival."[50] Wake work, as Sharpe calls it, is not about narratives of uplift or overcoming, nor is it about a sense of resurrection into the society that planned Black crucifixion. Rather, it is about attuning to the everyday climate of antiblackness and caring for those such weather hopes to drown. Here, we might recall Robin James's insistence of going into the death, her request that we stay melancholic in order to stay attentive to the care needed for all those who cannot or will-to-not overcome. To stay in the wake is to refuse the redemptions on offer—like Rhianna who floats on the water at the end of "Diamonds" without letting herself drown; like Jonah who sits persistently hot and angry in the midst of God's questioning; like the crip who refuses to lie straight in the end. But wake work is also more than this. Sharpe offers quotidian practices of care that move beyond the lamentant affects of melancholy and rage. She offers us what she calls "Black annotation" and "Black redaction."

To practice Black annotation and Black redaction is, through addition and extraction, to counter the dysgraphia and orthography of the wake. It is to refuse to leave the archives of the ditto ditto and multiplying holds undisturbed. Or as Sharpe puts it, "Redaction and annotation toward seeing and reading otherwise, toward reading and seeing something in excess of what is caught in the frame, toward seeing something beyond a visuality that is, as Nicholas Mirzoeff (2011) argues, subtended by the logics of the administered plantation."[51] Like the hearing on offer in Huffer's practices of erotic listening and the feeling on offer in my grave attending, such a reading and seeing otherwise is not about redeeming fugitive blackness, or the queer, or the mad. Sharpe is "not interested in rescuing the term *girl* (see "The Ship"), I am not interested in rescuing Black being(s) for the category of the 'Human,' misunderstood as 'Man,' or for the languages of development." Rather, she is "interested in ways of seeing and imagining responses to the terror visited on Black life and the ways we inhabit it, are inhabited by it, and refuse it. I am interested in the ways we live in and despite that terror."[52]

Black annotation and Black redaction are melancholic care work. Such work is slow, painful, and persistent work. For Black annotation, one must move past first sight and attend to a larger narrative of each member of the archive. As an example of Black annotation, Sharpe turns back to a photograph of a young Black girl lying on a stretcher in the wake of the 2010 Haitian Earthquake. On the girl's forehead someone had affixed a piece of tape that reads "Ship." Sharpe discusses being struck by the girl's eyes, but then thrown by the piece of tape. The word "ship" calls to mind other Black girls shipped in the holds of the middle passage, as well as where it might be that this girl is being shipped now, and what this mark might mean for the definition of her story. At first glance of this ditto in the archive, we can get stuck on her story as cargo, as suffering, as ship. But grave attending and Black annotation call us to more. Black annotation called Sharpe to re-look at the photograph. In doing so she notes, "I was looking for more than the violence of the slave ship. I saw that leaf in her hair, and with it I performed my own annotation that might open this image out into a life, however precarious, that was always there. *That leaf is stuck in her still neat braids.* And I think: *Somebody braided her hair before that earthquake hit.*"[53] A new part of the story comes to the fore: *Somebody* braided her hair. Through this wake work, through Black annotation, Sharpe has aspirated the part of this girl's story that runs counter to "the weather"; she is someone's, she has a life beyond the earthquake, and it is one of care. Black annotation is a refusal to let the hold, the ship, and the weather have the last word.

A further act of care work, this time through Black redaction, comes when Sharpe redacts lines in a *New York Times* article about Mikia Hutchings, a twelve-year-old Black girl, who, in 2014, was subjected to a juvenile criminal case for writing the word "Hi" on a wall at her school. After her Black redaction, all the lines are gone except the following: "'Hi' 'I only wrote one word, and I had to do all that,' 'It isn't fair.'"[54] Although the article is written in a sympathetic tone, as Sharpe points out, it still inadequately listens for Mikia's voice, and her point of view. Sharpe's redaction tries to bring Mikia to the fore. She shifts the climate of the piece. Sharpe aspirates the voice of a child. Sharpe makes clear that this is not an act of assumed representation of Mikia or a representational politics. Similarly, my grave attending for the murmurs of the unredeemed in the archive cannot be seen as a resurrection. These acts do not redeem the holds and ships that wove together the weather of the wake; rather they are acts that ask for other options. They are refusals of both crucifixion and narrowly defined resurrection.

In Excess of Redemption

In the concluding essay of *Stolen Life*, Moten performs an act of Black annotation to one particular case of the impossible domestic, whose story asks for other options. We might call these archives to which Moten listens, archives of the willfully unredeemed. To go willfully unredeemed might be

> to refuse what has been refused in a combination of disavowing, of not wanting, of withholding consent to be a subject and also of refusing the work, of withholding consent to do the work, that is supposed to bring the would-be subject online. It is to prefer not to, in stuttered, melismatic, gestural withdrawal from that subjectivity which is not itself, which is not one, which only shows up as a thwarted desire for itself, as the lurid auto-cathectic lure of an airy fiend that walks beside you in a storefront window. The experience of subjectivity is the would-be subject's thwarted desire for subjectivity, which we must keep on learning not to want, which we have to keep on practicing not wanting, as if in endless preparation for a recital that, insofar as it never comes, is always surreally present.[55]

Employability? I would prefer not to, I'm too sick to work. Resilient overcoming? I would prefer not to, I'm a bad investment. Straighten up in the end? I would prefer not to, I'm already too bent. In this allusion to a Bartlebyan politics, we should of course also hear Jonah's anger and prefer-ence not to go to Nineveh, and Martha's madness, her preference not to stop worrying over the needs of a this-worldly welcome. We should hear the hard everyday labor of Zamoria's "aspiration" that might break the windows of Wesleyan that enclose proper subjectivity. In these spaces of nonpreference, Moten finds the nonperformance of an impossible domes-tic, an enslaved woman named Betty. Following Moten in his acts of Black annotation, we hear the murmurs of the enslaved anew.

Listening to the haunting sounds of a juridical archive, Moten finds in Sora Han's essay, "Slavery as Contract: Betty's Case and the Question of Freedom," a figure of impossible domesticity, whose refusal performs sub-jective ruptures. Han's essay explores the 1857 Massachusetts Supreme Court case in which Chief Justice Lemuel Shaw declared Betty, an enslaved person brought by her masters from Tennessee to Massachusetts, to be free. Betty is granted a legal freedom, which she then refuses, choosing instead to return to Tennessee with her masters. For both Han and Moten, Betty, in preferring not to take the terms of freedom on offer, claims an excess of freedom. In her nonperformance, she performs the deformation of freedom such that we might see how freedom and slavery are less oppo-sitional stances than they are partners in the fortification of the "proper" terms of master-slave relations. In the refusal of the freedom on offer:

> The decision of unconditional responsibility shows up, at least on
> [Moten's] reading, as a reveling in an enacted threat of a freedom
> against freedom that haunts any and every promise of freedom the law
> both makes and guards. Her decision is an a priori fugivity to becom-
> ing a fugitive of the law of slave and free states. The force of this
> fugivity is what we might reference as blackness, a performative
> against all performances of freedom and unfreedom dependent on the
> historical dilemma of a lack of meaningful distinction between free-
> dom and slavery.[56]

Remaining fugitive even from the abolitionists, Betty embodies what Moten calls an ethics of the obscene.[57] Such obscenity calls to mind the methodol-ogy of the obscene in the "Indecent Theology" of Marcella Althaus-Reid, whose work has too rarely been counted as political theology, despite its deep resonance with the matrix of thinkers and subjects engaged in the field.[58] As I have argued elsewhere, Althaus-Reid, drawing on the definition of obscenity from Jean-Paul Sartre as that which reveals flesh to be flesh, indecents even the most liberal of theologies, revealing their orthodoxies and orthopraxis to be violent hardcore theologies.[59] Obscenity works similarly in the case of Betty. Betty's refusal reveals the flesh of the social contract, to be flesh—in particular the right of white propertied flesh to grant or seize the freedom of non-white flesh. Or as Moten puts it:

> [Betty's] decision is neither her submission to slavery, nor her permission to the state to enforce her legal freedom. It is a remnant legal act, or an unconditional responsibility to freedom a redoubled and redoubtable materialization of freedom that is otherwise known only in its relationship to the transcendent right of freedom driving modern law.[60]

To become a fugitive to both slave and free states is to refuse to participate in the proper standing of the states. Further, this fugivity is what Moten names as blackness; it is a performance of nonperformance that ruptures the terms of freedom and slavery on offer.

Still, as Moten makes clear, this improvisational rupture does not come through Betty's own words. Hers is a voice we do not and cannot hear. We do not have her testimony. Betty does not attend the decisive juridical decision in the judge's chambers, and there is no one who has properly attended to her singular story, nor to the multiplicity of interiorized fleshy histories to which her murmurs might attest. And yet, "Betty's story, which is not one, which she neither owns nor tells, in the very fact of its having been withheld from the court, obliterates the court."[61] Betty's nonperformance through the refusal of the freedom on offer, shakes the power of those doing the offering. In Moten's attention to Betty's ghost, he asks not just simply for the flight from histories of captivity, but more so for the unredemption of Western Civilization's conceptions of freedom to which we are supposed to flee. Indeed, to hear this unspeakable story is to "Listen to the ghosts of all these words, the ghost of the enslaved haunting these words, the enslaved as afterlife bearing a tremor, a solicitation, a black-and-blue blur of legal reason. It's Betty's blur, a promise kept and given in the contract's nonperformance."[62] The injunction to listen is a grave one; it is to erotically desire getting buried with the ghosts over and against being resurrected with the law and the proper.

We might hear Betty's murmur, once again, in the dialogue of the enslaved women in the play *An Octoroon* by Branden Jacobs-Jenkins. *An Octoroon* is the 2015 adaptation of Dion Boucicault's 1859 melodrama, *The Octoroon*. While both satirizing and honoring the form of melodrama, Jacobs-Jenkins's adaptation serves as a critique of the under-engaged assumptions about race and slavery in the original and the under-engaged racial attitudes of the contemporary audience. While there are several aspects of the adaptation to which we might turn in an attempt to undo our own assumptions of race and just how far we have(not) come, it is in the voice of the enslaved women where Jacobs-Jenkins breaks most starkly from Boucicault's original dialogue. In the breaking of dialogue, Jacobs-Jenkins reimagines, perhaps rememories and annotates, the possible subjectivities that might become again what they never were originally permitted to be. These characters, those in the position of the impossible domestic, murmur madly to us from within an archive of Black performance. While the enslaved characters Minnie (for Minerva) and Dido (appropriate names for the Greek chorus-like position the two inhabit for the play) speak in the "broken" English of black folksy vernacular reflective of the time of the original play's writing when addressing their white masters, they speak in contemporary vernacular when speaking to one another and other enslaved characters. The following lines illuminate the difference:

DIDO (speaking to the octoroon Zoe, a character, who while being one-eighth black has, to many degrees, "overcome" this "damage" and been welcomed as a member of the plantation family):

ZOE. Mammy! 'Tis I—Zoe.
DIDO. (*Taken aback by her word choice, then*): Missey Zoe! Why are you out in de swamp dis time ob night? And you is all wet! Missey Zoe, you catch de fever for sure!

DIDO and MINNIE (speaking about Dido's exchange with Zoe):

DIDO. And you know she kept calling me "Mammy"! And I was like, bitch, what? We are basically the same age!
MINNIE. Whaaaat?
DIDO. I can't believe that shit. Do I look that old to you?
MINNIE. No, girl. Black don't crack. That bitch is just crazy. That's what happens when you hang out wit all these damn white people all the damn time. Let it go.
DIDO. Naw, Minnie! Shit![63]

The dehumanized caricatures of the happy folksy slave as offered in the original play, are countered by Jacobs-Jenkins attention to the aurality of the sociality between Dido and Minnie. Such attention leads to a practice of Black annotation. In this case, the rememoried dialogue between the two and their laughter represent the murmur that undoes the moral of the play.

The original play ended variously with Zoe—the octoroon who, as octoroon, has her chance of love and freedom threatened when the plantation is sold, and as such represents the sympathetic core of the original play (and in some incarnations to Jacobs-Jenkins's version)—either killing herself or being saved. In the versions where Zoe lives, she is saved by the destruction of the evil new owner of the plantation who is revealed to be a murderer, and by proper papers that arrive to show she is actually free. In neither version do such papers arrive for the other enslaved characters. Dido and Minnie are beyond and before the law, they do not have proper standing, and there is no freedom on offer; they remain the impossible domestics. In Jacobs-Jenkins's version, however, we get a fifth and final act, quoted in part earlier. Instead of ending with Zoe's redemption or her tragic death, we end with the sociality between Dido and Minnie. Dido and Minnie, two of only four enslaved people on the plantation who are not part of a plot to run away before the sale, believe they have been sold at auction to a ship captain and are packing up their slave quarters. They do not know that the plantation sale has been thwarted and they must remain the other to Zoe's overcoming. In the last pages of the book, Dido complains of being de-sexed by Zoe's reference to her as "Mammy," and the following exchange ensues:

DIDO. *(Collecting herself.)* I'm sorry, Minnie. I just don't like when people be treating me like I'm some old woman. I am not a mammy! I'm not!

MINNIE. *(Realizes why Dido is upset, then):* It's okay, girl. I forgive you. *(Embraces her.)* But we gotta be good to one anutha. You know all we got is each other now.

DIDO. You right. *(They un-embrace.)* You think we should go tell somebody?

MINNIE. Tell somebody what?

DIDO. That Zoe is 'bout to poison herself . . .

MINNIE. Girl, stop. These people ain't our problem anymore. We 'bout to be livin' on a boat! *(Looks at Dido, who seems unexcited.)* I'm worried about you.

DIDO. Why?

MINNIE. I think you can get too worked up over small stuff. Stop being so sensitive and caring so much about other people and what they think about you or you gonna catch yourself a stroke, for real. You can't be bringing your work home with you. If Zoe's lightskinned ass wanna call you old and go poison herself over some white man, then you need to let her do that and move on. She's an adult. You can't change her. Shit. Same thing with Mrs. Peyton. And Miss Dora. And Mas'r George. And Mas'r M'Closky. *I know we slaves and evurthang, but you are not your job. You gotta take time out of your day to live life for you.* (Dido starts crying, softly.) Oh, girl! What's wrong?[64]

This scene is both comic and tragic. Minnie and Dido do not know that, in fact, they will not be going to live on a boat and that they will remain on the plantation. They do not know that they will remain in their current hold. And yet, when we attend to the feel of this scene, another kind of hold comes into view: the hold they have on one another. Sharpe illuminates the importance of such a hold when she asks of the reader: "In what ways might we enact a beholden-ness to each other, laterally? . . . How are we beholden to the beholders of each other in ways that change across time and place and space and yet remain? Beholden in the wake, as, at the very least, if we are lucky, an *opportunity* (back to the door) in our Black bodies to try to look, try to see."[65] In seeing beyond the story of Dido and Minnie in the original play where they are another ditto ditto in the archive of the enslaved, Jacobs-Jenikins asks for other options. There is a piercing irony, the whooping, wailing, whistle of a high-frequency contestation as care when Minnie tells Dido that the salvation of the white characters is not their job, and that even though they are slaves, they are not their jobs. This improper subjectivity of the property might be an improvisational rupture of the rights to cherished property. The refusal of the subjectivity of slavery on offer from Minnie to Dido is the murmur that exceeds speech. In the (humorous and tragic) breath shared between these two, a fugitive Black sociality that exceeds the slave-free binary, we can find a melancholic care work. They refuse to invest in the resilient narrative of Zoe; they go into her death. They refuse to do the salvific labor needed to redeem the white characters in the play. Instead they care for, remain with and good to, one another.

Unconcluded Care

The mode of witness offered by a political theology of and for the unredeemed does not seek to save white people—whiteness must take its poison pill. Nor does it request that we be frozen in shame. Knowing white people cannot be innocent, should not lead to more impotence. Nor does such witness portend to see no difference between forms of political and postsecular theology that wish to counter white supremacy and those whose purpose is to fortify it. It asks us to sit with pain, to be humiliated, to be undone by the horror of what white people, my people, have built. Instead of individual or denominational or disciplinary pardon, let us be ungrounded, let us be responsible for the active dismantling of the holds that have sheltered some while violating others for far too long.

The grave attention offered by Black studies and by the ghosts that haunt its archive remind me that, in all my calls to willful unredemption, I may have assumed we were all already inside the big big room full of every-body's hope. For Moten, the question of the city in Du Bois's work, which we might rewrite as the question of proper and propertied redemption, "demands that the questioner consider the one outside the house, be con-cerned with what the outside does to the one, explore the territories that have been thought to be outside the house of being, outside language. It requires an attempt to attune oneself to the outside language of the outside woman, the common-law outlaw, the shacked-up outside/r and, above all it, seeks to investigate and to inhabit that mode of interiority, that politico-aesthetic assertion, that inaugural, errant criminality that is the law of the outside, that the outside and everyday laboring growl and hum of everyday people enforces and allows."[66] It is my hope that the practice of grave attention gets us closer to such attunement, that it forces us to stay with Betty outside of the judge's chambers, and with Minnie and Dido outside of the house. I have hoped that in being brought down by the gravity of what is, and by attending to the growls of those who were supposed to stay buried, that we might rupture what has been in favor of what might be. We might breathe new life into the concrete utopian dreaming of the perhaps heard in a new word, and so a new world. We might hear the murmur that reminds us to ask for other options: "You are not your job."

Still, to listen for the impossible domestic and her improper improvisa-tional rupture must not be to claim ownership of such improvisational sound, to tune it to my own. As Ahmed, through Lorde, reminds us, we shall not have a common battle hymn. Rather, the request made by this archive, by the "Black mo'nin" of Moten and the Black annotation of Sharpe, is for those of us who have too often ignored the wakes and abysses on which our redemption was built to sit with the humiliation of not hav-ing been able to handle what has been handed down in our inheritance, both the inheritance of whiteness and that of the murmuring non-white flesh ransomed for our redemption. I have no clear answer to what this mode of holding the unholdable will bring. I have no happy ending, no stable ground to which we might all flee. There is no final port amidst the unreasoned storms. I have only the divine "perhaps"; the "what might be again, but never was"; the "yes, but" that comes in unconcluded care. To care incessantly is to let that which haunts—the mad murmurs and quotid-ian persistence of affect alien prophets—take hold.

ACKNOWLEDGMENTS

This book would not have been possible without the intellectual networks, emotional bonds, and mad collectives that have held and continue to hold me. In particular, I thank Catherine Keller, for whose support, guidance, and friendship I will be eternally grateful. I am indebted to Stephen Moore and Traci West, who nurtured this project in ways that made it more critically nuanced and ethically grounded. I am forever grateful to Richard Morrison, John Garza, and everyone at Fordham University Press for their incredible insight, time, and support.

Intellectual, theological, and ethical mentors, colleagues, and comrades have helped me to clarify ideas, struggle through lacunae, and keep going. Thank you in particular to: Christy Cobb, Holly Hillgardner, Natalie Williams, An Yountae, Beatrice Marovich, Terra Rowe, Sara Rosenau, Arminta Fox, Matthew Ketchum, Peter Mena, Jennifer Barry, Kathleen Elkins, Luke Higgens, Lydia York, Dhawn Martin, Geoff Pollick, Elijah Prewitt-Davis, Brandy Daniels, Kait Dugan, Lisa Gasson Gardner, Stephen Keating, Kyle Warren, Max Thornton, Jonathan Kocheski, Paige Rawson, Wade Mitchell, Anna Blaedel, Bo Eberle, Jordan Miller, Hollis Phelps, George Schmidt, Joseph Strife, Elizabeth Gish, Clayton Crockett, Jeffrey Robbins, Noelle Vahanian, Whitney Bauman, Mary Jane Rubenstein, J. Kameron Carter, Marion Grau, Anne Joh, Claudia Schippert, Meredith Doster, Meredith Coleman-Tobias, Carol Wayne White, Joerg Rieger, Kate Ott, Terry Todd, Chris Boesel, Melanie Johnson Debaufre, Mark Jordan, Susan Abraham, Shelly Rambo, Monica Maher, Maria Pilar Aquino, Amy Hollywood, Stephanie Paulsell, Dan McKannan, Nicole Kirk, Mike Hogue, Rebecca Parker, Kerry Sonia, Sonia Hazard, Kent Brintnall, Maia Kotrosits, Kathryn Tanner, Alan Jay Richard, Sarah Morice Brubaker, Mary Keller, Mike Grimshaw, Michael Zbaraschuk, Joshua Ramey, Brianne Jacobs, Jessica Coblentz, Jennifer Owens-Jofré, Eric Meyer, Donovan Schaefer, Steven Shakespeare, Jack Downey, Elana Jefferson Tatum, Gregory Seigworth, Kyle Lambelet, Jeremy Posadas, Eleanor Craig, Kevin Minister, Todd Willison, Karen O'Donnell, Katharine

Sarah Moody, Phil Snider, Marika Rose, Timothy McGee, Janna Hunter-Bowman, Luis Menéndez Antuña, Hillary Scarsella, Mark Larrimore, Michael Pettinger, Katherine Kurs, and Diana Kamin. An extra thank you to Natalie Williams, Joseph Strife, and Diana Kamin, who read chapters and helped me to get through the hardest of edits. An extra big thank you to Kent Brintnall and Maia Kotrosits, whose feedback on the full manuscript strengthened the project.

This book would also not have been possible without collectives of care and friendship woven across time and place. Thank you to friends near and far, who remained with me through both maddening and joyful moods, especially: Molly Housh Gordon, Daria Siegel, Laura Bellrose, Michelle Salerno, Rebecca Ackerman, Laura Scileppi, Julia Donahue, James Gordon, Audrey Brown Dickison, Scott Dickison, Tiffany Stanley, Alan Krill, Eva Payne, Evan Kingsley, Rebecca Curtin, Zachary Ugolnick, Kendra Goodson Plating, Chris Plating, Taylor Lewis Guthrie Hartman, Blair Hartman, Elizabeth Griswold, Elizabeth Ghedi-Ehrlich, Andi Winnette, Nathan Willard, Beth Yale, Elizabeth Pomerleau, Marcus McCullough, Andrew Forsyth, Josh Goodbaum, Allyson Lent, Emma Crossen, Andy Howard, Alyssa Cheadle, Garrett Fitzgerald, Marianne Tierney Fitzgerald, Tiffany Curtis, Julie Rogers, Kate Pyle, Heather Trobe, Carrie Dorn, Jessica Guy, Yael Bromberg, Iris Bromberg, Stephanie Kaliades, Sarah Johnson, Colleen Surlyn, Grant Surlyn, Nick Rudnick, Gary Carrion-Murayari, Meagan Haseman, Chris Haseman, Garret Kinsey, JP Hufnagel, Jaime Walker, Alan Lawn, James McDonnell, Daisuke O, Loren Crary, Matt Ellis, Ellen Zemelin, Greg Payan, Jason Starr, Joshua Takano Chambers-Letson, Jane Guyer, Renee Chudy, Jenny Fogarty, Pam Newton, Will O'Connor, Keith Newton, Jesse Lambert, Linda Ganjian, Zack Rice, Nicole Rice, Stephanie Rice, Jesse Rice, Michael Newton, Chris Wells, Clara Campos, Carly Beal, Sean Mack, Alice Rosenberg, Elizabeth Tenney, Rebecca Kruger, Paula Del Rio, Emily Kell, Charlie Thomas, Natalie Bourdon, Chris Smith, Sheree Keith, Tisha Simeral, Marnie Flanders, Erin Hall, Jake Hall, Eric Mayle, Enrico Bonatti, Merry Cai, Linda Schulze, and Christina Franke.

Thank you to all of my friends and colleagues from Wesleyan College; without their support and encouragement, this project could not have been completed. In particular, thank you to: Alexis Gregg, Tanner Coleman, Holly Cole, Barry Rhoades, Melanie Doherty, Randy Heaton, Kara Kostiuk, Tonya Parker, Melody Blake, Momo Yoshida, Karen Huber, Nick Steneck, Barbara Donovan, Tom Ellington, Mariana Furlin, Virginia Blake, Laura Lease, Joe Lease, Saralyn Desmet, Teresa Smotherman,

Shelly Martin, Jim Ferrari, Deidra Donmoyer, Brooke Bennet Day, James Ogden, Frazer Lively, and Patrick Pritchard. Finally, an extra big thank you to Tyler Schwaller, who has supported my growth for over a decade, and whom it is a blessing to call both a friend and a colleague.

This book was finished during my first years teaching at Wesleyan. Its pages were made more meaningful from my interactions with the Wesleyan students. I am thankful to them all. In particular, I want to thank the students of my Political Theology class whose discussions helped this book come to life: Zamoria Simpson, Sarah Belflower, Maddie Hobbs, Madison Giddings, Imani Somner, Brenda Wilkinson, Savanna Gowin, Jamie Fang, Lexi Mullaly, and Rongxin Sun.

Finally, I'd like to thank my family for the wells of support that have run deeper than I could ever repay. Thank you to: Jackie Bray, Alice Newton, Robert Newton, Michael Bray, Rose Marie Sherry, Kate Johnson, Meghan Reid, Ashley Walsh, Dylan Walsh, Jaiden Hatton, Emma Garneau, Matthew Garneau, Brynne Craig, Rick Johnson, Sarah Newton, Gabrielle Vincent, Joan Bray, Esther Newton, Holly Hughes, David Sprecher, Sean Sprecher, Paul Sprecher, Frances Simpson, John Macleod, Charlotte Macleod, Dylan Maclcod, Ian Macleod, Trudy Williams, Nicole Singer, Anne Swerdloff, Howie Swerdloff, Sasha Swerdloff, Samantha Swerdloff, Donald Smith, Mia Rublowski, Bob Machover, and Julia Deedee Agee Sprecher, whom we miss every day.

Material from this book has been presented and published in revised form elsewhere. Chapter 2 is adapted from a chapter in the volume *Sexual Disorientations: Queer Temporalities, Affects, Theologies*, published by Fordham University Press in 2017. Parts of Chapter 3 were first published in article form as "The Monstrosity of the Multitude: Unredeeming Radical Theology," in *Palgrave Communication*'s 2015 special issue on "Radical Theology." Finally, parts of Chapter 6 appeared as "Ungrounded Innocence: Confronting Christian Culpability in White Nationalism" in the volume *Doing Theology in the Age of Trump* (Cascade Books, 2018).

NOTES

1. UNBEGUN INTRODUCTIONS

1. Aura Bogado, "Listen: Ms. Lauryn Hill's 'Black Rage' Responds to Ferguson," *Color Lines*, August 21, 2014, http://colorlines.com/archives/2014/08/listen_ms_lauryn_hills_black_rage_responds_to_ferguson.html.

2. Sara Ahmed, *The Promise of Happiness* (Durham, N.C.: Duke University Press, 2010), 195.

3. Melissa Gregg and Gregory J. Seigworth, eds, *The Affect Theory Reader* (Durham, N.C.: Duke University, 2010), xi.

4. Gregg and Seigworth , *Affect Theory*, 3–4.

5. The psychobiological lens represented in the works of such thinkers as Eve Kosofsky Sedgwick, Adam Frank, and Silvan Tomkins (Tomkins first coined the term "affect theory" in 1962) looks to how feelings are psychobiologically structured in ways that shape human (and sometimes intra-human/nonhuman) experience. Psychobiological approaches can be, but are not always, investigations of affects that cut across histories and cultures. The prepersonal lens, found in work that draws on the philosophies of Alfred North Whitehead and Gilles Deleuze (Massumi, Clough, Manning, Shaviro), takes affect as a force or intensity: that moment on the mountaintop or before the first kiss. Affects are what we feel before we code emotions. It is important here to note that to understand affects as prepersonal is not to understand them as inconsequent to the social, or as unaffected by postpersonal emotion, but rather to understand affect as that which overflows the discursive production of emotional codes. And finally, the cultural approach to affect, which is most readily found in the work of queer and feminist cultural studies and critical race theory, resists categorizing affects as pre-social and focuses instead on how affects are produced through cultural and historical structures of power. Cultural theorists of affect look at which feelings stick to which bodies and which choices (to borrow from Ahmed). Again, we might note here the "Happy Housewife" versus the "Angry Black Woman."

6. Donovan O. Schaefer, *Religious Affects: Animality, Evolution, and Power* (Durham, N.C.: Duke University Press, 2015).

7. Ahmed, *Promise of Happiness*, 162.

8. Ahmed, 20.

9. Ahmed, 162.

10. Ann Cvetkovich, *Depression: A Public Feeling* (Durham, N.C.: Duke University Press, 2012), 109.

11. Cvetkovich, *Depression*, 5.

12. Cvetkovich, 11.

13. Cvetkovich, 167.

14. Cvetkovich, 206.

15. Cvetkovich, 21.

16. Schaefer, *Religious Affects*, 13.

17. Schaefer, 8.

18. Judith Halberstam, *The Queer Art of Failure* (Durham, N.C.: Duke University Press, 2011).

19. Prominent strains of disability studies focus on an acceptance and access model. This model aims at the inclusion of disabled people in mainstream society. While the importance of this work cannot be denied, other strains of disability studies known as crip theory or crip theology have challenged the field to expand into realms similar to those engaged by queer theory in its move beyond liberationist or identity politics. As with the reclamation of the word "queer," disability theorists who prefer the label "crip" seek to reclaim the derogatory "cripple" for their own critical work.

20. Robert McRuer, *Crip Theory: Cultural Signs of Queerness and Disability* (New York: New York University Press, 2006), 8.

21. Sharon V. Betcher, *Spirit and the Politics of Disablement* (Minneapolis, Minn.: Fortress Press, 2007), 14.

22. Tobin Siebers, *Disability Aesthetics* (Ann Arbor: University of Michigan Press, 2010).

23. Michael Hardt and Antonio Negri, *Multitude: War and Democracy in the Age of Empire* (New York: Penguin, 2004), 66.

24. Mike Grimshaw, *Palgrave Communications* Special Collection Introduction, http://www.palgrave-journals.com/palcomms/article-collections/radical-theologies.

25. We can include the following thinkers under the banner of radical political theologians and philosophers, postmodern theologians, and Process theologians (in this list I include a wide range of philosophers and theologians that can be traced back to the broad definition of radical theology given by the Palgrave editors) such as William Connolly, Catherine Keller, John Cobb, John D. Caputo, Jeffrey Robbins, Clayton Crockett, Noëlle Vahanian, Ward Blanton, Mark C. Taylor, Mark L. Taylor, and Richard Kearney who are engaged in theological reflection on the econo-political. These thinkers

rely heavily on the work of poststructuralists such as Derrida, Deleuze and Guattari, Malabou, Agamben, Žižek, Laclau, Laruelle, Lacan, Badiou, and Hardt and Negri, as well as on death-of-God philosophers such as Louis Altizer and Gabriel Vahanian. These thinkers refuse to counter secularized theologies, like those undergirding capitalism, with other absolutist theologies.

26. Mark L. Taylor, *The Theological and the Political: On the Weight of the World* (Minneapolis, Minn.: Fortress Press, 2011).

27. Mark C. Taylor, *Confidence Games: Moneys and Markets in a World without Redemption* (Chicago: University of Chicago Press, 2004), 331.

28. Sara Ahmed, "Not in the Mood," *New Formations* 82 (2014): 18.

29. Autonomist Marxism does not employ "autonomy" as a rejection of dependency or a synonym for independence. Rather, it uses its etymology to suggest the importance of self-rule. In this way it has deep ties not only to branches of socialism that sought to counter communist totalitarianism, but also to the development of anarchism. Autonomism, in the thought of Antonio Negri, should not be read as individualism, but rather as a critique of conformity and coercion.

30. Kathi Weeks, *The Problem with Work: Feminism, Marxism, Anti-Work Politics, and Postwork Imaginaries* (Durham, N.C.: Duke University Press, 2011), 13.

31. Alfred North Whitehead, *Process and Reality* (New York: The Free Press, 1978), 346.

32. Alfred North Whitehead, *Adventures of Ideas* (New York: The Free Press, 1967), 9.

33. Franco "Bifo" Berardi, *The Soul at Work: From Alienation to Autonomy* (Los Angeles: Semiotext(e), 2009).

34. That these books *felt* right to me does not mean that there is not a whole cannon of thinkers of madness, philosophers for whom the construction of subjectivities rely on violent exclusions of abjections. The works of Georges Bataille, Julia Kristeva, Saidiya Hartman, Hortense Spillers, and Luce Irigaray all come to mind as thinkers around whom this book could have been constructed. And yet, it was not to them that I got stuck.

35. Cvetkovich, *Depression*, 77.

36. Catherine Keller, "Uninteresting Truth? Tedium and Event in Postmodernity," in *Secrets of Becoming: Negotiating Whitehead, Deleuze, and Butler*, ed. Roland Faber and Andrea M. Stephenson (New York: Fordham University Press, 2011), 211.

37. Cvetkovich, *Depression*, 3.

38. Joerg Rieger, *No Rising Tide: Theology, Economics, and the Future* (Minneapolis, Minn.: Fortress Press, 2009), viii.

2. UNSAVED TIME

1. Lauren Berlant, *Cruel Optimism* (Durham, N.C.: Duke University Press, 2011), 1.

2. Phillip Goodchild, *Theology of Money* (Durham, N.C.: Duke University Press, 2009), 188.

3. I define radical political theology as a field of theology that takes postmodernism and postsecularism as a starting point for the writing of theology. It is interested in questions normally considered political—like that of sovereignty, economy, and agency. The field is greatly indebted to Carl Schmitt's famous assertion that "All significant concepts of the theory of the modern state are secularized theological concepts." Carl Schmitt, *Political Theology: Four Chapters on the Concept of Sovereignty* (Chicago: University of Chicago Press, 1985; originally published in German in 1922), 36. Radical political theology, for the purposes of this book, encompasses two strands of contemporary political theology: that often called just radical theology (which I will refer to as radical theology, or RT), and radical orthodox theology, or RO. Radical theology/radical democratic theology is a contemporary field of theology drawing on constructive theology, process theology, secular theology, and death-of-God theologies and is deeply influenced by continental thought—particularly the writings of Gilles Deleuze and Pierre-Félix Guattari, Alain Badiou, Slavoj Žižek, and Michael Hardt and Antonio Negri. It offers a theology that is written from within an immanent frame and is dependent on the potency of people over and against a transcendent God in whom rests ultimate sovereignty. Radical orthodox theologians, though similarly writing from within and in response to postsecularism and engaging in issues of sovereignty and economy, argue for a return to the transcendent sovereign God as a counter to what many see as the loss of value in a liberalism run amok in the wake of the death of God.

4. The discourse I refer to in this book as "radical democratic," or RD, often goes simply by "radical theology." However, in order to better distinguish this school from the radical orthodoxy, I have added "democratic" to the descriptor of the field.

5. John Milbank, *Theology and Social Theory: Beyond Secular Reason* (Oxford: Blackwell Publishing, 1990), 388.

6. Milbank, *Theology and Social Theory*, 359.

7. Milbank, 224.

8. Milbank, 246.

9. Milbank, 331; emphasis added.

10. Jeffrey W. Robbins, *Radical Democracy and Political Theology* (New York: Columbia University Press, 2011), 191.

11. Clayton Crockett, *Radical Political Theology: Religion and Politics after Liberalism* (New York: Columbia University Press, 2011).

12. Clayton Crockett, *Deleuze beyond Badiou: Ontology, Multiplicity, and Event* (New York: Columbia University Press, 2013), 97.

13. Crockett, *Deleuze beyond Badiou*, 99.

14. Gilles Deleuze, *Cinema II: The Time Image* (Minneapolis: University of Minnesota Press, 2003), 214.

15. Deleuze, *Cinema II*, 218.

16. Deleuze, 219.

17. Crockett, *Deleuze beyond Badiou*, 192.

18. Jacques Derrida's conception of the democracy to come, most prominently developed in *Specters of Marx* (1993), *The Politics of Friendship* (1994), and *Rogues: Two Essays on Reason* (2005), implies that full democracy is never present but always deferred or on its way. The democracy to come is a reminder that what we call democracy in the present is not full democracy. Democracy has never arrived.

19. Crockett, *Deleuze beyond Badiou*, 183.

20. Crockett, 192.

21. William T. Cavanaugh, *Being Consumed: Economics and Christian Desire* (Grand Rapids, Mich.: Wm. B. Eerdmans Publishing Co., 2008), Chap. 1.

22. Berlant, *Cruel Optimism*, 95.

23. Berlant, 95.

24. Steven Shakespeare, *Radical Orthodoxy: A Critical Introduction* (London: Society for Promoting Christian Knowledge, 2007), 127.

25. Shakespeare, *Radical Orthodoxy*, 163.

26. William E. Connolly, *Capitalism and Christianity, American Style* (Durham, N.C.: Duke University Press, 2008), 34.

27. Connolly, *Capitalism and Christianity*, 13.

28. Naomi Klein, *Shock Doctrine: The Rise of Disaster Capitalism* (New York: Picador, 2007).

29. Muñoz's work on queer futurity is essential to studies in queer temporality. Over the last decades, queer theory has taken a critical turn toward the "antisocial" thesis. In the queer turn to temporality, particularly in discourses arising around this thesis, we can find similar debates in terms of teleology, universalism, and value as those tackled by political theology. According to Robert L. Caserio, this thesis, first developed in Leo Bersani's 1995 work, *Homos*, proposes that "If there is anything 'politically indispensable' in homosexuality, it is its 'politically unacceptable' opposition to community." Robert L. Caserio, "The Antisocial Thesis in Queer Theory," *PMLA* 121, no. 3 (2006): 819. Antisociality represents a refusal to be a

productive or reproductive member of heteronormative society. The work
of Lee Edelman perhaps best represents the temporality proposed by the
antisocial thesis. For Edelman, politics rest on a reproductive futurism in
which the hopes of a better life are dependent on the figure of the Child
whom we are told we must fight for. As Edelman writes in his 2004 polemic
No Future: Queer Theory and the Death Drive (Durham, N.C.: Duke University Press, 2004), 2, queerness is what "names the side of those not 'fighting
for the children,' the side outside the consensus by which all politics con-
firms the absolute value of reproductive futurism." José Esteban Muñoz critiques such queer negativity for eclipsing the experiences of queer folks of
color and offers, instead, queer utopianism. (José Esteban Muñoz, "Thinking beyond Antirelationality and Antiutopianism in Queer Critique," *PMLA*
121, no. 3 [2006]: 825). For the purposes of this project, Muñoz's attention
to which queer bodies may have been ransomed for the formation of the
antisocial thesis matters for the ways in which he offers me a middle way
between a potentially crucifixionesque death drive and a resurrectionesque
optimism in an ephemeral utopia to come. That being said, one can read
Edelman as precisely the prophet of a middle day, of a Holy Saturday of
which I seek. Edelman, perhaps more so than Muñoz, refuses Sunday so as
to live more faithfully into what it has meant to be crucified. And yet, it is
not the hope of my particular political theology to reject the future; rather it
is to insist on a presentist-future never free of the hauntings and potentiali-
ties that come out of a moody past. Further, it is within a haunted and
expansive sociality that I find the most hope for a rejection of cruelly optimistic and neoliberal redemption narratives, and as such it is to the spaces of
queer collectivity embodied in Muñoz's concrete utopias that I find most
traction. Further, perhaps such a Holy Saturday temporality attentive to
both Edelman and Muñoz's positions resides in the complexity of a loss that
acts melancholically as a demand for a better future, à la the collection of
writings in *Loss: The Politics of Mourning*, edited by David L. Eng and David
Kazanjian (Berkeley and Los Angeles: University of California Press, 2003),
as discussed in this chapter.

    30. José Esteban Muñoz, *Cruising Utopia: The Then and There of Queer
Futurity* (New York: New York University Press, 2009), 1.

    31. Muñoz, *Cruising Utopia*.

    32. Muñoz, 3.

    33. José Esteban Muñoz, *Disidentifications: Queers of Color and the Perfor-
mance of Politics* (Minneapolis: University of Minnesota Press, 1999).

    34. Ann Cvetkovich, *Depression: A Public Feeling* (Durham, N.C.: Duke
University Press, 2012).

    35. Elizabeth Freeman, *Time Binds: Queer Temporalities, Queer Histories*
(Durham, N.C.: Duke University Press, 2010).

36. Shelly Rambo, *Spirit and Trauma: A Theology of Remaining* (Louisville, Ky.: Westminster John Knox Press, 2010), 3.

37. Rambo, *Spirit and Trauma*, 162.

38. Rambo, 46.

39. For Gilles Deleuze the new basis on which modern political cinema was founded is the acknowledgement that a people have been missing. According to Deleuze, political cinema's rejection of linear time or a historical narrative that has served to absent the people is represented through juxtapositions of old and new that create absurdities and point toward the cracks in history. Deleuze, *Cinema II*, 217–18.

40. Rambo, *Spirit and Trauma*, 48.

41. Rambo, 53.

42. Rambo, 43.

43. Rambo, 57.

44. Although I have chosen to focus on the writings of Heather Love, Robin James, and Elizabeth Freeman in order to illuminate the tie between certain theories of queer temporality, one could also look to the work of Jack Halberstam on queer failure in *The Queer Art of Failure* (2011) or to crip critiques of productivity such as those found in the work of Robert McRuer.

45. Heather Love, *Feeling Backward: Loss and the Politics of Queer History* (Cambridge, Mass.: Harvard University Press, 2007), 1.

46. Love, *Feeling Backward*, 13.

47. Love, 147.

48. Judith Butler, *The Psychic Life of Power: Theories in Subjection* (Stanford, Calif.: Stanford University Press, 1997), 139–40.

49. David L. Eng and David Kazanjian, "Introduction: Mourning Remains," in *Loss: The Politics of Mourning*, ed. David L. Eng and David Kazanjian (Berkeley and Los Angeles: University of California Press, 2003), 2.

50. Eng and Kazanjian, "Mourning Remains," 4.

51. Robin James, *Resilience and Melancholy: Pop Music, Feminism, Neoliberalism* (Alresford, UK: Zero Books, 2015), 4.

52. Naomi Klein, *The Shock Doctrine: The Rise of Disaster Capitalism* (New York: Picador, 2007).

53. James, *Resilience and Melancholy*, 135.

54. James, 135.

55. James, 56.

56. James, 9.

57. James, 162.

58. James, 13.

59. James, 15.

60. We might find some key differences in Beyoncé's more recent endeavors in "Lemonade" and "Formation," released after James's analyses.

However, I am still convinced by James's comparison between resilient pop songs and melancholic ones.

61. James, *Resilience and Melancholy*, 133.

62. James, 138.

63. James, 125.

64. James, 124.

65. James, 126.

66. James, 149.

67. James, 174.

68. James, 99.

69. Freeman, *Time Binds*, 137.

70. Freeman, 137–38.

71. Freeman, 147. Of course the play of pleasure and pain through ritual enactment is not unfamiliar to theologians and religious practitioners. There is a long history of Christian practice that involves bodily pleasure and pain in acts not only for worship, but also for the enactment of a different kind of time.

72. For instance, see George "Tink" Tinker's work on the problematic trope of exodus in liberation theology for Native Americans, for whom sticking with their land is politically and cosmologically crucial. George E. Tinker, *Spirit and Resistance: Political Theology and American Indian Liberation* (Minneapolis, Minn.: Augsburg Fortress, 2004).

73. Freeman, *Time Binds*, 145.

74. Freeman, 53.

75. Freeman, 149.

76. Freeman, 163–64; emphasis added.

77. Michel Foucault, *Hermeneutics of the Subject: Lectures at the Collège de France 1981–1982* (New York: Picador, 2001), 95.

78. Crockett, *Deleuze beyond Badiou*, 169.

79. Crockett, 169.

80. Cvetkovich, *Depression*.

81. Crip theory is a form of disability studies that seeks not for accessibility and acceptance, but rather, similar to queer theory, looks (through the experience of the disabled) to destabilize heteronormative and ableist systems of accessibility and acceptability. In *Crip Theory: Cultural Signs of Queerness and Disability* (New York: New York University Press, 2006), Robert McRuer explicates how compulsory heterosexuality is actually dependent on compulsory able-bodiedness because compulsory heterosexuality is built around concepts of normate bodies and sexualities.

82. In invoking bipolarity's pleasurable potential, I seek not to glorify depression or mania, but rather to uncover alternate desires for the world

produced in non-normate mental orientations. Additionally, I follow the work collected by editors Robert McRuer and Anna Mollow in *Sex and Disability* (Durham, N.C.: Duke University Press, 2012) to argue against the pathologization and desexualization of the crip (including the mentally crip).

83. Rambo, *Spirit and Trauma*, 77.

84. Freeman, *Time Binds*, 153.

85. Noëlle Vahanian, *The Rebellious No: Variations on a Secular Theology of Language* (New York: Fordham University Press, 2014), 71.

86. Vahanian, *Rebellious No*, 70.

87. Lynne Huffer, *Mad for Foucault: Rethinking the Foundations of Queer Theory* (New York: Columbia University Press, 2010), 92.

88. Huffer, *Mad for Foucault*, 56.

89. Huffer, 227.

90. Noëlle Vahanian, e-mail message to author, October 12, 2014.

91. McRuer and Mollow, *Sex and Disability*, 25.

92. "Feel Tank" names groups in Chicago, New York, and Toronto who have participated in the Public Feelings Project, which brings together activists, artists, and academics who do critical work in the study of theoretical, historical, and artistic materials engaged with political affects and the politics of affect.

93. Cvetkovich, *Depression*, 188.

94. Muñoz, *Cruising Utopia*, 186.

95. Muñoz, 189.

96. Dolly Parton, *9 to 5*, Dolly Parton © 1980 by RCA Nashville.

3. UNPRODUCTIVE WORTH

1. Michael Hardt and Antonio Negri, *Multitude: War and Democracy in the Age of Empire* (New York: Penguin, 2004), 135.

2. Crip theory is a form of disability studies that seeks not for accessibility and acceptance, but rather, similar to queer theory, looks (through the experience of the disabled) to destabilize heteronormative and ableist systems of accessibility and acceptability.

3. Kathi Weeks, *The Problem with Work: Feminism, Marxism, Anti-Work Politics, and Postwork Imaginaries* (Durham, N.C.: Duke University Press, 2011), 51.

4. Weeks, *Problem with Work*, 45.

5. Weeks, 70.

6. Autonomism is a school of thought and action most commonly traced back to the workerist (or operaismo) movement in Italy in the 1960s and '70s (a movement which Antonio Negri was a part of). In general, autonomism represents a stance toward capitalist labor in which, instead of seeking

reform of the system, one seeks autonomy from capitalist production. For instance, Franco "Bifo" Berardi, a leading voice in contemporary autonomist thought (and a primary theorist for the constructive work of this essay), has referred to autonomism as "out-onomy," which names the formation of ways of living that get one out of the capitalist economy.

7. Semiocapitalism is a neoliberal economy in which we are flooded with and dictated by an exhaustive flow of signs without referents. Franco "Bifo" Berardi, *The Soul at Work: From Alienation to Autonomy* (Los Angeles: Semiotext(e), 2009).

8. Joerg Rieger and Kwok Pui-lan, *Occupy Religion: Theology of the Multitude* (Plymouth, UK: Rowman and Littlefield, 2012), 67.

9. Recall from Chapter 2 that MRWaSP is Robin James's acronym for Multi-Racial White Supremacist Patriarchy. James uses MRWaSP to express how certain minoritized people are let into the neoliberal mainstream in part to justify the exclusion of other unproductive, or as I would say, "irredeemable" subjects.

10. Rieger and Kwok, *Occupy Religion*, 61.

11. By "singular" here, and by "singularity" elsewhere in this book, I refer not to an individualism, but rather back to the concept of singularity employed by Berardi (reading Gilles Deleuze's concept of singularity in which individuation [the uniqueness of each singularity] is not the same as individualism). It is a singularity that resists homogenization while keeping the uniqueness and creative potential of each entity within an assemblage of entities at the fore. Franco "Bifo" Berardi, *After the Future*, ed. Gary Genosko and Nicholas Thoburn (Edinburgh, Oakland, Baltimore: AK Press, 2011), 148.

12. Rieger and Kwok, *Occupy Religion*, 62.

13. Rieger and Kwok, 100.

14. Rieger and Kwok, 71.

15. Rieger and Kwok, 86.

16. Rieger and Kwok, 73.

17. My use of "willful" here, as well as later in this book, refers to Sara Ahmed's work on willfulness in *Willful Subjects* (Durham, N.C.: Duke University Press, 2014). According to Ahmed, certain forms of living are considered *willful* because they "pulse" with a desire directed away from that of the mainstream (Ahmed, 23). They willfully come apart and wander where they *will* (Ahmed, 50).

18. Weeks, *Problem with Work*, 68.

19. Weeks, 52.

20. Weeks, 64.

21. Weeks, 69.

22. Weeks, 69.

23. Hardt and Negri, *Multitude*, 66.

24. Hardt and Negri, 66.

25. Hardt and Negri, 66.

26. Weeks, *Problem with Work*, 70–71.

27. Dave Eggers, *The Circle* (San Francisco: McSweeney's, 2013).

28. Melissa Gregg, "On Friday Night Drinks: Workplace Affect in the Age of the Cubicle," in *The Affect Theory Reader*, ed. Melissa Gregg and Gregory J. Seigworth (Durham, N.C.: Duke University Press, 2010), 261.

29. Mark Tran, "Apple and Facebook Offer to Freeze Eggs for Female Employees," *Guardian*, October 15, 2004, http://www.theguardian.com/technology/2014/oct/15/apple-facebook-offer-freeze-eggs-female-employees.

30. Tran, "Apple and Facebook."

31. Jodi Kantor and David Streitfield, "Inside Amazon: Wrestling Big Ideas in a Bruising Workplace," *New York Times*, August 15, 2015, http://www.nytimes.com/2015/08/16/technology/inside-amazon-wrestling-big-ideas-in-a-bruising-workplace.html?_r=o.

32. Kantor and Streitfield, "Inside Amazon."

33. Kantor and Streitfield, "Inside Amazon."

34. "Amazon Leadership Principles," http://www.amazon.jobs/principles, accessed November 11, 2015.

35. Kantor and Streitfield, "Inside Amazon."

36. Kantor and Streitfield, "Inside Amazon."

37. Kantor and Streitfield, "Inside Amazon."

38. Kantor and Streitfield, "Inside Amazon."

39. Weeks, *Problem with Work*, 73.

40. Berardi, *Soul at Work*, 21.

41. Berardi, 23.

42. Berardi, 148.

43. Crockett, *Radical Political Theology: Religion and Politics after Liberalism* (New York: Columbia University Press, 2011), 102.

44. Berardi, *Soul at Work*, 148.

45. Berardi, 140.

46. Berardi, 179.

47. Berardi, *After the Future*, 135–38.

48. Berardi, 136.

49. See for instance Clayton Crockett and Jeffrey W. Robbins, *Religion, Politics, and the Earth: The New Materialism* (New York: Palgrave Macmillan, 2012); as well as essays by Randall Johnson and John Thibdeau in *The Future of Continental Philosophy of Religion*, ed. Clayton Crockett, B. Keith Putt, and Jeffrey W. Robbins (Bloomington: Indiana University Press, 2014).

50. I get the concept of bodymind from a virtual roundtable on "cripiste-mologies" convened and edited by Robert McRuer and Merri Lisa Johnson in which Margaret Price (who found the concept of bodymind in the work of Babette Rothschild) uses the term to represent how we can't talk about mind or brain split from the body. Robert McRuer and Merri Lisa Johnson, "Pro-liferating Cripistemologies: A Virtual Roundtable," *Journal of Literary and Culutral Disability Studies* 8, no. 2 (2014): 153.

51. Berardi, *After the Future*, 107.

52. Berardi, *Soul at Work*, 108.

53. Berardi, 160.

54. Love, *Feeling Backward*, 1.

55. See for example: Slavoj Žižek's work on revolution and his deploy-ment of the work of Badiou which spans across his work; Alain Badiou's *Being and Event* (2013), *Logics of Worlds: Being and Event II* (2013), and *Philosophy and the Event* (2013); Crockett's *Deleuze beyond Badiou* (2013) and *Radical Political Theology* (2011); Robbins's *Radical Democracy and Political Theology* (2011); the collected volume *Theology and the Political: The New Debate* (2005) edited by Davis, Milbank, and Žižek; and John D. Caputo's *The Weakness of God: A The-ology of the Event* (2006).

56. Speeding *up* change, moving *upward* might be reworked through slowing things *down* or moving *downward*.

57. Steven Shaviro, *No Speed Limit: Three Essays on Accelerationism* (Min-neapolis: University of Minnesota Press, 2015), 5–6.

58. Shaviro, *No Speed Limit*, 6.

59. Berardi, *After the Future*, 138.

60. Lauren Berlant, *Cruel Optimism* (Durham, N.C.: Duke University Press, 2011), Chap. 3.

61. Berlant, 276, n64.

62. Berlant, 276, n64.

63. Berardi, *After the Future*, 148.

64. Berardi, 152.

65. Berardi, 153–54.

66. Berardi, 163.

67. Berardi, 165–66.

68. Robert McRuer and Anna Mollow, eds., *Sex and Disability* (Durham, N.C.: Duke University Press, 2012), 32.

69. McRuer and Mollow, *Sex and Disability*, 31.

70. Robert McRuer, *Crip Theory: Cultural Signs of Queerness and Disability* (New York: New York University Press, 2006), 104.

71. McRuer, *Crip Theory*, 105.

72. McRuer, 112.

73. McRuer, 112.
74. McRuer, 144.
75. McRuer, 144.
76. Susan Schweik, "The Voice of 'Reason,'" in *Beauty Is a Verb: The New Poetry of Disability*, ed. Jennifer Bartlett, Sheila Black, and Michael Northern (El Paso, Tex.: Cinco Puntos Press, 2011), 70.
77. Hardt and Negri, *Multitude*, 332.
78. Hardt and Negri, 333.
79. Hardt and Negri, 332.
80. Slavoj Žižek, *The Parallax View* (Cambridge, Mass.: MIT Press, 2004).
81. Berardi, *After the Future*, 165.
82. Weeks, *Problem with Work*, 232.
83. Hardt and Negri, *Multitude*, 192.
84. Hardt and Negri, 190–95.
85. Cesare Casarino and Antonio Negri, *In Praise of the Common: A Conversation on Philosophy and Politics* (Minneapolis: University of Minnesota Press, 2008), 194.
86. Casarino and Negri, *In Praise of the Common*, 199.
87. Casarino and Negri, *In Praise of the Common*, 200–218.
88. Casarino and Negri, 203.
89. Hardt and Negri, *Multitude*, 196.
90. Berardi, *After the Future*, 166.
91. Jill Alexander Essbaum, "Swimming on Concrete: The Poetry of Vassar Miller," in *Beauty Is a Verb: The New Poetry of Disability*, ed. Jennifer Bartlett, Sheila Black, and Michael Northern (El Paso, Tex.: Cinco Puntos Press, 2011), 50.
92. Alexander Essbaum, "Swimming on Concrete" 50.
93. Here I refer (with a différance) to Jacques Derrida's *The Animal That Therefore I Am* (New York: Fordham University Press, 2008), which more accurately translated from the French would be *The Animal That Therefore I Am / I Follow*.
94. Berardi, *Soul at Work*, 129.
95. Cvetkovich, *Depression*, 3.
96. Cvetkovich, 60.
97. Cvetkovich, 154–202.
98. Berardi, *Soul at Work*, 138.
99. Weeks, *Problem with Work*, 221.
100. Berardi, *Soul at Work*, 207.
101. Berardi, 140.
102. Berardi, 99.

103. Berardi, 217.

104. Berardi, *After the Future*, 158.

105. Alexander Essbaum, "Swimming in Concrete," 51.

106. Alexander Essbaum, 51.

107. Berardi, *After the Future*, 162.

108. Stefano Harney and Fred Moten, *The Undercommons: Fugitive Planning and Black Study* (Wivenhoe, UK: Minor Compositions, 2013), 7.

109. Harney and Moten, *Undercommons*, 7.

110. Sara Ahmed, *Willful Subjects* (Durham, N.C.: Duke University Press, 2014), 184.

111. Ahmed, *Willful Subjects*, 199.

112. Berardi, *After the Future*, 166.

4. UNWILLING FEELING

1. Sara Ahmed, *The Promise of Happiness* (Durham, N.C.: Duke University Press, 2010), 20.

2. Melissa Gregg and Gregory J. Seigworth, eds., *The Affect Theory Reader* (Durham, N.C.: Duke University, 2009), 17; emphasis added.

3. This chapter should be viewed as a biblically inspired theology. However, it does not practice a strict fidelity to the definitions of redemption offered by early Christians and ancient Israelites, which often meant to be bought back from slavery. We might ask ourselves what it means for the concept of redemption to on the one hand, have shifted so dramatically for contemporary theological constructions, and on the other hand to have been so intimately tied with the process of buying back society's acknowledgment of one's status as a person and not property.

4. As thought experiments, my exegeses of Jonah and Martha are not meant to be canonical. Nor do they cover the depth of commentaries on each figure. Rather, in a constructive theological vein they hope to take seriously the hard work of biblical scholars and biblical interpretation while feeling free to wander where the affect in the text takes us, even if that is far afield from the field of biblical scholarship.

5. Ahmed, *Promise of Happiness*, 12.

6. Ahmed, 102.

7. Ahmed, 195.

8. Ahmed, 220.

9. The passage reads: "Now as they went on their way, he entered a certain village, where a woman named Martha welcomed him into her home. She had a sister named Mary, who sat at the Lord's feet and listened to what he was saying. But Martha was distracted by her many tasks; so she came to him and asked, 'Lord, do you not care that my sister has left me to do all the

work by myself? Tell her then to help me.' But the Lord answered her, 'Martha, Martha, you are worried and distracted by many things; there is need of only one thing. Mary has chosen the better part, which will not be taken away from her.'" (NRSV). Elsewhere in the New Testament, Martha is found only in John 11:1–44 passim and 12:2.

10. By rationale here I mean in no way the final word on or an expert exegesis of the pericopes explored here. Rather, I argue that each of these texts can be read against such expertise, against canons of interpretation. I argue that indeed to do so is to make reappear those parts of the biblical characters that have been disappeared from history. Additionally, given queer affect theories rejection of mastery, I seek to do anything but master the texts. Further, following Ben Highmore, who "suggests, the description of the ordinary (or depression) requires a science of the singular, which disrupts statistical and scientific understandings that operate through generalizations," I argue that the stories of Jonah and Martha's depressions (while simultaneously parabolic in function), must also be reading their singularity, such that they need not be the final word on a generalized theology of affect in the Bible or the only or defining characteristic of each character within their own stories.

11. Ahmed, *Promise of Happiness*, 22.

12. Ahmed, 22.

13. Ahmed, 311.

14. Ahmed, 223.

15. Ahmed, 219.

16. Ahmed, 220.

17. Ahmed, 183.

18. John D. Caputo, *The Insistence of God: A Theology of Perhaps* (Bloomington: Indiana University Press, 2013), 48.

19. Caputo, *Insistence of God*, 120.

20. Caputo, 40.

21. Caputo, 43.

22. According to Ahmed, "When I am saying that 'white men' is an institution I am referring not only to what has already been instituted or built but the *mechanisms* that ensure the persistence of that structure. A building is shaped by a series of regulative norms. 'White men' refers also to conduct; it is not simply who is there, who is here, who is given a place at the table, but how bodies are occupied once they have arrived; behaviour as bond." Sara Ahmed, "White Men" post on the *Feminist Killjoys Blog*, November 4, 2014, accessed December 2, 2015.

23. Judith Halberstam, *The Queer Art of Failure* (Durham, N.C.: Duke University Press, 2011), 119.

24. *Jonah: A VeggieTales Movie*. DVD, Directed by Mike Nawrocki and Phil Vischer (USA: Big Idea Productions, 2002); emphasis added.

25. *Jonah: A VeggieTales Movie.*

26. Justin Ryu Chesung, "Silence as Resistance: a postcolonial reading of the silence of Jonah in Jonah 4.1–11," *Journal for the Study of the Old Testament* 34, no. 2 (2009): 195–218, esp. 202.

27. Yvonne Sherwood, *A Biblical Text and Its Afterlives: The Survival of Jonah in Western Culture* (Cambridge: Cambridge University Press, 2000), 126.

28. Jione Havea, "First People, Minority Reading: Reading Jonah, From Oceania," in *The One Who Reads May Run: Essays in Honour of Edgar W. Conrad*, ed. Roland Boer, Michael Carden, and Julie Kelso (New York: T&T Clark, 2012).

29. Halberstam, *Queer Art of Failure*, 132.

30. Halberstam, 135.

31. Gerald O'Collins, SJ, *Salvation for All: God's Other Peoples* (Oxford: Oxford University Press, 2008), 38; emphasis added.

32. Daniel C. Timmer, *A Gracious and Compassionate God: Mission, Salvation, and Spirituality in the Book of Jonah* (Nottingham, England: Apollos, 2011), 101.

33. Jonah 4:3–11 (NRSV).

34. Sara Ahmed, *Willful Subjects* (Durham, N.C.: Duke University Press, 2014), 140.

35. Michael Snediker, *Queer Optimism* (Minneapolis: University of Minnesota Press, 2009), 18.

36. Snediker, *Queer Optimism*, 18–19.

37. Snediker, 19.

38. Albert Kamp, *Inner Worlds: A Cognitive Linguistic Approach to the Book of Jonah*, trans. David Orton (Leiden: Brill Academic Publishers, 2004), 147.

39. Sherwood, *Biblical Text*, 63.

40. Halberstam, *Queer Art of Failure*, 137.

41. Miguel A. De La Torre, *Liberating Jonah: Forming an Ethics of Reconciliation* (Maryknoll, N.Y.: Orbis Books, 2007), 1.

42. Sherwood, *Biblical Text*, 185.

43. Sherwood, 74.

44. Caputo, *Insistence of God*, 48.

45. Interpreters get this assignation of "better" to Mary's role from Luke 10:42, which follows Martha's complaint that Mary will not help her with the work of the household, but rather chooses to sit silently at Jesus' feet: ". . . there is need of only one thing. Mary has chosen the better part, which will not be taken away from her." (NRSV). As Kathleen E. Corley has pointed out, "Many consider this to be a story about discipleship or the

elevation of devotion to the word of God over other worldly concerns—even ministry." Kathleen E. Corley, *Private Women, Public Meals: Social Conflict in the Synoptic Tradition* (Peabody, Mass.: Hendrickson Publishers, 1993), 135. See also: Adams, *The Hidden Disciples*, 108; Elisabeth Schüssler Fiorenza, *In Memory of Her: A Feminist Theological Reconstruction of Christian Origins* (New York: The Crossroad Publishing Company, 1983), 330–33; Ben Witherington III, *Women in the Ministry of Jesus* (Cambridge: Cambridge University Press), 103.

46. Many interpreters concerned with feminist issues suggest that here Luke's positive concern for women as members of the Christian community can be discerned. Mary, seated as a disciple at the feet of Jesus the teacher, embodies the new, unique image of a woman who is allowed to learn from Jesus as a rabbinical student, a role denied to women within Judaism. Adams, *The Hidden Disciples*, 104; Mary Rose D'Angelo, "Images of Jesus and the Christian Call in the Gospels of Luke and John," *Spirituality Today* 37, no. 3 (Fall 1985): 204; Ellis, *Luke*, 160–61; Fitzmyer, *Luke*, 2:892–93; Robert J. Karris, *Luke: Artist and Theologian: Luke's Passion Account as Literature* (Eugene, Oreg.: Wipf and Stock Publishers, 2008; © 1985 by Paulist Press and licensed by special permission of Paulist Press), 135. While other feminist interpreters have rejected such a reading, complicating Luke's treatment of women (Schaberg, 1992; Seim, 2004; Schüssler Fiorenza, 1983; Alexander, 2002), even they have not fully engaged Martha's affect in as forceful a way as I argue here, and so have missed even more radical feminist potential within the character and her role in the Gospel story.

47. Caputo, *Insistence of God*, 65 and 248.

48. Schüssler Fiorenza, *In Memory of Her*.

49. Francois Bovon, *Luke 2: A Commentary on the Gospel of Luke 9:51–19:27* (Minneapolis, Minn.: Fortress Press, 2013), 70.

50. Bovon, *Luke 2*.

51. Blake R. Heffner, "Meister Eckhart and a Millennium with Mary and Martha," *Lutheran Quarterly* 5 (1991): 174.

52. Loveday C. Alexander, "Sisters in Adversity: Retelling Martha's Story," in *A Feminist Companion to Luke*, ed. Amy-Jill Levine (London: Sheffield Academic Press, 2002), 198–99.

53. Alexander, "Sisters in Adversity," 199.

54. "The second feature of this scene is *pollēn* ('numerous,' translated as 'many'), which Jesus contrasted with 'unique' (*enos*, translated as 'only one'). Martha did too much, with the result that her 'service' (*diakonia*), which could and should have been positive, was thereby affected negatively. Whatever criticism of Martha there might have been was not directed at either her hospitality or her desire to serve but rather at her excess activity and the worries that occasioned it." Bovon, *Luke 2*, 71.

55. We might see this double-bind further reflected in Luke 8:1–3. In these passages even though three women, Mary, Joanna, and Susana, are named as being with Jesus along with the twelve, they are also listed as providing for the twelve "out of their resources" (8:3). If discipleship requires the giving up of material possessions (14:33), then perhaps while these women were necessary supports for the disciples they were denied the better part of discipleship.

56. Schüssler Fiorenza, *In Memory of Her*.

57. Alexander, "Sisters in Adversity," 199–200.

58. By drawing on John I do not intend to imply that the two versions of Martha need to converge, but rather to continue to trace the character as she might murmur to us from within both texts.

59. Caputo, *Insistence of God*, 232.

60. Bovon, *Luke 2*, 70.

61. Bovon, 73–74.

62. Bovon, 73.

63. Bovon, 72; emphasis added.

64. Bovon, 73; emphasis added.

65. Alexander, "Sisters in Adversity," 212.

66. Caputo, *Insistence of God*, 48; emphasis added.

67. Caputo, 135.

68. Caputo, 65.

69. Bovon, *Luke 2*, 74.

70. Caputo, *Insistence of God*, 65.

71. Meister Eckhart, *Meister Eckhart: Teacher and Preacher* (Mahwah, N.J.: Paulist Press, 1986), 338.

72. Eckhart, *Teacher and Preacher*, 339.

73. Eckhart, 340.

74. Eckhart, 340.

75. Caputo, *Insistence of God*, 45.

76. Eckhart, *Teacher and Preacher*, 344.

77. Eckhart, 342.

78. Eckhart, 342.

79. Eckhart, 344.

80. Caputo, *Insistence of God*, 44.

81. Caputo, 45.

82. Caputo, 178–79.

83. Meister Eckhart, *Meister Eckhart: The Essential Sermons, Commentaries, Treatises and Defense* (Mahwah, N.J.: Paulist Press, 1981), 285.

84. Sara Ahmed, "Not in the Mood," *New Formations* 82 (2014): 18.

85. Ann Cvetkovich, *Depression: A Public Feeling* (Durham, N.C.: Duke University Press, 2012), 155.

86. Cvetkovich, *Depression*, 154.

87. Cvetkovich, Chap. 3.

88. Cvetkovich, 197.

89. Cvetkovich, 74.

90. Cvetkovich, 190.

91. Bovon, *Luke* 2, 42; emphasis added.

92. Ahmed, *Willful Subjects*, 1.

93. Ahmed, 175.

94. Ahmed, 175.

95. Ahmed, 176.

96. Ahmed, 176.

97. Jack Halberstam, "Riots and Occupations: The Fall of the United States," *Make/Shift* (Spring/Summer 2012): 14.

98. Ahmed, *Willful Subjects*, 160.

99. Ahmed, 139.

100. Ahmed, 140.

5 · UNREASONED CARE

1. Lynne Huffer, *Mad for Foucault: Rethinking the Foundations of Queer Theory* (New York: Columbia University Press, 2010), 23.

2. Michel Foucault, *The Hermeneutics of the Subject: Lectures at the Collège de France 1981–1982* (New York: Picador, 2001), 95.

3. Isabelle Stengers, *Thinking with Whitehead: A Free and Wild Creation of Concepts*, trans. Michael Chase (Cambridge, Mass.: Harvard University Press, 2011), 461.

4. Alfred North Whitehead, *Process and Reality* (New York: Free Press, 1978), 343.

5. Michel Foucault, *History of Madness* (Abingdon, Oxon: Routledge, 2006), 443.

6. Huffer, *Mad for Foucault*, 144.

7. According to Huffer, "If returning to the Greeks was Foucault's way of getting out from under Christian morality, turning to the moment of splitting in the Age of Reason was Foucault's way of getting out from under philosophy's despotic moralizing power." Huffer, *Mad for Foucault*, xvi.

8. Huffer, *Mad for Foucault*, 92.

9. Foucault, *History of Madness*, 345.

10. For Huffer, "This is where eros becomes important, for in its etymology eros refers not only to a notion of passionate love but also to a life force, what Audre Lorde calls, like Nietzsche, 'the *yes* within ourselves.'" Hence she asks, "Might an ethics of eros be articulated as a possibility of life to transform the violence of biopower?" Huffer, *Mad for Foucault*, 256.

11. Foucault, *History of Madness*, 9.

12. Foucault, 10.

13. Foucault, 9.

14. Gilles Deleuze, *Foucault* (London: Continuum, 1999), 97.

15. Huffer, *Mad for Foucault*, 102.

16. Huffer, 59.

17. Huffer, 51.

18. Henri-Jacques Stiker, *A History of Disability*, trans. William Sayers (Ann Arbor: University of Michigan Press, 1999), 134.

19. Noëlle Vahanian, *The Rebellious No: Variations on a Secular Theology of Language* (New York: Fordham University Press, 2014), 71.

20. Huffer, *Mad for Foucault*, xvi.

21. Huffer, 487.

22. Huffer, 227.

23. Foucault, *History of Madness*; Huffer, *Mad for Foucault*.

24. Alfred North Whitehead, *Modes of Thought* (New York: Free Press, 1968), 26.

25. Whitehead, *Process and Reality*, 149.

26. Whitehead, 133.

27. Huffer, *Mad for Foucault*, 43.

28. Huffer, 43.

29. Whitehead, *Modes of Thought*, 57.

30. Whitehead, 57.

31. Whitehead, 57.

32. Whitehead, 57.

33. Whitehead, *Process and Reality*, 346.

34. Foucault, *History of Madness*, 79–80.

35. Foucault, 373.

36. Foucault, 373; emphasis added.

37. Foucault, 373.

38. Foucault, 373; emphasis added.

39. Foucault, 368; emphasis added.

40. Foucault, 71.

41. Foucault, 448.

42. Foucault, 106.

43. Foucault, 361.

44. Huffer, *Mad for Foucault*, 52.

45. Huffer, 53.

46. Huffer, 80.

47. Foucault, *History of Madness*, 532.

48. Huffer, *Mad for Foucault*, 275.

49. Huffer, 118; emphasis added.

50. Foucault, *Hermeneutics of the Subject*, 95; emphasis added.

51. Foucault, 93.

52. Michel Foucault, *The Courage of Truth: The Government of Self and Others II: Lectures at the Collège de France, 1983–1984* (New York: Palgrave Macmillan, 2012), 246; emphasis added.

53. Mark D. Jordan, *Convulsing Bodies: Religion and Resistance in Foucault* (Stanford, Calif.: University of Stanford Press, 2015), 174.

54. Foucault, *Courage of Truth*, 180.

55. Foucault, *Hermeneutics of the Subject*, 95.

56. Huffer, *Mad for Foucault*, 243.

57. Foucault, *Courage of Truth*, 183.

58. Jordan, *Convulsing Bodies*, 175.

59. Foucault, *Courage of Truth*, 184.

60. Whitehead, *Modes of Thought*, 45.

61. Whitehead, *Process and Reality*, 7–8.

62. Huffer, *Mad for Foucault*, 249.

63. Huffer, 243.

64. Huffer, 243.

65. Foucault, *Courage of Truth*, 166.

66. Foucault, 43.

67. Foucault, 43.

68. Foucault, 43.

69. Huffer, *Mad for Foucault*, xvii.

70. Stengers, *Thinking with Whitehead*, 315.

71. Catherine Keller, "Uninteresting Truth? Tedium and Event in Postmodernity," in *Secrets of Becoming: Negotiating Whitehead, Deleuze, and Butler*, ed. Roland Faber and Andrea M. Stephenson (New York: Fordham University Press, 2011), 211.

72. Keller, "Uninteresting Truth?", 211.

73. Foucault, *Courage of Truth*, 169.

74. Keller, "Uninteresting Truth?", 213.

75. In Whitehead's cosmology there exists a similar resistance to rational moral order as in Foucault's poetic style. According to Steven Shaviro: "Whitehead posits God on the basis of 'aesthetic experience,' rather than morality. To the extent that we make 'decisions'—and, for Whitehead, decision 'constitutes the very meaning of actuality' (1929/1978, 43)—we are engaged in a process of selection. We 'feel' (or positively prehend) certain data, and 'eliminate from feeling' (or negatively prehend) certain others (23). But this process of selection is an aesthetic one. It is felt, rather than thought (or felt before it is thought); and it is freely chosen, rather than being obligatory." Steven Shaviro, *Without Criteria: Kant, Whitehead, Deleuze, and Aesthetics*

(Cambridge, Mass.: MIT Press, 2009), 139. While Shaviro takes Whitehead's aesthetic as precluding an ethical style, I take it as exactly that which nurtures a Whiteheadian ethic, one this chapter hopes to reveal as being in concert with a Foucauldian one of eros.

76. Roland Faber, *Divine Manifold* (Maryland: Lexington Books, 2014), 365.

77. Foucault, *Courage of Truth*, 170.

78. Stengers, *Thinking with Whitehead*, 476.

79. Whitehead, *Modes of Thought*, 102.

80. Whitehead, *Process and Reality*, 110–11.

81. Eugenie Brinkema, *The Forms of the Affects* (Durham, N.C.: Duke University Press, 2014), 244–45.

82. Stengers, *Thinking with Whitehead*, 456.

83. Faber, *Divine Manifold*, 24.

84. Shaviro, *Without Criteria*, 123.

85. Whitehead, *Process and Reality*, 244.

86. Stengers, *Thinking with Whitehead*, 476.

87. Whitehead, *Process and Reality*, 351.

88. Faber, *Divine Manifold*, 383.

89. Faber, 383.

90. Faber, 108.

91. Faber, 469–70.

92. Huffer, *Mad for Foucault*, 118.

93. Huffer, 202.

94. Jordan, *Convulsing Bodies*, 191.

95. Jordan, 191.

96. Whitehead, *Modes of Thought*, 174.

97. Stengers, *Thinking with Whitehead*, 244.

98. Jasbir Puar ed., "Precarity Talk: A Virtual Roundtable with Lauren Berlant, Judith Butler, Bojana Cvejic, Isabell Lorey, Jasbir Puar, and Ana Vujanovic," *Drama Review* 56, no. 4 (T216) (Winter 2012): 168.

99. Puar, "Precarity Talk," 168.

100. Puar, 168.

101. Stengers, *Thinking with Whitehead*, 476.

102. Huffer, *Mad for Foucault*, 33.

103. Whitehead, *Modes of Thought*, 87.

104. Brinkema, *Forms of the Affects*, 243.

105. Brinkema, 243.

106. Huffer, *Mad for Foucault*, 120–21.

107. Huffer, 121.

108. Faber, *Divine Manifold*, 374.

109. Jack Halberstam, introduction to *The Undercommons: Fugitive Planning and Black Study* by Stefano Harney and Fred Moten (Wivenhoe, UK: Minor Compositions, 2013), 6.

110. Halberstam, introduction to *Undercommons*, 6–8.

111. Huffer, *Mad for Foucault*, 120.

6. UNATTENDED AFFECT

1. Christina Sharpe, *In the Wake: On Blackness and Being* (Durham, N.C.: Duke University Press, 2016), 113.

2. Sharpe, *In the Wake*, 106.

3. Sharpe, 27.

4. Sharpe, 7.

5. Sharpe, 11.

6. Kelly Brown Douglas, *Stand Your Ground: Black Bodies and the Justice of God* (Maryknoll, N.Y.: Orbis Books, 2015), 10.

7. Brown Douglas, *Stand Your Ground*, 41–42.

8. Brown Douglas, 14.

9. Brown Douglas, 5.

10. Brown Douglas, 36.

11. Jonathon S. Kahn, "Conclusion: James Baldwin and a Theology of Justice in a Secular Age," in *Race and Secularism in America*, ed. Jonathon S. Kahn and Vincent W. Lloyd (New York: Columbia University Press, 2016), 244.

12. George Shulman, "From Political Theology to Vernacular Prophecy," in *Race and Political Theology*, ed. Vincent W. Lloyd (Stanford, Calif.: Stanford University Press, 2012), 242.

13. For coverage of Wesleyan's racial history see Brad Schrade, "Macon Women's College Seeks to Atone for Ku Klux Klan's Legacy," *Atlanta Journal-Constitution*, June 22, 2017, http://www.myajc.com/news/state—regional/macon-women-college-seeks-atone-for-klux-klan-legacy/g7C2fxlEtmmV7ge4f7znCK/; and Brad Schrade, "Ga. College Linked to Klan Rituals Apologizes for 'Pain' of Its History," *Atlanta Journal-Constitution*, June 22, 2017, http://www.ajc.com/news/breaking-news/college-linked-klan-rituals-apologizes-for-pain-its-history/nYbpXM8wKncDM6AMv9VkKK/.

14. James Cone, interview by Bill Moyers, *Bill Moyers: The Journal*, November 23, 2007, http://billmoyers.com/content/james-cone-on-the-cross-and-the-lynching-tree/.

15. Brown Douglas, *Stand Your Ground*, 42.

16. Stefano Harney and Fred Moten, *The Undercommons: Fugitive Planning and Black Study* (Wivenhoe, UK: Minor Compositions, 2013), 65.

17. Roxane Gay, "No One Is Coming to Save Us from Trump's Racism," *New York Times*, January 12, 2018, https://www.nytimes.com/2018/01/12/

opinion/trump-shithole-countries-haiti-el-salvador-african-countries
-immigration-racism.html?_r=0.

18. Fred Moten, *Stolen Life* (Durham, N.C.: Duke University, 2018), 155.

19. Moten, *Stolen Life*, 155.

20. Moten, 160.

21. Moten, 160.

22. Fred Moten, "Black Mo'nin'," in *Loss: The Politics of Mourning*, ed. David L. Eng and David Kazanjian (Berkeley and Los Angeles: University of California Press, 2003), 73.

23. Ashon Crawley, "Breathing Flesh and the Sound of Black Pentecostalism," in *Theology & Sexuality* 19, no. 1 (2015): 49–60, https://doi.org/10 .1179/1355835814Z.00000000021.

24. Crawley, "Breathing Flesh," 49–60.

25. Crawley, 57

26. Crawley, 57.

27. Sharpe, *In the Wake*, 73.

28. Sharpe, 87.

29. A prime example of such narrative can be found in an article by Julie Irwin Zimmerman titled, "I Failed the Covington Catholic Test," *Atlantic*, January 21, 2019, https://www.theatlantic.com/ideas/archive/2019/01/julie -irwin-zimmerman-i-failed-covington-catholic-test/580897/. In the article Irwin Zimmerman apologizes for too hastily condemning the teens in her coverage of the event and asks us to consider the larger picture, which includes that these boys were only teenagers.

30. Elie Mystal, "Black Children Don't Have Nick Sandmann's Rights: And They Definitely Don't Get the Chance to Redeem Themselves on National TV with the Help of Savannah Guthrie," *Nation*, January 24, 2019, https://www.thenation.com/article/black-children-nick-sandmann-savannah -guthrie/.

31. Sharpe, *In the Wake*, 109.

32. Moten, *Stolen Life*, 135.

33. Sharpe, *In the Wake*, 111.

34. Sharpe, 73.

35. Moten, *Stolen Life*, xii.

36. Moten, 155.

37. Moten, 130.

38. Moten, 130.

39. Moten, 130.

40. Moten, 128.

41. Moten, 129.

42. Moten, 130.

43. Moten, 133.

44. Moten, 133.

45. Moten, 137–38.

46. Moten, 138.

47. Moten, 138–39.

48. Monica A. Coleman, *Making a Way Out of No Way: A Womanist Theology* (Minneapolis, Minn.: Fortress Press, 2008).

49. Sharpe, *In the Wake*, 131.

50. Sharpe, 14.

51. Sharpe, 117.

52. Sharpe, 116.

53. Sharpe, 120.

54. Sharpe, 123.

55. Moten, *Stolen Life*, 243–44.

56. Moten, 247.

57. Moten, 247.

58. Marcella Althaus-Reid, *Indecent Theology: Theological Perversions in Sex, Gender, and Politics* (New York: Routledge, 2000), 110.

59. Karen Bray, "The Common Good of the Flesh: An Indecent Invitation to William E. Connolly, Joerg Rieger, and Political Theology," in *Common Goods: Economy, Ecology, and Political Theology*, ed. Melanie Johnson-DeBaufre, Catherine Keller, and Elias Ortega-Aponte (New York: Fordham University Press, 2015), 387.

60. Moten, *Stolen Life*, 247.

61. Moten, 251.

62. Moten, 258.

63. Branden Jacobs-Jenkins, *An Octoroon* (New York: Dramatist Play Service, 2015), 55–57.

64. Jacobs-Jenkins, *Octoroon*, 57–58; emphasis added.

65. Sharpe, *In the Wake*, 100–101.

66. Moten, *Stolen Life*, 135.

Ahmed, Sara. "Not in the Mood." *New Formations* 82 (2014): 13–28.

———. *The Promise of Happiness*. Durham, N.C.: Duke University Press, 2010.

———. *Willful Subjects*. Durham, N.C.: Duke University Press, 2014.

Alexander, Loveday C. "Sisters in Adversity: Retelling Martha's Story." In *A Feminist Companion to Luke*. Edited by Amy-Jill Levine. London: Sheffield Academic Press, 2002.

Althaus-Reid, Marcella. *Indecent Theology: Theological Perversions in Sex, Gender, and Politics*. New York: Routledge, 2000.

Betcher, Sharon V. *Spirit and the Politics of Disablement*. Minneapolis, Minn.: Fortress Press, 2007.

Bennett, Jane. "Powers of the Hoard: Further Notes on Material Agency." In *Animal, Vegetable, Mineral: Ethics and Objects*. Edited by Jeffrey Jerome Cohen. Washington, D.C.: Oliphaunt Books, 2012.

Berardi, Franco "Bifo." *After the Future*. Edited by Gary Genosko and Nicholas Thoburn. Edinburgh, Oakland, Baltimore: AK Press, 2011.

———. *The Soul at Work: From Alienation to Autonomy*. Los Angeles: Semiotext(e), 2009.

Berlant, Lauren. *Cruel Optimism*. Durham, N.C.: Duke University Press, 2011.

Betcher, Sharon V. *Spirit and the Politics of Disablement*. Minneapolis, Minn.: Fortress Press, 2007.

Bovon, Francois. *Luke 2: A Commentary on the Gospel of Luke, 9:51–19:27*. Minneapolis, Minn.: Fortress Press, 2013.

Bray, Karen. "The Common Good of the Flesh: An Indecent Invitation to William E. Connolly, Joerg Rieger, and Political Theology." In *Common Goods: Economy, Ecology, and Political Theology*. Edited by Melanie Johnson-DeBaufre, Catherine Keller, and Elias Ortega-Aponte. New York: Fordham University Press, 2015.

Brinkema, Eugenie. *The Forms of the Affects*. Durham, N.C.: Duke University Press, 2014.

Brown Douglas, Kelly. *Stand Your Ground: Black Bodies and the Justice of God*. Maryknoll, NY: Orbis Books, 2015.

Brueggemann, Walter. "The Costly Loss of Lament." *Journal for the Study of the Old Testament* 36:10 (1986).

Butler, Judith. *The Psychic Life of Power: Theories in Subjection.* Stanford, Calif.: Stanford University Press, 1997.

Caputo, John D. *The Insistence of God: A Theology of Perhaps.* Bloomington: Indiana University Press, 2013.

Casarino, Cesare, and Antonio Negri. *In Praise of the Common: A Conversation on Philosophy and Politics.* Minneapolis: University of Minnesota Press, 2008.

Caserio, Robert L. "The Antisocial Thesis in Queer Theory." *PMLA: Publications of the Modern Language Association of America* 121, no. 3 (2006).

Cavanaugh, William T. *Being Consumed: Economics and Christian Desire.* Grand Rapids, Mich.: Wm. B. Eerdmans Publishing Co., 2008.

Chesung, Justin Ryu. "Silence as resistance: a postcolonial reading of the silence of Jonah in Jonah 4.1–11." *Journal for the Study of the Old Testament* 34, No .2 (2009): 195–218.

Cobb, John B., and David Ray Griffin, eds. *Process Theology: An Introductory Exposition.* Louisville, Ky.: Westminster John Knox Press, 1976.

Coleman, Monica A. *Making a Way Out of No Way: A Womanist Theology.* Minneapolis, Minn.: Fortress Press, 2008.

Cone, James. Interview by Bill Moyers. *Bill Moyers: The Journal*, November 23, 2007. http://billmoyers.com/content/james-cone-on-the-cross-and-the-lynching-tree/.

Connolly, William E. *Capitalism and Christianity, American Style.* Durham, N.C.: Duke University Press, 2008.

Corley, Kathleen E. *Private Women, Public Meals: Social Conflict in the Synoptic Tradition.* Peabody, Mass.: Hendrickson Publishers, 1993.

Crawley, Ashon. "Breathing Flesh and the Sound of BlackPentecostalism." *Theology and Sexuality*, 19, no. 1 (2015): 49–60. https://doi.org/10.1179/1355835814Z.00000000021.

Crockett, Clayton. *Deleuze beyond Badiou: Ontology, Multiplicity, and Event.* New York: Columbia University Press, 2013.

———. *Radical Political Theology: Religion and Politics after Liberalism.* New York: Columbia University Press, 2011.

Crockett, Clayton, B. Keith Putt, and Jeffrey W. Robbins, eds. *The Future of Continental Philosophy of Religion* (Bloomington: Indiana University Press, 2014).

Crockett, Clayton, and Jeffrey W. Robbins. *Religion, Politics, and the Earth: The New Materialism.* New York: Palgrave Macmillan, 2012.

Cvetkovich, Ann. *Depression: A Public Feeling.* Durham, N.C.: Duke University Press, 2012.

De La Torre, Miguel A. *Liberating Jonah: Forming an Ethics of Reconciliation.* Maryknoll, N.Y.: Orbis Books, 2007.

Dean, Tim. "An Impossible Embrace: Queerness, Futurity, and the Death Drive." In *A Time for the Humanities: Futurity and the Limits of Autonomy*. Edited by James J. Bono, Time Dean, and Ewa Plonowska Ziarek. New York: Fordham University Press, 2008.

Deleuze, Gilles. *Cinema II: The Time Image*. Minneapolis: University of Minnesota Press, 2003.

———. *Foucault*. Translated by Seán Hand. London: Continuum, 1999.

Derrida, Jacques. *The Animal That Thefore I Am*. New York: Fordham University Press, 2008.

Eckhart, Meister. *Meister Eckhart: The Essential Sermons, Commentaries, Treatises, and Defense*. Mahwah, N.J.: Paulist Press, 1981.

———. *Meister Eckhart: Teacher and Preacher*. Mahwah, N.J.: Paulist Press, 1986.

Edelman, Lee. *No Future: Queer Theory and the Death Drive*. Durham, N.C.: Duke University Press, 2004.

Eggers, Dave. *The Circle*. San Francisco: McSweeney's, 2013.

Eng, David L., and David Kazanjian, eds. *Loss: The Politics of Mourning*. Berkeley and Los Angeles: University of California Press, 2003.

Essbaum, Jill Alexander. "Swimming on Concrete: The Poetry of Vassar Miller." In *Beauty Is a Verb: The New Poetry of Disability*. Edited by Jennifer Bartlett, Sheila Black, and Michael Northern. El Paso, Tex.: Cinco Puntos Press, 2011.

Faber, Roland. *Divine Manifold*. Maryland: Lexington Books, 2014.

———. *God as Poet of the World: Exploring Process Theologies*. Louisville, Ky.: Westminster John Knox Press, 2008.

Foucault, Michel. *The Courage of Truth: The Government of Self and Others II: Lectures at the Collège de France, 1983–1984*. New York: Palgrave Macmillan, 2012.

———. *The Hermeneutics of the Subject: Lectures at the Collège de France 1981–1982*. New York: Picador, 2001.

———. *History of Madness*. Abingdon, Oxon: Routledge, 2006.

Freeman, Elizabeth. *Time Binds: Queer Temporalities, Queer Histories*. Durham, N.C.: Duke University Press, 2010.

Gay, Roxane. "No One Is Coming to Save Us from Trump's Racism." *New York Times*, January 12, 2018. https://www.nytimes.com/2018/01/12/opinion/trump-shithole-countries-haiti-el-salvador-african-countries-immigration-racism.html?_r=0.

Goodchild, Phillip. *Theology of Money*. Durham, N.C.: Duke University Press, 2009.

Gregg, Melissa. "On Friday Night Drinks: Workplace Affect in the Age of the Cubicle." In *The Affect Theory Reader*. Edited by and Melissa Gregg and Gregory J. Seigworth. Durham, N.C.: Duke University Press, 2010.

Gregg, Melissa, and Gregory J. Seigworth, eds. *The Affect Theory Reader*. Durham, N.C.: Duke University, 2009.

Grimshaw, Mike. *Palgrave Communications* Special Collection Introduction. Accessed December 2, 2015. https://www.nature.com/articles/palcomms 201532

Halberstam, Jack. Introduction to *The Undercommons: Fugitive Planning and Black Study* by Stefano Harney and Fred Moten, 2–12. Wivenhoe, UK: Minor Compositions, 2013.

Halberstam, Judith. *The Queer Art of Failure*. Durham, N.C.: Duke University Press, 2011.

Hardt, Michael, and Antonio Negri. *Multitude: War and Democracy in the Age of Empire*. New York: Penguin, 2004.

Harney, Stefano, and Fred Moten. *The Undercommons: Fugitive Planning and Black Study*. Wivenhoe, UK: Minor Compositions, 2013.

Hartman, Saidiya V. *Scenes of Subjection: Terror, Slavery, and Self-Making in Nineteenth-Century America*. New York: Oxford University Press, 1997.

Jione Havea, "First People, Minority Reading: Reading Jonah, From Oceania," in *The One Who Reads May Run: Essays in Honour of Edgar W. Conrad*, ed. Roland Boer, Michael Carden, and Julie Kelso (New York: T&T Clark, 2012).

Heffner, Blake R. "Meister Eckhart and a Millennium with Mary and Martha." *Lutheran Quarterly* 5 (1991).

Huffer, Lynne. *Mad for Foucault: Rethinking the Foundations of Queer Theory*. New York: Columbia University Press, 2010.

Jacobs-Jenkins, Branden. *An Octoroon*. New York: Dramatist Play Service, 2015.

James, Robin. *Resilience and Melancholy: Pop Music, Feminism, Neoliberalism*. Alresford, UK: Zero Books, 2015.

Jonah: A VeggieTales Movie. DVD. Directed by Mike Nawrocki and Phil Vischer. USA: Big Idea Productions, 2002.

Jordan, Mark D. *Convulsing Bodies: Religion and Resistance in Foucault*. Stanford, Calif.: University of Stanford Press, 2015.

Kahn, Jonathon S. "Conclusion: James Baldwin and a Theology of Justice in a Secular Age." In *Race and Secularism in America*. Edited by Jonathon S. Kahn and Vincent W. Lloyd. New York: Columbia University Press, 2016.

Kamp, Albert. *Inner Worlds: A Cognitive Linguistic Approach to the Book of Jonah*. Translated by David Orton. Leiden: Brill Academic Publishers, 2004.

Kantor, Jodi, and David Streitfield. "Inside Amazon: Wrestling Big Ideas in a Bruising Workplace." *New York Times*, August 15, 2015. http://www.nytimes.com/2015/08/16/technology/inside-amazon-wrestlingbig-ideas-in-a-bruising-workplace.html?_r=0.

Keller, Catherine. "Uninteresting Truth? Tedium and Event in Postmodernity." In *Secrets of Becoming: Negotiating Whitehead, Deleuze, and Butler.* Edited by Roland Faber and Andrea M. Stephenson. New York: Fordham University Press, 2011.

Klein, Naomi. *The Shock Doctrine: The Rise of Disaster Capitalism.* New York: Picador, 2007.

———. *This Changes Everything: Capital vs. the Climate.* New York: Simon and Schuster, 2014.

Leibniz, G. W. *Philosophical Writings.* London: Everyman's Library, 1973.

Long, D. Stephen, and Nancy Ruth Fox. *Calculated Futures: Theology, Ethics, and Economics.* Waco, Tex.: Baylor University Press, 2007.

Love, Heather. *Feeling Backward: Loss and the Politics of Queer History.* Cambridge, Mass.: Harvard University Press, 2007.

McRuer, Robert. *Crip Theory: Cultural Signs of Queerness and Disability.* New York: New York University Press, 2006.

McRuer, Robert, and Anna Mollow, eds. *Sex and Disability.* Durham, N.C.: Duke University Press, 2012.

McRuer, Robert, and Merri Lisa Johnson. "Proliferating Cripistemologies: A Virtual Roundtable." *Journal of Literary and Culutral Disability Studies* 8, no. 2 (2014): 149–69.

Milbank, John. *Theology and Social Theory: Beyond Secular Reason.* Oxford: Blackwell Publishing, 1990.

Morton, Timothy. *Ecology without Nature: Rethinking Environmental Aesthetics.* Cambridge, Mass.: Harvard University Press, 2009.

Moten, Fred. "Black Mo'nin'." In *Loss: The Politics of Mourning.* Edited by David L. Eng and David Kazanjian. Berkeley and Los Angeles: University of California Press, 2003.

———. *Stolen Life.* Durham, N.C.: Duke University, 2018.

Muñoz, José Esteban. *Cruising Utopia: The Then and There of Queer Futurity.* New York: New York University Press, 2009.

———. *Disidentifications: Queers of Color and the Performance of Politics.* Minneapolis: University of Minnesota Press, 1999.

———. "Thinking Beyond Antirelationality and Antiutopianism in Queer Critique." *PMLA: Publications of the Modern Language Association of America* 121, no. 3 (2006).

Mystal, Elie. "Black Children Don't Have Nick Sandmann's Rights: And they definitely don't get the chance to redeem themselves on national TV with the help of Savannah Guthrie." *Nation,* January 24, 2019. https://www.thenation.com/article/black-children-nick-sandmann-savannah-guthrie/.

O'Collins, Gerald, SJ. *Salvation for All: God's Other Peoples.* Oxford: Oxford University Press, 2008.

Puar, Jasbir, ed. "Precarity Talk: A Virtual Roundtable with Lauren Berlant, Judith Butler, Bojana Cvejic, Isabell Lorey, Jasbir Puar, and Ana Vujanovic." *Drama Review* 56, no. 4 (T216) (Winter 2012).

Parton, Dolly. *9 to 5*, Dolly Parton © 1980 by RCA Nashville.

Rambo, Shelly. *Spirit and Trauma: A Theology of Remaining.* Louisville, Ky.: Westminster John Knox Press: 2010.

Rieger, Joerg. *No Rising Tide: Theology, Economics, and the Future.* Minneapolis, Minn.: Fortress Press, 2009.

Rieger, Joerg, and Kwok Pui-lan. *Occupy Religion: Theology of the Multitude.* Plymouth, UK: Rowman and Littlefield, 2012.

Robbins, Jeffrey W. *Radical Democracy and Political Theology.* New York: Columbia University Press, 2011.

Schaefer, Donovan O. *Religious Affects: Animality, Evolution, and Power.* Durham, N.C.: Duke University Press, 2015.

Schildrik, Magrit. *Dangerous Discourses of Disability, Subjectivity, and Sexuality.* London: Palgrave Macmillan, 2009.

Schmitt, Carl. *Political Theology: Four Chapters on the Concept of Sovereignty.* Chicago: University of Chicago Press, 1985.

Schrade, Brad. "Ga. College Linked to Klan Rituals Apologizes for 'Pain' of Its History." *Atlanta Journal-Constitution*, June 22, 2017. http://www.ajc .com/news/breaking-news/college-linked-klan-rituals-apologizes-for -pain-its-history/nYbpXM8wKncDM6AMv9VkKK/.

———. "Macon Women's College Seeks to Atone for Ku Klux Klan's Legacy." *Atlanta Journal-Constitution*, June 22, 2017. http://www.myajc.com/news/ state—regional/macon-women-college-seeks-atone-for-klux-klan-legacy/ g7C2fxlEtmmV7ge4f7znCK/.

Schüssler Fiorenza, Elisabeth. *In Memory of Her: A Feminist Theological Reconstruction of Christian Origins.* New York: The Crossroad Publishing Company, 1983.

Schweik, Susan. "The Voice of 'Reason.'" In *Beauty Is a Verb: The New Poetry of Disability.* Edited by Jennifer Bartlett, Sheila Black, and Michael Northern. El Paso, Tex.: Cinco Puntos Press, 2011.

Sedgwick, Eve Kosofsky. *Touching Feeling: Affect, Pedagogy, Performativity.* Durham, N.C.: Duke University, 2003.

Shakespeare, Steven. *Radical Orthodoxy: A Critical Introduction.* London: Society for Promoting Christian Knowledge, 2007.

Sharpe, Christina. *In the Wake: On Blackness and Being.* Durham, N.C.: Duke University Press, 2016.

Shaviro, Steven. *No Speed Limit: Three Essays on Accelerationism.* Minneapolis: University of Minnesota Press, 2015.

———. *Without Criteria: Kant, Whitehead, Deleuze, and Aesthetics.* Cambridge, Mass.: MIT Press, 2009.

Sherwood, Yvonne. *A Biblical Text and Its Afterlives: The Survival of Jonah in Western Culture.* Cambridge: Cambridge University Press, 2000.

Shulman, George. "From Political Theology to Vernacular Prophecy: Rethinking Redemption." In *Race and Political Theology.* Edited by Vincent W. Lloyd. Stanford, Calif.: Stanford University Press, 2012.

Siebers, Tobin. *Disability Aesthetics.* Ann Arbor: University of Michigan Press, 2010.

Smith, James K. A. *Introducing Radical Orthodoxy: Mapping a Post-Secular Theology.* Grand Rapids, Mich.: Baker Academic, 2004.

Snediker, Michael. *Queer Optimism.* Minneapolis: University of Minnesota Press, 2009.

Stengers, Isabelle. *Thinking with Whitehead: A Free and Wild Creation of Concepts.* Translated by Michael Chase. Cambridge, Mass.: Harvard University Press, 2011.

Stiker, Henri-Jacques. *A History of Disability.* Translated by William Sayers. Ann Arbor: University of Michigan Press, 1999.

Taylor, Mark C. *Confidence Games: Moneys and Markets in a World without Redemption.* Chicago: University of Chicago Press, 2004.

Taylor, Mark L. *The Theological and the Political: On the Weight of the World.* Minneapolis, Minn.: Fortress Press, 2011.

Timmer, Daniel C. *A Gracious and Compassionate God: Mission, Salvation and Spirituality in the Book of Jonah.* Nottingham, England: Apollos, 2011.

Tran, Mark. "Apple and Facebook Offer to Freeze Eggs for Female Employees." *Guardian*, October 15, 2004. http://www.theguardian.com/technology/2014/oct/15/apple-facebook-offer-freeze-eggs-female-employees.

Vahanian, Noëlle. *The Rebellious No: Variations on a Secular Theology of Language.* New York: Fordham University Press, 2014.

Weeks, Kathi. *The Problem with Work: Feminism, Marxism, Antiwork Politics, and Postwork Imaginaries.* Durham, N.C.: Duke University Press, 2011.

Weheliye, Alexander G. *Habeas Viscus: Racializing Assemblages, Biopolitics, and Black Feminist Theories of the Human.* Durham, N.C.: Duke University Press, 2014.

Whitehead, Alfred North. *Adventures of Ideas.* New York: Free Press, 1967.

———. *Modes of Thought.* New York: Free Press, 1968.

———. *Process and Reality.* New York: Free Press, 1978.

Wilson, Elizabeth A. *Gut Feminism.* Durham, N.C.: Duke University Press, 2015.

Zimmerman, Julie Irwin. "I Failed the Covington Catholic Test." *Atlantic*, January 21, 2019. https://www.theatlantic.com/ideas/archive/2019/01/julie-irwin-zimmerman-i-failed-covington-catholic-test/580897/.

Žižek, Slavoj. *The Parallax View.* Cambridge, Mass.: MIT Press, 2004.

Index

ableism, 11–12, 25–26, 60, 156. *See also* crip theory

Adventures of Ideas (Whitehead), 178

affect alienation: Ahmed on, 105–6; anger and, 116, 117–24, 125; bipolarity and, 110–11, 124–25; counter-flow and, 110, 111–12, 124–25; crip theory and, 150; defined, 6, 105; depression and, 98, 110, 111, 125–27; double bind of, 127–32, 234n55; freedom to be unhappy and, 3, 6, 107, 109–10, 150–51; grave attending to, 106–7, 150–51; hap-ness and, 112, 117, 143–44, 146, 148; of Hebrew and Christian bibles (*see* Jonah; Martha); killjoys and, 106–7, 110, 111, 119–20, 142, 145–48; madness and, 136–45; overview, 6–7, 28; perhap-ness and, 112, 117, 118, 146, 148; of postcolonialism, 115–17; as prayers of lament, 108; prophetic potential of, 109–14; shame of, 25, 120–21, 123–24; willfulness and, 28, 111–12, 145–51; worries and, 132–36. *See also* killjoys

affect economy, 14, 75–76

affect theology, 9–11

affect theory: about, 4–5, 107–8; attunement and, 16; domestic spheres and, 8; Marxism and, 18; methodology for examination of, 23–29 (*see also* affect alienation; temporal structures; unproductive worth; unreasoned care; willfulness and willingness); political theology and, 4, 5–6, 9, 11–13; post-theological concept and, 15–16; on redemption narratives, 11–12, 15, 41, 186–87; religious studies and, 9–11

The Affect Theory Reader (Gregg), 4–5, 107

After the Future (Berardi), 70, 80, 81, 102

agency: of bipolar time, 61–63; discipleship as, 73, 127–32, 140, 142–44, 232–33n45; process theology on, 21

Ahmed, Sara: on affect alienation, 28, 105–6, 110, 111–12; on affect theory, 9–10; on attunement, 16, 141; on freedom to be unhappy, 3, 6, 107, 109–10; on hap-ness, 113–14, 146, 148; on happiness, 6–7, 105–6, 109–10, 112–13, 114, 149; on "institution of White Men," 114, 231n22; on killjoys, 6, 106, 110; on redemption, 211; *The Promise of Happiness*, 6–7, 105, 106, 110, 146; on The *Promise of Happiness*, 106; on willfulness and willingness, 103, 111–12, 120, 145–46, 148, 149, 158, 226n17; *Willful Subjects*, 145

Alcibiades, 168

Alexander, Loveday, 127, 129–31, 133–34, 135–36, 139, 141

alienation. *See* affect alienation

Althaus-Reid, Marcella, 206–7

Amazon, as a workplace, 77–79

antisociality, 221–22n29

anxiety: affect alienation and, 125–26, 136–37, 144; bipolar time and, 62; God as Eros on, 182–83; as killjoy lament, 136–37; as neoliberal economic interpretation, 19–20; productivity and, 94–97, 99–100; as societal diagnosis, 6

Apple, as a workplace, 77

Aristide, Jean-Betrand, 37

Aronowitz, Stanley, 91

Artaud, Antonin, 166–67

"The Attendant" (Julien), 56–58

Augustine (saint), 38, 129

Autobiography of My Mother (Kincaid), 116

autonomism, 18, 28, 70, 80–86, 225–26n6

"Baby One More Time" (Spears), 65

backward future, 47–48, 84

Karen Bray is an Assistant Professor of Religious Studies and Philosophy, and the Chair of Religious Studies and Philosophy, at Wesleyan College. Her research areas include continental philosophy of religion; feminist, critical disability, and black studies; and queer, political, and decolonial theories and theologies. Her work has appeared in such journals as the *American Journal of Theology and Philosophy*, the *Journal for Cultural and Religious Theory*, and *Palgrave Communications*, and in several edited volumes.

CPSIA information can be obtained
at www.ICGtesting.com
Printed in the USA
JSHW021643051219
2814JS00001B/12